Resurrection
Myth or Reality?

OTHER BOOKS BY JOHN SHELBY SPONG

Resurrection
Myth or Reality?

A Bishop's Search for the Origins
of Christianity

JOHN SHELBY SPONG

 HarperSanFrancisco
A Division of HarperCollins*Publishers*

FIRST EDITION

Library of Congress Cataloging-in-Publication Data

Spong, John Shelby.
    Resurrection : myth or reality? / John Shelby Spong. — 1st ed.
      p. cm.
    Includes bibliographical references and index.
    ISBN 0–06–067546–2 (cloth : alk. paper)
    ISBN 0–06–067547–0 (Int'l pbk)
    1. Jesus Christ—Resurrection—Controversial literature.
  2. Christianity—Origin.   3. Future life—Christianity.
  I. Title.
BT481.S684   1994
232'.5—dc20   93–25114
                                        CIP

94 95 96 97 ❖ CWI 10 9 8 7 6 5 4 3 2 1

This edition is printed on acid-free paper that meets the American National Standards Institute Z39.48 Standard.

For Wanda Corwin Hollenbeck,

*without whom my professional life would not be
complete, either as a bishop or as an author, and for
whom my gratitude is overwhelming, my respect
genuine, and my affection real.*

Contents

Part Four: Clues That Lead Us Toward Easter

Part Five: Reconstructing the Easter Moment

Preface

The subject of the resurrection of Jesus of Nazareth lies at the foundation of Christianity itself. It was the experience that came to be called Easter that propelled the Christian movement into history. This focal point in my religious tradition has captured my attention for many decades. I remember first treating this subject in 1957 in a series of lectures at Kanuga, a conference center in Hendersonville, North Carolina. Those lectures evolved until they were published, in 1980, in a book called *The Easter Moment*. Most authors have a tendency to put aside a subject once they have completed a book and to assume that they have no further significant contributions to make to the subject beyond wishing that they had included this or that point in the original work.

However, for reasons that I cannot always fathom, such an abdication of interest has never been possible for me in regard to the resurrection. Through the years the Easter narratives have continued to demand and to receive my attention in significant ways. Perhaps it could be said that resurrection and the meaning of life are, for me, so deeply intertwined that every experience is finally incorporated into this interest.

In 1983, through a unique friendship I was privileged to develop with Senator Claiborne E. Pell, Democrat of Rhode Island, I became part of an interdisciplinary seminar, held at Georgetown University, on the question of survival after biological death. Through that experience I was forced to look at these issues from beyond the boundaries of the ecclesiastical tradition that had been until that moment my only frame of reference. Those who shared that stage with me did not share my religious context nor even, in several cases, my Western mentality. Rather, I tested my ideas in interaction with such people as physicist Paul Davies, now of the faculty of the University of Adelaide in Australia; Rupert Sheldrake, an English biologist; Anthony Flew, a British philosopher and atheist; Stanlislav Grof, a neurologist; and Sogyal Rinpoche, a Buddhist mystic.

My thoughts on Easter and life after death had to grow to accommodate new angles of vision. Those new angles continued to expand as my widening orbit of travel carried me in ever-broadening ways to parts of the world such as Africa, India, and China. In these places I sought out those who lived in and articulated the faith traditions of their people. While in Kenya I made a study of the early African religious traditions and how they first made their transitions into both Christianity and Islam. From my perspective the transitions were not profound changes but verbal veneers put over the easily recognizable indigenous beliefs. The superstitious elements in this tradition clearly indicated the fears that the people's religious system was called on to meet.

In 1984 I journeyed to south India, where, in the small town of Kottayam, in the state of Kerala, I had the opportunity to engage in a wide-ranging, day-long public dialogue with three Hindu scholars sponsored by the seminary of the Mar Thoma tradition. As each one of us sought to address the critical issues and questions universally raised by human life, this dialogue allowed me to begin identifying common traditions within the various religious systems of the world.

In 1988, traveling in the New Territories of China, I participated in a dialogue with the Reverend Yuen Quing, a Buddhist monk and holy man. He not only expanded my comprehension of another great religious tradition but also opened my eyes to the way in which a Christianity united with Western imperialism was perceived in other parts of the world.

My vision, enlarged and informed by these experiences, compelled me to look again and to look far more deeply at my own faith tradition, but it also demanded that I look through a broader and perhaps even different lens. One person who helped to create that lens for me was Joseph Campbell, the scholar of human mythology who was discovered by American television viewers in the late 1970s and early 1980s. In both his televised interviews with Bill Moyers and *The Power of Myth*, the book that grew out of that series, I was touched by Campbell's ability to see the truth of myths while refusing to literalize the rational explanation of those myths, which found permanent places in religion and liturgy. Campbell enabled me to appreciate such timeless themes as virgin births, incarnations, physical resurrections, and cosmic ascensions, which appear again and again in the religious histories of the world's peoples. Slowly, ever so slowly, but equally ever so surely, a separation began to occur for me between the experience captured for us Christians in the word *Easter* and the interpretation of that experience found in both the Christian Scriptures and the developing Christian traditions, which have borrowed freely, if not always consciously, from the mythology of the ages. When that separation was complete, I had to face the fact that my thinking had moved to a new place and that I had to examine the Easter claim once again from this new perspective. It was a compelling vocational call that I could not put aside.

I still assert with deep conviction that my understanding of Christianity is rooted firmly in the reality of Easter. My faith in Jesus' resurrection, however, does not today demand that I claim a nonmythological literalness for the words I use to talk about that resurrection. Nor do I insist that Easter be understood as an objective supernatural event that occurred inside human history. I do maintain that the effects of that experience called Easter are demonstrably objective. I believe and affirm that Jesus, in the experience called Easter, transcended the limits of human finitude expressed in the ultimate symbol of that finitude—death. I do believe that those of us who are called by this Jesus to live in him and in the Spirit that he made available to us will also transcend that final barrier. Furthermore I believe that what we Christians call heaven is in fact real.

But, having said that, I must also state that I today approach and understand that critical moment in the life of Jesus called Easter and the Christian hope of life after death quite differently from the way I once did. I would describe that difference as both less literal and more real, and both parts of that statement are equally important. I wrote this book to give content to those words and to place my convictions before both the church and society in a way that transcends the sterile debates of the past and offers a new starting point for faith.

Since I first wrote a book on Easter my intellectual and spiritual life has been stretched in some other wonderful directions. I have written *Into the Whirlwind: The Future of the Church,* which called me to walk into new frontiers. I have contributed to and served as editor for a volume called *Consciousness and Survival,* which grew out of the interdisciplinary conference at Georgetown University— a result of my friendship with Senator Pell. I have coauthored a treatment of the Ten Commandments, entitled *Beyond Moralism,* in which ancient ethical rules may be examined in the light of modern circumstances. Most significantly, and beyond my wildest imagination, I have written the three books that together have lifted me as an author onto both a national and international stage. They are *Living in Sin? A Bishop Rethinks Human Sexuality; Rescuing the Bible from Fundamentalism: A Bishop Rethinks the Meaning of Scripture;* and *Born of a Woman: A Bishop Rethinks the Birth of Jesus.*

I have also read deeply in the area of the physical sciences and in the works of those theologians who dare to take seriously in their theological writings the full panoply of contemporary thought—Don Cupitt, Thomas Sheehan, Hans Küng, Rosemary Ruether, Arthur Peacock, David Jenkins, Diogenes Allen, Teilhard de Chardin, and Elisabeth Schüssler-Fiorenza, to name just a few. Beyond that, I have never ceased to make the Bible my primary textbook, with Raymond Brown, Michael Goulder, Edward Schillebeeckx, Phyllis Trible, Jane

Schaberg, and Elaine Pagels, among others, expanding dramatically my knowledge of and excitement for the Bible.

I cannot escape the interior tension created by my dual roles. By vocation I am a bishop; by avocation I seek to be a scholar and an author. For me the combination has generated the richest and most exciting possibilities imaginable. Scholars who are authors have said for years in learned volumes most of the things about which I have written. But their insights have never moved beyond the circles of academia. A bishop, because he or she belongs to the people, is a public self, a symbol of the church's life, its order and unity. As a bishop who offers the insights of the scholars to public awareness, who makes accessible the various speculative theories for public debate, who openly explores areas of ethical concern, and who invites both the church and the world into a dialogue that seeks, and perhaps even demands, a new theological or faith consensus, my vocation has proved to be both feared and welcomed by my audience.

Those whose primary response is fear tend to use the symbols of their religious persuasion as a security system in which to hide from the churning tides of the modern world. When that system is disturbed and the certainty that they assume to be self-evidently true is challenged and perhaps even relativized, they express their anxiety as overt hostility. Literalistic religious convictions, thinly stretched over gaping anxieties and unanswered questions, and in some cases even over unasked questions, exist in their own hidden inner tabernacles. For many people the church has become a port of call that one does not leave lest he or she be caught amid the swirling storms of life. Some of the fearful ones are ordained persons who are unconsciously attempting to build in their ecclesiastical jurisdictions safe havens for the frightened and the insecure, among whom they are surprised to discover they themselves are included. The fearful ones are also numbered among those ecclesiastical professionals who measure success only in terms of institutional unity. These people seem to believe that honest questions should never be raised because they might disturb the peace of mind of many of their members. For them the task of seeking the truth of God has become a secondary goal, and they ignore the fact that both scholarship and integrity are sacrificed by that process.

The ones who, on the other hand, welcome my writing and my theological and ethical speculations are, by and large, drawn from the ranks of those who find themselves alienated from institutional forms of religion but who are still deeply attached to the truth to which religion itself seems to point. My life in the church and, even more important, my life as a bishop, proclaims that there might yet be a place for them inside the structures of the Christian institution. They are the ones put off by forms, by tactics of control, by dogmatic assertions, and by those who dare to draw lines beyond which they seem to believe the love of God cannot move. Such alienated people are unlikely to read the scholars' tomes but they are fascinated by a bishop's ideas, for somehow the bishop belongs to them. If a bishop can think these thoughts and can say or write them publicly, then possibly these thoughts can be more widely entertained. Perhaps even the doors of the church might crack open to beckon someone like them to listen once more to the old, old story. Perhaps that story can be believed once again with passion and integrity by those who have thought of themselves as forever outside the church.

So it is that I find myself hated and feared by some and at the same time a kind of religious folk hero for others. Frankly, I have coveted neither response. My only desire is to walk the path opened for me by my study of the Bible as a Christian who, by the grace of God, has been called to be a bishop. To stand in this special place is a vocation I commend to the next generation of the church's bishops. I am certain that within that body there is already at this moment the one upon whom the mantle of this style of leadership will fall. It is a role that I will be happy to lay aside when this century passes into history and my writing vocation has been completed.

As I have grown older it has increasingly been my desire to be more than a critic of the literalizing religious traditions of the past. I have wanted to state a positive case for a broad religious understanding, and to call people into a living religious future that is rich and engaging.

So quite deliberately in my books *Living in Sin?, Rescuing the Bible from Fundamentalism* and *Born of a Woman,* I focused on the positive themes. What does sexual morality look like when your deepest conviction is that every human being bears God's image? What does the Bible mean when it is freed from debilitating literalism? How can the feminine aspect of God and human life both be celebrated in a dawning new century?

I sought in those volumes to create some space where the church of tomorrow might live, especially since the space occupied by the church of yesterday has proved to be inadequate. That effort continues in this volume. I seek here to articulate the transcendent and eternal meanings that I believe reside in God and inside each of us, and which make the concept of Easter both believable and real. Readers of this book will have to be willing to engage the content of the Bible seriously. A Christian who is either ignorant of the biblical text or unwilling to delve beneath the level of literalism will find it difficult to follow the nuances of my argument as it develops. My readers must be able to see new possibilities, some threatening and others exhilarating, but, above all else, possibilities that open the doors to new truth. I hope that walking through those doors will lead my readers to an ever-deeper commitment to the one we Christians call Lord and Christ. I am convinced that if this Jesus can be for us the doorway into God, as he seems to have been for Peter and others in that critical moment when Easter dawned in human history, then this faith story of ours can live in dramatic new ways in the challenging future of the human enterprise. At least that is my intention in this volume.

I hope to take this intention even further in my next book, which will seek to discover how contemporary Christians can say the historic creeds with integrity and still live in a world shaped by Copernicus, Galileo, Newton, Darwin, Freud, and Einstein. My working title for that book is *A Believer in Exile.* Both key words in that title are important to me. I am a believer in the Christian creeds. I am also in exile, as I believe all thinking Christians are, from the worldview in which those creeds were formed and in which its concepts are easily translatable. Most of us therefore face a difficult choice. We can either literalize the creeds and thereby become irrelevant, or we can abandon our creeds and become non-believers. I hope to offer a better alternative.

When I think of those institutions that made this book possible, two come immediately to mind. They are the Diocese of Newark in the United States and Cambridge University in England. The laity and clergy of the Diocese of Newark have opened door after door to me in my years as their bishop, enabling me to grow in count-less ways. Everything I have published since I entered the episco-pal office in 1976 has lived first as a lecture to the people of the Diocese of Newark. Behind this book, for example, are Lenten lec-tures given in 1992 at St. Peter's Church in Morristown, New Jer-sey, where I developed the three chapters that show how the Jesus of the resurrection was seen in terms of Hebrew images as atoning sacrifice, suffering servant, and Son of man. My thanks go to the Reverend David Hegg, rector, the Reverend Marisa Herrera, assis-tant to the rector, and the Reverend Dr. Charles Rice, priest associ-ate, as well as to the Morris Convocation and its president, the Reverend Phillip Wilson, who cosponsored that event.

There were also the New Dimensions lectures in the fall of 1992, where the themes of this book were once again pursued with an audience of clergy and laypeople. Those lectures were held at St. Peter's Church, Essex Fells, New Jersey, and I wish to thank espe-cially the Reverend Gordon Tremaine, rector, and his congregation, for hosting that event. Next there were the Diocesan Lenten lec-tures of 1993, where I pressed this story further. They were held at St. Paul's Church, Englewood, New Jersey, where the Reverend Kenneth Near is rector, and they were cosponsored by the churches of the East Bergen Convocation, whose president was the Reverend Richard Demarest. Finally, I completed my first public journey through the content of this book in the fall of 1993, in the New Dimension lectures held at Christ Church in Ridgewood, New Jersey. Once again, to the Reverend Margaret Gunness, rector, and the Reverend Mark Lewis, assistant rector, I express my grati-tude.

Beyond these specific events, the Diocese of Newark has always encouraged my vocation as a scholar-bishop dedicated to a teaching ministry. They did this not only with their support and attendance but also by inviting me countless times to add an adult forum hour to my confirmation visitations to our some 130 churches. Furthermore this diocese created for me a sabbatical program that enabled me to take a month each year from 1988 to 1991 to be in residence at an academic center for reading and study. In those four years I spent a month each at Union Theological Seminary in New York City; at Yale Divinity School in New Haven, Connecticut; at Harvard Divinity School in Cambridge, Massachusetts; and at Magdalen College at Oxford University in the United Kingdom. In 1992 the diocese gave me a three-month sabbatical, and Emmanuel College of Cambridge University elected me a Quatercentenary Research Fellow, thus opening to me the time and the resources to write this book. I am particularly grateful to the master at Emmanuel College, Lord St. John of Fawsley; to the lecturer in theology and religious studies at Emmanuel, the Reverend Don Cupitt; to the dean of Emmanuel College, the Reverend Brendon Clover; and to the assistant librarian at the Theological Library in Cambridge, Dr. Peta Dunstan. It was a rich experience for me to take advantage of three wonderful libraries, to have my own study suite, expert counsel as I perused various subjects, and the stimulation of daily meals with the faculty and vigorous interaction with students at the graduate and undergraduate levels. Cambridge University in general and Emmanuel College in particular will forever be among my life's happiest memories.

The person to whom this book is dedicated has been the unsung hero of my writing career for a decade. I could never have been an effective author without her. She has worked with me now on six books and three major revisions of books. She combines patience with competence, sweetness with toughness, dedication with grace. I count it a privilege to know her, to trust her, to love her, and to admire her. Nothing gives me more pleasure than to dedicate this volume to Wanda Hollenbeck. Everyone in the Diocese of Newark is aware of the contribution she has made to our corporate life.

Other members of our staff who greatly enrich my life are my partner in the episcopacy, the Right Reverend Jack M. McKelvey; our chief financial officer and director of our housing programs, John Zinn; our chief administrative officer, Michael Francaviglia;

our communications, program, and personnel officer, Karen Lindley; and the dean of our Cathedral, the Very Reverend Petero Sabune. Working with this wonderful combination of decisive and talented people has always been an expanding experience for me both personally and professionally.

Other people who work in our diocesan office are Cecil Broner, Rupert Cole, Gail Deckenbach, Sulmarie Duncan, Margaret Gat, Gloria Gerrman, Jeffrey Kittross, Robert Lanterman, Carla Lerman, Barbara Lescota, Patricia McGuire, Bradley Moor, the Reverend David Norgard, Eric Nefstead, William Quinlan, Joyce Riley, Lucy Sprague, Elizabeth Stone, and Teresa Wilder. I salute each of them with both my appreciation and my admiration.

Most important and above all, I thank my wife, Christine, who graces my life with so much love that I am constantly being re-created by it. Words cannot adequately convey the depth of my love for her. Suffice it to say that to be married to Christine is the culminating joy of my whole life.

Finally, my special thanks go to the members of our family: to our daughters and sons, Ellen Spong and Gus Epps, Katharine Spong and Jack Catlett, Jaquelin Spong and Todd Hylton, Brian Barney and Rachel Barney; to our grandchildren Shelby Catlett, Jay Catlett, and John Lanier Hylton; to the menagerie of granddogs Flosshilde, Repo, Headstrong Samson, and Axel Rodriguez Beasley; and to our grandcats Nina, Annie, and Big Boy, who invigorate the lives of each of us.

I have been sustained by this wonderful family during the ups and downs of my life with a particular kind of gentle strength. I have loved every role—husband, father, grandfather, stepfather, and pet trainer. Only in the last of these roles do I confess total failure, for let it be noted for the records of history that my granddog Repo (short for Repurchase) not only flunked out of dog obedience school but was actually expelled as a hopeless case.

I also acknowledge with special joy my eighty-seven-year-old mother, Doolie Boyce Griffith Spong, of Charlotte, North Carolina; my mother-in-law, Ina Chase Bridger, of Worthing, Sussex, England; my brother, Will Spong, and his wife, Nancy, of Austin,

Texas; my brother-in-law, Bill Bridger, and his wife, Doris, of Finham, near Coventry, England; and my sister, Betty Spong Marshall, of Charlotte. The greatest gift of grace, I believe, comes in the sustaining love of one's primary family. I have lived as the recipient of such grace.

Part One

Approaching the Resurrection

Chapter 1

The Method Called
Midrash

When I was doing my theological training in the 1950s, the word *midrash* was not heard with any frequency. If employed at all, it referred to a running commentary on the Hebrew Scriptures done by the rabbis throughout history. This commentary was voluminous, and the manuscripts that contained it would fill libraries. Commentaries by the rabbis thought to be the greatest would be particularly noteworthy, we were told, and would be studied in more detail and referred to more frequently by contemporary Jewish teachers in a continuing effort to illumine their sacred sources. Midrash was not presented as a method by which the Bible was written and not, hence, as a method by which the Bible was to be understood. So it was that midrash was deemed not terribly important to the study of the Christian Scriptures.

I am amazed today at this blindness in those who taught me Scripture. I no longer accept the proposition that anyone can understand the Bible, and most especially the New Testament, without understanding the method of midrash.

HAS CHRISTIAN SCHOLARSHIP BEEN ROOTED
IN ANTI-SEMITISM?

When I begin to explore why Christian scholars failed to see the midrash method of the Jewish tradition as the very style in which the Gospels were written, I run headfirst into both the official and the unofficial anti-Semitism that has engulfed the church from the latter years of the first century of the Christian era until this very moment. This anti-Semitism reached its crescendo in the middle of the twentieth century in the Holocaust in Germany, but it found a significant expression in this same period of history in the United States and Great Britain, the leading nations of this so-called Christian West.

These three major Western political powers, Germany, the United States, and Great Britain, were centers of the most important and influential Christian scholarship. These three nations produced the vast majority of the world's theologians and the experts in biblical studies. Unconscious of its Western anti-Semitism, however, Christian scholarship developed with little openness to the primary midrashic outlines of the Christian story or to the basic midrashic content of the Christian Gospels. The original Jewish roots of the Christian tradition were simply not acknowledged. Seldom was it said with any sense of pride that every writer in the New Testament, with the possible exception of Luke, was Jewish. Seldom was the context of the Jewish world or the thinking processes of the Jewish mind given more than a cursory tip of the hat when scholars sought to explicate Christian texts.

When scholars pored over the Christian Scriptures, the language they worked with was Greek, not Hebrew. When they studied the biblical roots of Christian theology, they inevitably looked through the lens of Greek philosophy, which had shaped Christianity's creeds, and primarily through that lens did they begin to illumine the New Testament. Even when they read the Old Testament they almost always used a Greek translation rather than the Hebrew original.

Of course they could not ignore the New Testament's references to Jewish prophecy, thought to be fulfilled in the story of the Jesus of history. But, beginning at least with Polycarp and Justin Martyr in the second century, the typical Christian understanding of this tradition was that the Jewish prophets had simply predicted concrete events in the life of the messiah who was to come, and Jesus had fulfilled these predictions in an almost literal way as a sign of his divine origin. "The Jews," a term spoken with undertones of derision in Christian circles, had failed, so the argument went, to understand their own messiah, and God had consequently created a new Israel, called the Christian church, to take the place of the old Israel, which had been composed only of Jews.

The people of the first covenant, it was asserted, were given their chance, and they had failed. The promise now was to be given to the people of the second covenant. By naming the parts of the Bible the Old Testament and the New Testament, Christians incorporated this prejudice into the very title of the sacred Scriptures. The Bible of the Jews was the Old Testament, now replaced by the Bible of the Christians, which was the New Testament. The twelve tribes of Israel were superseded by the twelve apostles. Jesus had fulfilled all the law and the prophets, and this validated his messianic claim. It was a neat and complete system, and in the triumphal confidence of these conclusions, Christianity began its life as the unchallenged dominant religion of the Western world.

Christianity's rationale for its overt anti-Semitism was to blame the Jews themselves as the cause—even for Christian hostility. It was a classic example of blaming the victim. The Jews had, after all, rejected the Christ. What could a people expect from God (in whose name Christians assumed that they both spoke and acted) when they had rejected God's own Son and their own messiah? The Jews were quoted in the Gospel narratives as even willingly accepting this blame: "His [Jesus'] blood be upon us and upon our children" (Matt. 27:25). These words were destined to echo through the centuries as justification for one wretched deed after another.

In spite of eyes blinded by prejudice, the close connection between Jesus and the Hebrew Scriptures could not be limited only to those texts that obviously referred to the fulfillment in Jesus of prophetic expectations. There were other Gospel stories whose parallels in Hebrew Scripture were too conspicuous to be over-looked. The story of King Herod trying to remove God's promised deliverer by killing all the Jewish male babies in Bethlehem simply had too many echoes of the pharaoh ordering the death of all the Jewish male babies in Egypt in his attempt not only to rid his realm of his "Jewish problem" but also to destroy in his infancy God's di-vinely promised deliverer, Moses.

There was also a connection, too deep in Scripture to be denied, between the Last Supper and the Jewish Passover. Gentile Chris-tians, not fully understanding Jewish worship traditions, blended Passover with Yom Kippur and identified Jesus with both the Paschal Lamb and the sacrificial lamb of the Day of Atonement. Once this was accomplished, both Passover and Yom Kippur could and did disappear from Christian consciousness, and the Eucharist developed its own gentile theological meaning. The only conclu-sion that was consistent was that as Christians had replaced Jews as God's people, so the Eucharist had replaced Passover as the cen-tral liturgy of the people of God, while Yom Kippur, for all practi-cal purposes, was abandoned. It might be argued that the themes of Yom Kippur reemerged later as the themes of the Christian sea-son of Lent, but any Jewish origin would have been stoutly denied.

When Christians read Luke's story of Pentecost in the Book of Acts, it occurs to very few of us that Pentecost was in fact a Jewish festival called Shabu'ot (or Shavu'ot), which Luke used (mistak-enly, I believe) as the context in which to tell the story of the mo-ment when the Christian movement broke out publicly in the holy city of Jerusalem. Luke's account of Pentecost was simply lifted out of its Jewish context, and few recognized that the symbol of fire had a long Jewish history—from the pillar of fire in the wilderness to the fire associated with the prophet Elijah—or that the mighty rush-ing wind that indicated the presence of the Spirit came out of the desert people's concept of a God who was Spirit and out of their understanding of the wind as the breath (Hebrew *ruach*) of God. The disappearance of language barriers in Luke's Pentecost narra-tive did get connected with that ancient story of the tower of Babel, where God was said to have confused the languages of the people to prevent the completion of the tower to heaven (Gen. 11:1ff).

It was primarily the preachers of the day who made these connections. These biblical stories constituted basic, easy-to-remember contrasts. However, these stories were generally interpreted as simply the fulfillment of expectations that had been expressed in the Old Testament. This interpretation served to demonstrate anew the superiority of the new covenant to the old covenant. Little did these early Christian expositors know that they were discovering the method of midrash in the Scriptures of Christian people, all of which were written by Jewish people, with but the one possible exception of Luke, who, though he might have been a Gentile, was also a devotee of synagogue worship and was thereby heavily influenced by Jewish thinking.

CENTURIES OF SIMPLISTIC ANSWERS TO LOGICAL QUESTIONS

The church invested the Christian Scriptures with such literal authority that centuries would pass before some questions were even allowed to be raised. To these questions the most simplistic answers were immediately offered to calm the questioners' anxiety. Were the details of the birth stories historically accurate? Since none of the authors of the Gospels had been in Bethlehem at the time of Jesus' birth, the details of that event had to have been supplied to the Gospel writers by the parents of Jesus, it was said. Indeed Luke was thought to have been given some special access to Mary so that he would know of such details as mangers and swaddling cloths, and that she "kept all these things, pondering them in her heart" (Luke 2:19). Matthew must have had some access to Joseph, it was suggested, for how else would he have known the content of Joseph's dreams? Such simple answers sufficed in an uncritical era.

Since the events of the episode that we call the temptation in the wilderness happened while Jesus was alone, according to the texts (Matthew 4, Luke 4), it was assumed that Jesus himself told someone about these things so that they could be recorded with accuracy. Similarly the content of Jesus' prayer in the Garden of Gethsemane, which he uttered after leaving Peter, James, and John and going "a stone's throw away" (Luke 22:41), was something that Jesus himself must have told the disciples. It was a bit more difficult in this latter episode to determine just when this transmission of the content of Jesus' prayer took place, since upon Jesus' return he found his disciples asleep and he was immediately thereafter betrayed, arrested, tried, convicted, and crucified. It was suggested without embarrassment in that believing and literal world that perhaps the risen Christ was the source of these details.

In a similar manner the Gospels tell us that all of the disciples forsook Jesus and fled when he was arrested, yet we are given in the accounts of the crucifixion intimate details as to what Jesus said, what the crowd said, what the penitent thief said, what the nonpenitent thief said, and what the centurion said. Who recorded all of that conversation? Who transmitted it? We are also told what the soldiers did, what Pilate did, what Herod did, and what Simon of Cyrene did. Did any of these people give transcripts to the Gospel writers?

For most of Christian history no one raised questions about the authenticity of these accounts. Hence no one entertained the possibility that they were quite obviously and simply the products of the Jewish tradition called midrash.

THE LOSS OF MIDRASH TO LITERALISM

What is midrash? It is both a collection of the interpretations of sacred Scripture and a method for the continued expansion of the sacred Scripture. It comes in three forms: Halakah, Haggadah, and Pesiqta. Halakah is an interpretation of the law—the sacred Torah. Haggadah is the interpretation of a story or an event by relating it to another story or event in sacred history. Pesiqta is a whole sermon or an exhortation written midrashically to capture themes of the past to enable them to be perceived as operative in the present. The sermons of Peter and Paul in the Book of Acts, as well as the long speech of Stephen, are examples in the New Testament of Pesiqta.

Midrash is the Jewish way of saying that everything to be venerated in the present must somehow be connected with a sacred moment in the past. It is the ability to rework an ancient theme in a new context. It is the affirmation of a timeless truth found in the faith journey of a people so that this truth can be experienced afresh in every generation. It is the recognition that the truth of God is not bound within the limits of time but that its eternal echoes can be and are heard anew in every generation. It is the means whereby the experience of the present can be affirmed and asserted as true inside the symbols of yesterday.

Midrash occurred again and again in the Hebrew sacred Scriptures as they were compiled over the centuries. Indeed the authority to bring the present into the sacred story was actually claimed by adopting the midrash tradition. The power of God working through Moses was seen in the parting of the waters to allow the Hebrew people to walk into God's promised future beyond the Red Sea. But Moses died, and God's people needed to validate God's continuing presence in Moses' successor, Joshua. That validation was established by retelling the parting of the waters story in the saga of Joshua. This time it was the waters of the Jordan River rather than the Red Sea, but the affirmation of the parting of the waters was equally real. God was still at work among God's people in the time of Joshua, still calling them into God's promised future. The midrash tradition continued when Elijah was also said to have parted the waters of the Jordan River when he exercised his authority as the leader of God's people (2 Kings 2:7, 8). When Elijah died, the story was repeated in the cycle of stories about Elisha (2 Kings 2:14). The ability to part the waters told the Jewish people that Israel's history was one continuous story.

This same midrash tradition sought to tell the story of Jesus, who was believed by his followers to have both fulfilled and expanded the symbols of the Jewish tradition. The Gospel writers had Jesus begin his public career by walking into the waters of the Jordan River and parting, not the waters, but the heavens themselves so that the Spirit of God, which was linked with heaven and water in both Jewish mythology (Gen. 1:7) and in the Gospel tradition (John 7:39), could visibly descend, rest on, and validate Jesus as the new expression of God in the ongoing story of God's people.

The question to ask of this midrash tradition is not, Did it really happen? That is a Western question tied to a Western mind-set that seeks by sensory perception to measure and describe those things defined as objectively real. That Western question sets up a yes-or-no answer, for it either happened or it did not; it was either real or it was not. In the premodern period of Western history it was maintained with great authority that the details of this event of Jesus' baptism were actual, historical details. The heavens in that time of human history were thought to be but a dome over the earth, separating God from the life of the world. God was intensely interested in this earth, however, and from the divine residence would intervene with some frequency in human affairs. Since Jesus was God's Son, a literal validating action that linked heaven and earth was not only comprehensible but also quite normal and expected. No one asked how the sky, which turned out to be not a blue canopy stretched across the heavens but a permeable atmosphere of various chemical components through which someday human beings would fly and ultimately even escape as they journeyed into space, could be split or opened to allow God's Spirit to descend like a dove and light on the newly baptized Jesus. Similarly no one asked what language the heavenly voice used when God pronounced Jesus to be God's Son.

When Copernicus and Galileo managed to recast the shape of the world so that the literal details of this story began to be questioned, the church, which had lost touch with the midrash tradition and had claimed too much by literalizing everything in the first place, fought a slow but inevitable rear-guard retreat. First it drew back from objectivity, then from subjectivity, and finally from reality. This stance resulted in the creation of a new category called symbolic truth, or mythological truth, which meant very little in a world that knew only the objectively real or the unreal. This category therefore had very little power to persuade modern people of anything. The Western mind had already separated the dominant religion of the Western world from the tradition that gave birth to this religion. The only options were to see something as literally true or as an untrue fantasy. Many people still seem to live as if there are no other choices.

In today's world evangelical and fundamentalist elements of the Christian church, Catholic and Protestant, cling to the fading possibility of a literal truth being present in the details of their faith story. Sometimes they cling with the intensity of fanaticism while the unbelieving world of postmodern men and women dismisses most of the content of organized religion as sheer nonsense. The liberal religious establishment, having seen the turf it tried to defend shrink to nonexistence, is barely audible when it seeks to speak about the reality of God or the power of Christ. That is the inevitable result of asking the wrong questions of a tradition that employs midrash to tell its story.

The proper question of the midrash tradition is, What was the experience that led, or even compelled, the compilers of sacred tradition to include this moment, this life, or this event inside the interpretive framework of their sacred past? What was there about Jesus of Nazareth that required the meaning of his life to be interpreted through the stories of Abraham and Isaac, Moses and Passover, Exodus and wilderness, Sinai and promised land, Hannah and Samuel, David and Solomon, Elijah and Elisha, the servant figure and the Son of man, Pentecost and Tabernacles, and a thousand other choices that served to incorporate the life of Jesus into the meaning of God known in the history of the Jewish people? That is the midrash question of which we were ignorant for so long, the question that could not be asked in any substantive way until we developed Jewish eyes and Jewish minds with which to read and understand our own holy gospel.

FROM HIGHER CRITICISM BACK TO MIDRASH

Before turning to that option, however, we had to experience our literal understanding of the Bible as no longer trustworthy. In the reverberations of the knowledge explosion that began with Copernicus and continued through Galileo, Newton, Darwin, Freud, and Einstein, among others, the literal Bible disintegrated. When a literal view of Scripture became no longer tenable, the Bible itself came to be looked at and studied in a new way, albeit still not in a Jewish way.

The task was first to find the concrete, historical realities that underlay the biblical story. This pursuit of truth was called biblical higher criticism. Born first in Germany in the nineteenth century, it produced the liberal Protestant alternative to literalism that was to mark mainline churches as both advocates of this position and re-actors against this position, into our very day. It was to prove not a lasting or satisfying alternative, however, and has generally passed out of existence in the common mind as the contemporary church declines into secularity. It is preserved in the particular enclave of academic Christian scholarship and is thought to be too unfruitful to share with the average pew-sitter, for it raises more questions than the church can adequately answer. So the leaders of the church would protect the simple believers from concepts they were not trained to understand. In this way that ever-widening gap between academic Christians and the average pew-sitter made its first appearance.

Clergy were introduced in their theological training to this new way of reading and understanding the Bible, to these new theories about how the Bible came to be written, and to new ways of inter-preting the tales of the supernatural; but they were encouraged not to use this new knowledge when speaking from the pulpit to their congregations. Far better, they were told, simply to keep on telling the old, old story with only an occasional slightly modern accent.

As this gap widened, however, it spawned tensions within church structures between those who were called liberals and those who were called conservatives. In the Roman Catholic tradi-tion, Pope John XXIII, who occupied the See of Peter from 1958 to 1963, opened that venerable institution to the modern winds of change. Those gales proved so powerful, however, that every pope since has sought to repress the modern spirit in the name of "the unchanging and infallible truth of God mediated through God's divine instrument, the Catholic Church." Creative Roman Catholic scholars, like Teilhard de Chardin, Hans Küng, Charles Curran, Edward Schillebeeckx, Matthew Fox, Leonardo Boff, Rosemary Ruether, Elisabeth Schüssler-Fiorenza, Joseph Fitzmyer, Raymond Brown, and David Tracy, just to name some, found themselves re-moved, silenced, harassed, or compromised in some way. This treatment was based on the gap between the conclusions of their research and the authoritative statements of their faith system.

Protestant Christianity was no better served by this new schol-arship. This community of faith soon split into mainline churches and evangelical or fundamentalist churches. The message of the mainline churches came to stand for less and less theologically because the ground disappeared from under it. The evangelical or fundamentalist churches refused even to raise the modern questions, choosing rather defiantly to affirm the literal conclusions to which they were driven by their presuppositions. In time they came to view the modern world and knowledge itself as their enemy. The literalists threw themselves into this struggle to save their rigid version of God's truth with the passion of soldiers at the Battle of Armageddon.

A generation of people perceptive enough to fear that if they listened to competent research they might find themselves faithless, first gave to these reactionary elements, in both its Catholic and Protestant forms, a momentary boost in statistics of all sorts. The messageless liberal traditions, meanwhile, experienced a steady decline. But this trend was not to last, for one can artificially resuscitate the dead corpse of yesterday's religious conclusions only so many times. Eventually they will not hold air. That is the moment in which either a new starting place is found or the final chapter in the history of a long, but now exhausted, faith story is written.

Inspired by John A. T. Robinson, an Anglican bishop and Cambridge New Testament scholar, whose 1963 book *Honest to God*, had launched a theological revolution, I began my first tentative ventures into seeking that new starting point where the integrity of my religious affirmations could remain intact. I did not know at the time that someday I also would stand in the office of bishop, as one of John Robinson's spiritual heirs, to give this movement a mighty shove into the twenty-first century.

Knowing so little about midrash that I never used the word, I nevertheless began to explore my faith story by looking at the Jewish tradition that had given it birth. My first major book, *This Hebrew Lord*, first published in 1974, was the result of my intuitive feeling that only in this context was the meaning of Christianity going to unfold for me in a new way. I explored the images of Elijah, Moses, and the suffering servant, which played such important roles in the way Jesus was understood in the Gospels. My book touched something deep in me and apparently in those who read it. It was not that the book became a major best-seller so much as that it refused to die. Year after year it sold about a thousand copies, enough to keep it on the backlist. Very few religious books have a published life of twenty years. I revised that book in 1986 and again in 1992. But more important, I worked off it in new directions.

What was the relationship, I wondered, of the Books of Chronicles to the Books of Kings in the Hebrew Scriptures? They both covered much the same history and material, but they did it with very different and sometimes contradictory detail. The possibility that Chronicles was an example of Jewish midrash on the Book of Kings had not yet dawned in me.

I began to see midrash in the Gospels without quite realizing what it was. Was Jesus' feeding of the five thousand in the wilderness related to the story of God's providing bread for Israel through Moses while they wandered in the wilderness? Was the story of Jesus' ascension but the retelling of the story of Elijah's ascension? Was the story of Jesus' raising of the widow's son at Nain related to Elijah's raising of the widow's son in the Book of Kings (1 Kings 17:17ff)? Did Jesus preach the Sermon on the Mount, or was it an attempt to portray Jesus as the new Moses? After all, much of what constitutes Matthew's Sermon on the Mount is in Luke taught by Jesus on the plains of Galilee.

Then my attention was captured by the crucial question of the historical reality of those narratives that surround Jesus' entry into and departure from human life. What was the level of history that could be located in these Gospel narratives? As I first studied the birth narratives, it was clear that no major scholar of any persuasion took them literally. I read with wide-eyed fascination works by Raymond Brown, Joseph Fitzmyer, and Hermann Hendrickx, Roman Catholics all. The birth narratives consumed me, and far from this study destroying their meaning, the Christmas stories grew in power and significance for me. I still, however, did not have the vocabulary of midrash to open the final door into my study of the New Testament.

The word was finally supplied to me by Jeffrey John, New Testament scholar and dean at Magdalen College, Oxford. He simply said, "The birth narratives are quite obviously Haggadic midrash."[1] Haggadic midrash indeed! The door opened, and for me the birth narratives would never be the same. And ultimately neither would the Bible. I was now ready to enter fully the mind of those wonderful Jewish people who would provide me with a new starting place in my study of the Gospels—a starting place that had long been obscured by Christian prejudice.

Midrash is described in *The Jewish Encyclopedia* as "the attempt to penetrate into the spirit of the text, to examine the text from all sides, to derive interpretations not immediately obvious, to illumine the future by appealing to the past."[2] With this wondrous new tool I began to see that the location of Jesus' birth in Bethlehem was shaped not by a fact of history but by an expectation, planted in the Jewish tradition by the prophet Micah, of a Davidic savior who was to hail from Bethlehem, like King David of old. The wise men came out of the sixtieth chapter of Isaiah, where kings were said to come to the brightness of God's rising. They came on camels and brought gold and frankincense. This developing narrative was then combined with elements from the visit of the queen of Sheba, who brought spices (myrrh?) to honor the king of the Jews (Solomon) (1 Kings 10:1–13), and the story of Balaam, a seer from the East who saw the star of David rise and came to bless the king of the Jews (Numbers 22–24). The guiding star had appeared earlier in the midrashic tradition in the stories of the birth of Abraham, Isaac, and even of Moses. The song of Mary was patterned on the song of Hannah. The story of Zechariah and Elizabeth, childless in their old age, was a retelling of the story of Abraham and Sarah, childless in their old age. The vision of Zechariah in the temple speaking with Gabriel was a retelling of the story of Daniel in the temple speaking with Gabriel.

Jesus' flight to Egypt was a reliving of Israel's history. Jesus' father, Joseph, was created out of the whole cloth of the ancient patriarch to whom God also spoke in dreams, and who also served God's promise by fleeing to Egypt. Luke's shepherds came out of Bethlehem, home of the shepherd king, David, and the tower-of-the-flocks story in Micah 2–5. The story of the young Jesus in the temple was patterned after Samuel and his experience in the temple.

Haggadic midrash! You do not ask of midrash, Did it happen? You ask, What was there about Jesus that caused him to be incorporated into the midrash tradition?[3]

Jeffrey John also introduced me to the work of Michael Goulder, who expanded my vision of midrash beyond the birth narratives and into the Gospels as a whole. Goulder presented Matthew to me as a midrashic expansion of Mark.[4] Then Goulder argued that Luke was but a midrashic reworking of both Mark and Matthew in a new context.[5] Sometime later Walter Righter, my colleague in the episcopacy, introduced me to the work of Dale Miller, an isolated, entrepreneurial religion professor at Drake, a midwestern American university, who had developed midrash in some fascinating and sometimes, I believe, overly enthusiastic ways. Nonetheless, his work had the effect of breaking open some biblical texts in startling directions for me.[6]

With this newfound tool and toy, I went back to the great commentaries that had so enriched my life in years past and reread them in the light of my understanding of midrash. Names like Westcott, Hort, Lightfoot, Hoskins, Dodd, Brown, Nineham, Childs, Fuller, Albright, and even Bultmann shone with a new luster.

For me midrash was a way in which transcendent human experiences could be processed and incorporated in an ever-developing faith story that knew no closed chapters and claimed no frozen infallibility. It was a way to think mythologically about dimensions of reality for which the language of time and space were simply not appropriate. It was an attempt to gather rational words and concepts around those moments when eternity broke into the consciousness of men and women living in time. The appropriate language for talking about the meaning of Jesus was the language of midrash, because that was the language of the living Jewish sacred tradition. In this way I came to believe that in order to enter the meaning of the Gospels one had to enter the tradition of midrash.

Because the center of the Jewish world, Jerusalem, was destroyed in 70 C.E. by the Roman army, the Christian story born in that Jewish context soon thereafter began to float exclusively in a gentile sea. Before the end of the first century all the Gospels had been written, each deeply shaped by the midrash tradition. But beginning in the second century, these Gospels were interpreted almost exclusively by non-Jewish people who knew nothing of midrash. Early on, one gentile Christian leader, Marcion, even tried to cut the Hebrew Scriptures out of the Christian Bible entirely. Officially the church resisted this idea, but unofficially it adopted a Marcionite attitude that relegated the first covenant to a place of near-obscurity. Certainly that was not the literature to which one was taught to turn to illumine the Christian story, unless the Old Testament was seen to predict that which was realized in the New Testament.

So it was that Christianity entered its gentile exile, denied its Jewish roots, ignored its Jewish womb, and, in the process, distorted its own deepest insights. In time this resulted in extravagant literal claims for the historicity of what were in fact midrashic retellings of ancient themes in new moments of history. When the explosion of scientific knowledge in the sixteenth century began its relentless march to our day, it left in its path the debris of a literalized religious system. In rapid succession the literalness of the story of creation, the supernatural context of most of the biblical drama and the words of miracle and magic disintegrated. The religious arena was left with the sterile choice of trying to maintain credibility inside a literalizing tradition or giving up all belief in any religious system that assumes a sense of transcendence.

The last stages of the liberal fight to defend the Bible's honor were desperate. First the miraculous elements of the Old Testament were questioned. Then even some of the moral elements of that part of our heritage were challenged. Already gone were the dietary laws, polygamous marriages, and such cultic practices as circumcision and Sabbath Day observance. Next questioned was the appropriateness of an intervening deity who could rejoice in the drowning of those Egyptians unable to escape the returning waters of the Red Sea. When this same God was portrayed as stopping the sun in the sky to allow more daylight for Joshua to continue to annihilate the Amorites (Josh. 10:12ff), that God was seen to be not just unbelievable but actually immoral.

Then slowly and with fear the challenge began to turn to the New Testament. First the miraculous elements of the Gospels were interpreted in terms of natural phenomena that occurred with divinely inspired coincidence. Thus the generosity of the lad who gave up his lunch of five loaves and two fish to feed the hungry crowd inspired the others to bring out their hidden food supplies, and that's how the five thousand were actually fed. It was a feeble attempt to make believable once again what had become unbelievable. The story of Jesus walking on water was said to be a misunderstanding of the Greek preposition, which could mean "on" or "alongside of." The psychological power of Jesus that could give courage to the psychologically crippled was said to be the means by which New Testament healing events were achieved. So it went, until there was not much supernatural substance left to the faith story of Christians. New knowledge drove people to liberal solutions that finally were so flat that they satisfied no one. In turn this approach also sparked the reactions of a threatened and militant evangelical fundamentalism, which decided to assert its version of truth by screaming it defiantly into the ears of the modern world in churches, over radio, and on television. Their message was sent much in the style of the old country preacher who marked on the edge of his sermon notes, "Argument weak; yell like hell!"

When critical scholarship began to suggest that the birth narratives of Jesus could not be understood literally, conservative religious circles became anxious and angry. Many believers considered the birth stories the great line of defense against the erosion of the divinity of Jesus. But how long could the educated folk of the twentieth century continue to be literal about such things as a conception that occurred for a couple when both were well beyond menopause, the visit of the angel Gabriel, a pregnancy without a male agent, an angelic choir that sang in the sky, a star that roamed through the heavens, shepherds that had no trouble finding a baby in a city crowded with people called to a special census, and a king named Herod who would rely on three men he had never met before to bring him an intelligence report about a pretender to his throne who was said to have been born just six miles away? If the divinity of Jesus was attached to the literal details of the birth tradition, then it was a doomed concept. When the birth narratives were separated from literalism, however, the divinity of Christ did not die; indeed it was enhanced.

Similarly, when the attention of biblical scholarship was turned to the narratives of Jesus' resurrection, the anxiety of believers intensified a hundredfold. If there was no literal resurrection, then, it was feared, the whole faith system called Christianity would collapse. As one prelate observed when this battle broke into the British media in the early 1990s, the resurrection is so central to the Christian faith that without it there is no Christianity.[7] But the real question of what constituted "the resurrection" was left unanswered.

Does Christianity depend on a grave that was empty, on a body that has been resuscitated, on angels that descend in earthquakes and roll massive stones away from the mouth of a tomb, or on a figure who can disappear into thin air after the breaking of bread? Does it not bother the literal believer that the details in the Gospels are as contradictory about what happened after Jesus' death as they are about what happened at the time of his birth? Is this not the last frontier? Since the liberals have, by and large, vacated the arena by rejecting the miraculous elements and thus reducing Easter to a pale subjectivity, the only battle to be waged is between hysterical literalism confronting an unbelieving modern mentality that says miracles cannot and do not happen. In that battle literalism will vanish, but the winning reality will be an enormous emptiness, a vacuum at the heart of human life. Surely there must be a better alternative.

I believe that there can be a new scenario for a Christian future. It requires neither a literal victory nor a liberal revival. It cannot begin, however, with a literal biblical text that describes either the birth of the transcendent reality found in Jesus of Nazareth or in the rebirth of that transcendent reality in the moment called resurrection. I recognize the presence of midrash not only in the birth narratives but now more especially in the resurrection narratives.

Beyond that I have finally begun to see the midrashic element of timelessness in the entire corpus of the canonical Gospels. When transcendence is experienced in history, time is frequently the casualty. Because something dramatic occurred in the life of Jesus when he went up to Jerusalem on one occasion, every time we read in the Bible about another journey to Jerusalem we are being given another dimension of that same revelatory moment. Time collapses and every journey in Scripture reflects the memory of that defining revelatory journey. In that way the Bible is not a chronology. It is layer after layer of timelessness. Every reference to Jesus going up to Jerusalem, every mention of three days, every place where bread is taken, blessed, broken, and given, every account of the rebuilding of the temple—these are but midrashic traditions that seek to communicate the meaning of Easter. Affirmations of Jesus, reached after a generation of processing the experience of Jesus, also are read back into history to be Jesus' very words. Surely Jesus never called himself the bread of life or the source of "living water," but when people came to know the transcendent meaning of his life as that which fed their deepest human hunger and satisfied their deepest thirst for God, it became appropriate for believers to place these words upon the lips of Jesus himself. There is a timelessness about the midrashic approach to the Bible. The approach to truth through midrash thus became my doorway into this study of the moment of Easter.

Midrash means that when one enters the Scriptures, one must abandon linear time. This also means one must abandon literal certainty in favor of a living, open-ended faith tradition, where God is seen as past, present, and future, all at once as if the three were inseparable. It was Jaroslav Pelikan who helped me see that tradition is the living faith of dead people to which we must add our chapter while we have the gift of life. But traditionalism is the dead faith of living people who fear that if any jot or tittle changes, the whole enterprise will crumble.[8] Traditions, however, always change. That is the meaning of midrash.

The Gospels of Mark, Matthew, Luke, and John are products of the tradition of midrash far more than most Christians have ever imagined. The question we must address to the Gospels is not, Is this detail literally true? Rather we must ask, What happened in that life, or in that moment or detail, that forced the tradition of midrash to embrace and interpret it in that way at that time?

I would not want to be literal about most of the content of the Gospel tradition that purports to describe the dawn of Easter. But I do not want to deny for a moment the reality that drove those early Christian writers to describe what happened in the way that they did. They employed the language and the style of midrash, for that was the only language and style they had at their disposal to capture the intensity of the realm of God being experienced in the human arena. In some ways midrash was mythology wedded to religious traditions and universal themes. Above all it was language that could not be literalized being employed to process an experience that could not be denied. It was designed to portray a truth that could not be captured in the vocabulary of time and space but that employed this vocabulary in the hope that the meaning would be understood, because there was no other vocabulary at their disposal.

At its very core the story of Easter has nothing to do with angelic announcements or empty tombs. It has nothing to do with time periods, whether three days, forty days, or fifty days. It has nothing to do with resuscitated bodies that appear and disappear or that finally exit this world in a heavenly ascension. Those are but the human, midrashic vehicles employed to carry the transcendent meaning of Easter by those who must speak of the unspeakable and describe the indescribable because the power of the event was undeniably real.

I seek now to enter the experience of Easter. I believe that this experience is both real and true but that the details that describe it cannot be literalized. My journey will carry me first deep into the biblical texts, but then ultimately it must carry me beyond those texts into a dimension of timelessness in which a presence I call God ultimately resides. My access to that presence is through a life referred to in history as Jesus of Nazareth but called, by faith and in the language of midrash and mythology, the Christ of God. I believe that this Jesus journeyed through time into timelessness and through finitude into infinity. Beyond that, I believe that those of us who have found our lives inside his life can also make that journey and can know this Christ as our way, our truth, and our life, through whom we too can approach the presence of God, and in that presence we also may know the timelessness of eternity. Yes, I even mean to state that I believe that this life I have in this Christ is beyond the power of death to extinguish or even to diminish.

I offer those in my world, who are willing, a journey that many of my fearful religious brothers and sisters, hanging so desperately to the last vestige of their literal affirmations, are too afraid to take.

Because they are not willing to risk anything, they will be forced to surrender everything. The best way to lose all is to cling with desperation to that which cannot possibly be sustained literally. Literalistic Christians will learn that a God or a faith system that has to be defended daily is finally no god or faith system at all. They will learn that any god who can be killed ought to be killed. Ultimately they will discover that all their claims to represent the historical, traditional, or biblical truth of Christianity cannot stop the advance of knowledge that will render every historic claim for a literal religious system questionable at best, null and void at worst.

To those who know that this literal system is filled with terminal leaks and who are ready to risk some new possibilities, I open another door. I offer them another point of entry, called by the names of midrash, mythology, and symbol. My witness is that by journeying through this new door, by risking the loss of yesterday's certainties that are already in such decline, my readers might discover, as I have, a path that leads in new and powerful ways to the confession of an ancient faith tradition:

"Jesus is Lord!"
"Come Lord Jesus!"
"Death cannot contain him!"
"We have seen the Lord!"

I invite my reading audience to lay aside religious security blankets and come with me into this adventure that will, in part, be like a detective story as we explore the midrash tradition that leads us into the heart of Easter.

Chapter 2

The Impact of Easter—
A Place to Begin

In the first half of the first century of this common era, an enormous burst of energy erupted in the Mediterranean world. It had its roots in the religion of the Jews, but somehow it transcended those roots sufficiently to appeal to Gentiles on the one side even while incurring Jewish hostility on the other side.

The force of this movement's explosion was to prove so great that all of Western history would be shaped by it. Before four centuries were over, this force had exerted its influence over every political structure in the Mediterranean. In time, all of Western art, architecture, and music would develop as the servants of this movement. Poets, kings, nobles, and peasants bowed before this vibrant power. Even today, almost two thousand years later, stories about this movement can be found on the front pages of such venerable publications as the *London Times* and the *Wall Street Journal*.[1] Competing views as to the truth of this movement, even at the dawn of the twenty-first century, still set Catholic against Protestant in a deadly duel in a place like Ireland, while in nations shaped by this movement politicians to this day pay it lip service with regularity.

What accounts for such a phenomenon? This question can, of course, be answered on many levels. But what I am asking at this moment is the question of the movement's origin. What happened that gave Christianity its birth? In what reality lies its powerful beginning?

CHANGED LIVES—THE SUPREME EVIDENCE

The dawn of Christianity was connected with the life of one known as Jesus of Nazareth. But there are almost no objective records anywhere that can verify a single fact of his life. There are only things called Christian Scriptures, written by passionate believers, through which we can gain access to this man's life. Are these sources accurate? At the very least it must be said that none of these Christian writings has either the quality or the advantage of being an eyewitness account. The earliest of these writings are called epistles. Basically they are letters written by disciples of this Jesus, some dated within as few as twenty years after the end of this Jesus' life, but others as late as one hundred years after his life.

These letters, whether early or late, however, tell us almost nothing of the details of this man's life. From them one would learn only something of the basic claims his followers made for him: This Jesus had been crucified, but God raised him to life. Those who wrote these letters claimed that they had seen this risen life. Names associated with these letters were Paul, Peter, John, James, and Jude. Later studies reveal the probability that Paul was the only actual author of the letters that bear various disciples' names and that even some of those that bear Paul's name are not authentic.[2] Only those called Romans, 1 and 2 Corinthians, Galatians, 1 and 2 Thessalonians, Philemon, and Philippians remain without dispute today as Paul's genuine writings. Paul never claimed in any of his letters that he knew the Jesus who lived in history.

Books about the life of this Jesus did not appear before the seventh decade of the common era at the earliest, and many would dispute that date, maintaining that it was the eighth decade before any Gospel appeared. The range for dating these books, called Gospels, would be 65 C.E. to 100 C.E. Many details recorded about this Jesus in these books are contradictory. There are serious conflicts about dates, names, places, and events. The Gospels make claims to contain the words Jesus spoke. However, none is written in the language he spoke. They are all written in Greek. Jesus seems to have spoken Aramaic.

These books do, however, share one affirmation: Jesus was put to death. His life seemed to end in tragedy, and yet out of somewhere came the conviction that in some way this death had been overcome and Jesus had been raised to life anew. The power of this movement was connected to the reality of that claim.

With various kinds of words and images the Gospel narratives tried to describe that moment. It was not easy. How could something thought to be the act of God be talked about in the secular language of men and women? How could something thought to be of heavenly origin be described in earthly terms? How could that which was believed to be timeless find expression inside time? Yet how could one ignore this eruption of power? How could one deny that something gave birth to this movement that was destined to change the face of human history?

So we look at the writings we have and seek to understand what they point to, what they reveal, what truth they convey. They all point to one consistent conclusion. Something happened! Whatever that something was, it had power! Incredible power!

These writings tell us of an incipient Jesus movement that gathered around this man during the course of his earthly life. It is hard to determine what the hopes and expectations of his followers were, but they certainly did not seem to expect his death. These narratives feature very unflattering portraits of the followers of this Jesus. They seem to have responded to the crisis of Jesus' arrest with weak and cowardly behavior. Rumors abounded about the betrayal coming from his inner circle, though even the details of that betrayal are confused and contradictory.

There was a unanimous assertion, however, that the first deputy of this movement, a man named Simon, acquitted himself very poorly. To save his own life Simon denied even knowing this Jesus.

This unflattering material about Simon had about it the ring of authenticity. One must wonder how it was that this man who lied about Jesus, who denied even knowing him, could have acquired the nickname Cephas, or Petras (the Rock). But that was what occurred, the story asserts. There is some external evidence that Simon, now called Peter, actually rallied this movement and brought it back into existence after Jesus had been executed.

What brought about the change in Simon? How does a coward turn into a leader? How does a man who denied ever knowing this Jesus get changed into being the one who proclaimed this Jesus as the ultimate meaning of his life? That is the data that cries out for some explanation. What happened to Simon to turn him around? What stands between the frightened, denying Simon at Jesus' arrest and execution and the courageous, fearless Simon who became the leader of the Christian movement? The change in this man was measurable and objective even if the cause of this change is debated. The change was a part of that first-century explosion of power that cannot be denied by any student of history.

Simon was not the only one whose life was changed. The record of the Christian movement presents us with a picture of Jesus' disciples forsaking him when he was arrested and fleeing for their lives. One reference suggests that they were scattered, each to his own home. The experience of abandonment in this crisis was so acute that the image of a flock of sheep running crazily in every direction when their shepherd was slain was employed with regularity until those very words found a place in the Christian story.

Yet before many months had passed these same unheroic people who had acted so weakly that they inspired no confidence in anyone were back in Jerusalem acting quite differently. They were now courageous, assured, and heroic. They were now willing to bear abuse, be imprisoned, beaten, and even put to death with not the slightest hesitancy. They were now people possessed. Some new reality had touched them, embraced them, and transformed them. People who forsook their leader and fled in panic when he was executed were now transformed into courageous folk willing to die for the one they proclaimed. Where did this transformation come from? What caused it? What explains it? What was the moment when flight stopped and risky public witness began? What occurred to turn fear into strength?

The burst of enormous energy that erupted out of the Jewish world in the early years of the first century had to do with the reconstitution of this cowardly, fleeing, fearful group of men. The sacred writings of this community, which viewed these men with reverence, not only as leaders of their movement but as direct links to the one they called Lord, would hardly create negative material about them out of nothing. This negative image of cowardly, less-than-admirable behavior was the kind of memory that would be suppressed if possible. It was not suppressed because it was not possible to suppress it. It was truth bound into the consciousness of those who acted this way. It was powerful evidence that change had occurred in their lives—radical, reorienting change that cried out for an explanation. Something happened! What was it?

THE MOVEMENT'S JEWISH CONTEXT

Other data are still lurking in this enigmatic crevice that defined the before and after of the moment of erupting energy that came to be called Christianity. This movement had its inception inside Judaism. That fact lends incredible weight to the necessity of explaining dramatic changes. What would cause a people shaped by Abraham and Moses to turn in such a new direction?

The worship of the Jewish people was best epitomized by their liturgical chant known as the Shema: "Hear, O Israel, the Lord, the Lord your God is one Lord and you shall worship the Lord your God with your heart, mind, soul, and strength and him only shall you serve." At the heart of Jewish worship was the oneness of God, a God who could not be compromised by another loyalty.

In the Jewish code of conduct that we today call the Ten Commandments, the first law proclaimed that God was one. God could not be imaged by any human creation, and, for the Jews, no human authority could stand competitively before this God's authority. When the Roman overlords sought to impose the religion of Caesar on the conquered provinces of the empire, the symbol chosen to represent submission was the requirement that the heads of the conquered people must bow at the name of Caesar. Among the people of the empire's provinces, the Jews alone refused to submit. They would bow their heads to no one save to their holy God. Threats, beatings, imprisonments, and even executions brought no bending of the Jewish will. God was the one, the only sovereign to whom their heads would bow. Finally Rome relented and no longer tried to enforce this practice in Judea. This refusal to bow to Caesar earned the Jews their reputation as a "stiff-necked people." It was a label that they wore with pride.

All of the disciples of this Jesus were Jewish. The official twelve were Jewish males. The oneness of God was among the highest values of their lives, and acting out that value in worship was the highest religious virtue of their tradition. Yet some dramatic experience inspired these Jewish people to believe that a man named Jesus of Nazareth was somehow inside the very definition of God. All the ins and outs of explaining just how this could be took years, even centuries, before it was finally defined, although the experience itself was seemingly instantaneous. Jesus appears to have been quickly turned into an object of worship, which for Jews meant that Jesus was incorporated into the meaning of God. That was a shocking new experience.

Within three decades of Jesus' death, a well-trained and disciplined Jewish leader named Saul of Tarsus wrote to his followers in Philippi, commending to them this Jesus by suggesting that "at the name of Jesus every knee should bow, in heaven and on earth and under the earth, and every tongue confess that Jesus Christ is Lord, to the glory of God the Father" (Phil. 2:10–11). That was a stunning, revolutionary statement for any Jewish man to make about any human life. It was even more incredible to have been stated by a man who prided himself on his devotion to the traditions of his fathers, one who claimed that he was "as to righteousness under the law blameless" (Phil. 3:6). For this to be said about a person who had been publicly executed made it all the more incredible. This Pauline attitude was rooted in the earliest, most primitive Christian practices. Something created a revolution in the consciousness of Jewish people in the first century that meant that those among them who shared in that experience could no longer think of God without including Jesus in their very definition of the word, and they could no longer think of a man named Jesus without his being a part of the meaning of God.

Had these people come out of a pluralistic tradition of polytheism it would not have been nearly so dramatic or powerful a moment of redefinition. But these were Jews, nurtured in the understanding of God as one, holy and indivisible. It was inside that religious frame of reference that this revolutionary concept was born. Something happened! Something forced this change, something that now demands both explanation and definition. Its effects were awesome. Its marks had an objective presence to them.

There was yet another change begun in that first-century eruption of energy that demands an explanation. It is the tradition known as the first day of the week. It is called the Christian Sunday, sometimes the Christian Sabbath, sometimes simply the Lord's day.

Next to the belief in God's oneness, the second most defining Jewish custom was the observance of the Sabbath Day. From the Babylonian exile, in the early years of the seventh century B.C.E., the practice of keeping Sabbath became part of the public definition of what it meant to be a Jew. This custom served to keep Jewish people separate and distinct. It also created havoc in Babylonian work projects, for every seventh day the Jewish members of the crew refused to work, meaning that work either limped along or ceased altogether if a full complement of "hands" was required. During the exile the priestly writers strove to codify the Sabbath Day restriction so that no Jewish man or woman was in doubt as to what constituted a proper observance of this holy day. The Sabbath was deep in the hearts and emotions of Jewish people.

Yet the movement from within the first-century Jewish world that came to be called Christianity focused its story on the day after the Sabbath, the first day of the week. Exactly how that day came to be designated, or chosen, as the inaugurating moment of the Christian experience will be the subject of a later discussion. Right now it is essential only to state that the explosion of power was so enormous that in time the day on which it was thought to have occurred was established even in Jewish Christian circles as the Lord's day. Within thirty years it was referred to by the Jewish Paul as the day on which the people gathered for worship (1 Cor. 16:2). Paul's reference is so casual as to assume that this gathering was the common practice of the Christians and had been so for a long time. But those of us who understand the depth of emotion that people link to holy days and sacred traditions are astonished beyond measure, first, that a new holy day came into being at all and, second, that in a relatively short time it had eclipsed the Sabbath tradition in importance even among those Jewish people who called Jesus Lord.

TRACKING THE VERBAL CLUES

These are the signs that can be identified, examined, measured, and codified—signs pointing to a dramatic moment in the first-century Jewish world when something unprecedented and unexpected erupted in human history. In the power of that experience cowards were turned into heroes, a scattered and demoralized group was reconstituted with new purpose and self-possessed drive, the deepest and most sacred definition of God was expanded instantaneously to incorporate the reality of the new experience, and a new holy day was created that challenged the ancient holy tradition of the Sabbath and that today, two thousand years later, organizes the week for Christians, non-Christians, and post-Christians in the Western world.

We observe this evidence that appears to be real, objective, and discernible within history. We try to follow this evidence to its source, but can get only so close. After that we hit a wall, an impenetrable barrier beyond which we cannot roam.

In some ways those of us who seek the moment of Christianity's origin are like physicists seeking the moment of the birth of the universe. We can return only so close to the moment of creation. We start with the given. Both the Christian church and the visible universe exist. Then we drive both back in time. The ever-expanding universe can be driven mathematically by computers, in a process that reverses time and space, to a moment billions of years ago when the incredible density, beyond the power of the imagination to contemplate, exploded in a burst of energy known very flippantly as "the big bang." Physicists today are able to enter that bang to within minuscule fractions of that first second of the explosion. But their inability to penetrate that final momentary fragment of a second at the dawn of creation continues to keep the element of mystery around that which is not now otherwise considered quite so mysterious.

In a similar fashion, but working with different measures of time, I will seek to probe the ultimate moment that gave birth to the Christian story. Like the physicist, I must begin with the given and examine the artifacts. I will look for clues that will enable me to move toward the origins. The physicists use the language of mathematics and rightly claim for their language a higher level of objectivity. I am forced to use the language of words: frail, symbolic, highly subjective words that are capable of being distorted either in the giving or in the receiving of every transmission. But words are all we human beings have to process any powerful experience for transmission from one life to another. If one does not participate directly in a particular experience, one can receive and enter that experience only through the medium of words. One person's words will open that experience to another person, and, through the impregnation of idea and consciousness by memory and form, the transmission of human content is achieved.

Before we can claim to have captured some objectively real moment with our words, we need to cleanse and scrape those words, examine their history, cross-reference their nuances, and be carried on their backs as closely as we can get to the reality those words seek to describe. Finally we are forced to admit that words cannot capture truth. They can only point to truth. We will seek to go to the limits of verbal rationality; there we can stare into the mystery we cannot comprehend and decide what our response to that moment will be.

A journey into, through, and beyond words awaits us as we seek to illumine a reality that words cannot finally describe. We

31

journey in time seeking a moment that is quite clearly timeless. We look in history for a reality that breaks in on us from outside history. We probe the thought processes of those who appear to have been the primary receivers of what they believed to be an ultimate revelation. It all leads us toward Easter and toward that experience that forced people to say that this Jesus, who was crucified, was now their living Lord.

It will be a disturbing journey to those who literalize the symbols of their religious story. I hope it also will be disturbing to those who long ago dismissed as nonsense the literalized version of this tradition. My hope is to call traditional believer and hostile critic alike to new possibilities that challenge the conclusions both sides have made about the moment in which Christianity was born in human history.

Chapter 3

The Vehicle of Words—
An Unsteady Ship

We begin our investigation of the resurrection in a modest way and at a modest place.

When a person experiences a transforming reality, one filled with integrity and incapable of being denied, that experience has to be processed. The processing involves first recalling, reliving, and re-creating the context, and varied attempts, usually in a liturgical or ceremonial format, to revisit the moment. In time this experience is described, understood, and interpreted within the context of the life of the processing one or the processing community. In this way the transforming reality passes into the history of the people, tribe, nation, and civilization of which this person is a member. The words used to explain the ecstatic moment are drawn from the language spoken by those people. That language grew in and was shaped by the members of that tribe. It embraces the presuppositions alive in their bit of history. It reflects the worldview and the level of knowledge available to that generation living in that place. It also contains the values and the prejudices by which that tribe lives.

Once this experience is put into words, with all of the limitations that this implies, the words themselves take on a life of their own. No word is objective; hence no word ever passes from the lips of one person into the hearing of another without being changed in meaning. The hearing person always interprets that message internally, and in that process the message is subjected to the limitations of another person's history, experience, knowledge, likes and dislikes, and vocabulary. Identical words, therefore, are never passed on with identical meaning to two different persons, even in the same tribe. When the words pass to a person outside the tribe, and therefore outside the shared meanings of a common history, the changes in meaning are even more dramatic.

The word *God* is a powerful illustration of this reality. In ancient Egypt God was associated with and primarily defined by the presence of the sun and the Nile River. Among the Sumerians, a people who lived in a mountainous region, God was identified with that high ground, and the clouds that seemed to hover at the mountaintop were thought to be the visible sign of God's presence.

Among the primitive Canaanite people, who had developed a settled agrarian life, God was seen in the fertility cycle of nature's birth, death, and rebirth. The offspring lamb and the planted seed that grew were the primary content of the religious tradition of their gods Asherah and Baal.

For the Hebrew people, whose national life was shaped by the wilderness, God was thought of after the analogy of the fierce desert wind. In the desert the wind would arise suddenly, prove incapable of being bound, possess enormous power, and then mysteriously disappear. This wind was called the *ruach*. It was understood by the Hebrew people to be nothing less than the breath of God. This God was known and worshiped by a tribe of people who, at that time, had no fixed land to call their own and who lived under the vastness of a limitless sky that ultimately pointed them toward ideas of universality. Because of this definition of God, the Hebrews' settled life in Canaan, when it finally came, did not bring a permanent temple for this God for at least three hundred years. The symbolic dwelling place of this God was a tabernacle that moved with the people and had no fixed location. Only when the people of Israel moved into their new identity as a nation with known boundaries during the reign of Solomon (960–920

B.C.E.) did they proceed to build a temple. Now that they were settled, their God had to become settled also. The Jerusalem temple then became both possible and desirable and was, in fact, erected.

When these tribes interacted, whether in war, trade, or slavery, their particular ideas of the divine were shared. So time after time the words by which one people defined God were reshaped in and through the hearing of another people whose history, and therefore whose definitions, was different. Tribal identity grew out of tribal history, which was but the arena of common learned definitions. Every nation had a word for God, and when that word was translated from one tribe into the word for God in another tribe, one cannot assume that the same content was also translated.

Words are never neutral or objective. Therefore words can never be used as if they themselves were the truth of the experience that one is trying to relate. Words are never the truth. They are only the medium of the truth, the means of communication used by one person to convey to another the experiences that have defined and given meaning to the one speaking. Words become the vehicles by which experiences are shared. Words point to reality; they do not capture reality. So it is that no words employed by anyone at any time can be objective, infallible, inerrant, or strictly literal. To apprehend them as such is to destroy, distort, bind, and violate the content of the experience that those words seek to communicate.

These linguistic facts present serious problems and challenges to every institutional religious system in every age. Every religious system has historically built and maintained its authority on the claim that its tradition was different and somehow spoke objectively for a God who was perceived to be both eternal and unchanging. When employed in religious history, this argument has proved to be both powerful and wondrously circular. Its component parts include, first, the claim that the God acknowledged in a particular religious tradition is the only true God and, thus, that all other gods are false. It asserts, second, that this true God has been made known in a direct way to a particular faith community by divine revelation, the veracity of which can be challenged no more than God can be challenged. Finally, since this religious tradition is portrayed as the sole recipient of the divine revelation, and since its leaders are the primary interpreters of this God, they alone can relate to the people the truth they have received. The circle is complete, and these designated religious leaders now make the claim that they speak with the infallible voice of God and that this voice brooks no challenge and will entertain no debate.

To buttress these circular arguments, some historical process is frequently built in to authenticate the leaders' claims to power. It might be said, for example, that at the originating point in this religious faith story God had spoken directly to the founder of this tradition and had given the founder exclusive authorization to set up the religious system itself and to provide a means by which the authority that God had conveyed to the founder could be passed on to successive generations. A hierarchy of authority was thereby established, guaranteeing that only the leaders and their designated successors could be the guardians of this eternal and changeless truth.

Vestiges of this ancient process can be seen today in the Western Christian tradition in such claims as the infallibility of the papacy and the inerrancy of Scripture, with the caveat added that only those who are in the line of authority can interpret the Scriptures properly. It is also seen in the claims that certain people or church institutions possess something called apostolic succession, and that such authorities have the right to impose "orthodoxy" on the interpretations of the historic creeds. Understanding this mind-set helps us begin to understand why religious systems attempt to defuse internal and external challenges by leveling charges of heresy or false teaching.

Excommunication, religious trials, execution, and religious wars are all part of the arsenal that has been used to defend the claims of institutional religious power throughout history. Well did Sigmund Freud suggest that such behavior revealed not conviction but the hysteria of fear and unbelief that has marked the world's religious traditions.[1] Such powerful lines of defense are not erected if one has confidence in the truth by which one claims to live. These fortifications, built to avert challenges to faith, would not be necessary unless belief itself was fragile and weak, unless the believers were convinced that they could not endure the anxiety present in this world without this belief, and unless they convinced themselves that they were possessed by this absolute certainty. Such certainty, however, has never in fact been a religious reality. It has only been a religious illusion. It has always been in the overextension of religious claims that the weakness of institutional religious systems is primarily revealed.

THE CERTAINTY OF EXPERIENCE

What is real, however, is that behind our religious systems, our holy words, our power claims, and even behind our fears lies an experience that transforms, deepens, and calls us into what Paul Tillich has called "the new being."[2] It is that experience which demands of us an openness, a probing, questioning mind, a capacity to process willingly every new bit of data, and, most significant of all, a yearning to be led into what the Jesus of the Fourth Gospel called "the abundant life" (John 10:10).

Religion, if it is to live for me and for my generation, must not be based on a system of propositional, creedal statements framed in a limited context of time and space. Religion must be a doorway into the transcendence of an expanded vision. It must point us to a truth deeper, far deeper, than even the truths of our religious system. Religion cannot be static, unchanging, or imposed.

Above all, words must be recognized as symbolic pointers to truth, not objective containers of truth. So the first thing to note about words is that they are inevitably subjective and cannot ever be otherwise. Second, words that gather around religious experiences quickly become mythological. This must be understood before we begin to examine the narratives of the resurrection and their sometimes excessive claims.

This Easter moment broke upon the stage of human history in a particular place and at a particular time, yet it was an event of which the secular world took no notice. It was not covered by the media of its day, not only because press, radio, and television did not exist, but because this movement at its inception was not deemed to have been inaugurated by an external event of history. It was merely an experience that transformed those who shared in it, opening up the possibility, which in fact did occur, that through these changed people history itself would be transformed. They affirmed that reality, and yet the subjective side of that experience was never suppressed. They even proclaimed the subjectivity in the way their sacred writings, which came to be called Scriptures, talked about Easter.

One biblical narrative even went so far as to state overtly that this experience of Jesus alive was not so objective that he was seen by just anyone or by everyone. Jesus was visible after his death, this text stated, only to those who were especially prepared, whose eyes had been spiritually opened, and whose lives had been spiritually fed (Acts 10:34ff). How can the standards of objectivity be applied to a description of that kind of truth? In time, probably to keep questions from being asked, more and more objective claims were made for this moment. For our purposes, the important thing to note is that none of the literalized claims were capable of obliterating finally this original nonobjective, yet profoundly moving, indescribable experience called resurrection.

Easter for the disciples, and indeed for the first generation of Christians, seemed to hover on that borderline between the divine and the human, the finite and the infinite, the objectively real and the transcendentally unreal. Somehow this moment was something beyond history, but it always made its meaning felt inside history. It was both something that happened at a particular time and something that was always happening. To say it differently, the essence of this event had about it much of the nature of a timeless myth. When this reality was put into words, it slipped almost immediately into literalizing tendencies and then into mythological symbols.

Transforming moments or life-changing experiences that by definition touch the deepest wells of the human psyche are always and inevitably captured by the eternal and therefore by the mythological themes of human life. The tale of an exodus that leads to the founding of a new nation, the search for paradise or the Holy Grail, the mythic hero or heroine who goes into the realm of the unknown and returns to tell of it, the miraculous birth of such a hero or heroine that presages his or her larger-than-life destiny, and even the translation of such figures from earth and heaven—this is the very stuff of mythology. It is primarily in terms of these constant and ever-present human themes that the sacred source we call the Bible tells us about the Christian Lord who was identified with the historical life known as Jesus of Nazareth. Yet when Rudolf Bultmann coined the word *demythologize* as a way to approach the Christian story, and when Albert Schweitzer finally concluded his search for the historical Jesus with the assertion that the Jesus of history could never be found,[3] those who did not understand the world in which religious vocabulary is formed sent up howls of protest. Every faith story is by nature enshrouded in mythic elements. Were it not so, that faith story would long ago have ceased to be repeated.

Religious traditions are strange combinations of subjective descriptions of actual events plus mythological interpretations of those events. It is only when an actual event enters into and is carried by a mythological interpretation that the event is finally remembered at all. Whatever it was that resided in that moment when Christianity was born had to have been caught up in a mythological framework almost at once or it would have perished. Legends, symbols, and myths gathered around the moment, as they do whenever time and eternity appear to intersect.

Joseph Campbell, the great American student of mythology, observed that most people have no difficulty seeing the mythological elements in a religious system other than their own. The problem, he suggested, comes when looking at one's own traditions. Most of us are too close to our own faith to see clearly, and too invested in the meaning of that faith to have any objectivity about the beliefs that finally undergird our life. The suggestion that key elements of our faith tradition have been caught up in and are interpreted by the mythological patterns of the ages disturbs some people, even while it promises new insights for others. A senior fellow at Emmanuel College, Cambridge, told me that he thought mythology could not be in one's own religion. "Once you see your own religion as myth, it dies," he asserted. Not so, I countered. Your religion does not really live until you allow it to enter, touch, and illumine the great mythological themes of the ages.[4] To enter into such mythology does not compromise any truth except literal truth. Only when literal truth is challenged are we able to float in the profound and limitless sea of ultimate truth. I assume that when I explore Easter I will have to explore mythologies, legends, symbols. I must also continue to assert that they are mythologies, legends, and symbols that are connected to a moment that I believe is real.

THE TELLING OF A HERO'S STORY AND
THE PREMODERN PERSPECTIVE

With this thought in mind, we must start our search for the truth of Easter by recognizing the presence of mythological narratives in the Christian story. They were designed to capture the meaning of both the origin and the destiny of Jesus of Nazareth, who was cast as the mythic hero. The dominant myth of his origin was expressed in the story of the virgin birth—a theme that has been repeated countless times in almost every religious system, from Zoroaster to Romulus and Remus. The ultimate destiny of this Jesus was portrayed in the mythological account of his return to God in a cosmic ascension, another theme that is quite popular in many religious traditions. Buddha and Osiris come immediately to mind in this context.

Between the narratives of the virgin birth and the cosmic ascension there was the story of a life lived in history upon whom the Christian religious tradition rests. But even the part of the story that purports to be history is fragile by our contemporary standards. It was, as I have already suggested, a narrative richly shaped and embellished with themes from the Jewish past that were interpretative, not literal. Ancient stories were retold in Jewish circles as a way of authenticating Jesus' life and incorporating it into that ancient heritage.

To the tradition of midrash we have to add not only the subjectivity of all words but also the dimension of mythology. Recapturing truth from the ancient world is not nearly so easy as simple people like to imagine. Nor do the difficulties stop here. When we get to the words used by people two thousand years ago to process the reality they called Easter, when we journey beyond midrash, subjectivity, and mythology, we must confront one remaining barrier to understanding what makes literalization impossible and objectivity an illusion.

First-century people wrote with certain presuppositions that were then universally assumed to be true. With the march of knowledge and science, however, those assumptions have been abandoned and are regarded today as relics from a world of premodern ignorance. In that period of human history, miracle and magic were assumed by the general population to be both normal and commonplace. This planet Earth was not thought of as a planet at all but as a flat space at the very center of the created order. A blue canopy called the sky was believed to separate the earth, the realm of the human, from heaven, the realm of the divine. Their cosmology was based on their earth-bound observations. God lived beyond that blue canopy, they assumed, watching over the earth, employing the stars as peepholes through which, even in the dark, divine eyes could see and judge human behavior. Not infrequently it was assumed that this God from beyond that sky would intervene in human history to perform a miracle, heal a sickness, win a battle, call a prophet, or establish rules for human conduct. For this God to come down to earth to sojourn among humans was neither so commonplace as to be mundane nor so unusual as to be unimaginable. Certainly this divine invasion and the subsequent return to heaven was not ruled out as a major or unthinkable achievement.

It was in this kind of world and inside this interpretive framework that the life of Jesus was lived. But people at the dawn of the twenty-first century cannot possibly accept this frame of reference. The question is, Can the truth embedded in that story, interpreted in that ancient context, escape those limitations and find a way to live in our generation?

EYEWITNESS EXPERIENCES AND THE FILTER OF WORDS

So we must journey beyond midrash, subjectivity, mythology, and premodern assumptions before we can turn our attention to the fragile vehicle we call words, which were used to capture the moment we call resurrection. Even after making that journey, we are not allowed to rest secure. We must still seek to understand why the earlier details of the life of this Jesus came to be written in the first place.

When the claim of resurrection was made for the crucified one, the sometimes excited, sometimes incredulous hearers wanted to know "Who was this Jesus?" To that question the disciples began to offer answers. He was a Galilean, a man from Nazareth. He was a teacher, and we remember things he said and stories he told. He was a healer, and we saw people restored to health by his touch. He was a free man who honored the sacred Torah but who did not make an idol of it. He set aside the Torah in the face of human need because no human being was made for the Sabbath (or the law); the Sabbath (and the rest of the law) was in fact made for human beings.

It was only as these stories were told by the disciples that the shape of Jesus' life began to emerge out of their memories. The ultimate authority in this developing tradition was that of the eyewitness. Those who had been with the Lord during the days of his life were the honored ones in the movement. They were the historical link, the teachers, the keepers of the memory, the correctors of the tradition. Whenever there was a dispute over what Jesus had said or done, the word of the eyewitnesses was final.

It was in this way that the Jesus tradition came out of a private experience and into public memory. It lived in public memory, being shaped and formed, expanded and contracted, heightened and forgotten, as always occurs in oral transmission, for some thirty-five to seventy years before becoming set and bound in written form. If that were not complicated enough, one other, and final, transition occurred to those words.

The tradition passed into another language. The historical life of Jesus was lived in the land of the Jews. Aramaic was the version of the Hebrew language that Jesus and his disciples spoke. The story of Jesus was told first in this original language, but the story did not move far before it confronted a Greek-speaking world and required translation. No translation of an event, concept, or experience from one language to another can be made without distortion. It matters not how quickly the translation occurs or how dedicated and skilled the translator is. There are no absolutely accurate translations, and no absolutely identical meanings given to words of different languages.

So we trace the process and begin to embrace our fragile hold on objective reality present in the words we use. First, there was the experience that the disciples had with the life of this Jesus, focused as it was in the last week of his life and culminating as it did in whatever Easter was. Second, this experience was interpreted by words. They were originally Jewish words, carrying a Jewish mind-set and a Jewish frame of reference. These words entered the world of universal myths as the realm of the divine was incorporated into the realm of the human. These were also first-century words, bound by the level of knowledge available to first-century people and thus reflecting concepts no longer believed two thousand years later.

Transcending the Jewish origin of this faith story, the narrative then entered the Mediterranean world, was translated into the Greek language, and began to be shaped and distorted by the prejudices, presuppositions, history, knowledge, and mythology of the Greek world. Still later it passed first into Latin and then into the tribal languages of the nation-states that emerged in the Western world. This religious system survived the period of persecution by the Roman Empire, enjoyed a period of time as the world's ultimate authority, entered transition, and endured challenge in the period of history known as the Renaissance, which was marked by the demise of universal authority, the rise of protestantism, nation-states, democracy, and the middle class. It witnessed the emergence of scientific discoveries and modern technologies. At every stage the meaning of the words this story used and the concepts by which it defined itself were changed.

Keep in mind that by the time these words of the Bible come to us, there has been a translation from Greek to English, a third new language into which the story has been set. The Christ we seek was born in and originally interpreted by a premodern Jewish mentality. Doctrines, creeds, and orthodoxy were established in a premodern Greek world, redefined in the Renaissance, and reincarnated in national churches at the beginning of the modern period. Now, at the dawn of the twenty-first century, we find ourselves seeking words from a postmodern world that will still make contact with the subterranean truth that we believe flows deep in the recesses of the Christian story and that will continue to carry the eternal myth into the hearts of postmodern men and women. To find that truth and to speak it is our task as we proclaim the reality of Easter and the meaning of resurrection in our day.

Something happened. That something had dramatic power. That power changed lives. Those affected by that power processed it with words so that they could tell others what had happened to them. In time, out of their memory, they re-created the story of the one whose life lay at the heart of their experience. That re-creation was achieved by utilizing the tradition of midrash, legend, and mythology. Their story floated through history, being translated into new languages and redefined by new concepts.

We must now take those original words and examine, probe, and research them, seeking clues within them, demythologizing them, and journeying on their wings. Through them we may finally come to gaze at the truth, the power, the experience they sought originally to define. Ultimately it is the wordless experience beyond every verbal form that we seek. But we can travel there only on the limited vehicle of words.

Aware of the pitfalls of our not-always-trustworthy vessel of human words, we set sail to explore the heart of the Christian story, the exploding power experience we call the resurrection.

Part Two

Examining the
Biblical Texts

Chapter 4

The Witness of Paul

"Have I not seen Jesus our Lord?" (1 Cor. 9:1). These words contain the most overt first-person statement about the founding moment of the Christian faith in all of the Christian sacred writings. It is uttered by a man named Paul as part of an argument against those Christians who discounted both Paul's ministry and his message. It was written sometime near the midpoint of the sixth decade of the Christian movement, which would place the writing within twenty-five or thirty years of the final events in the life of Jesus of Nazareth. Such a straightforward, first-person claim for seeing the risen Lord is stated nowhere else in Scripture.

This is all the more fascinating for there is no hint anywhere that Paul ever actually knew the earthly Jesus of Nazareth. What Paul knew of the Jesus of history he had learned through others. He tells us in this same epistle that he [Paul] "received from the Lord" the account of the night of betrayal when Jesus was inaugurating the common meal (1 Cor. 11:23ff). Paul also asserts in this same letter that he received from others the crucial formula that stands at the heart of the Christian story. It is written as if it has already been standardized and made part of a creedal or liturgical statement: "that Christ died for our sins in accordance with the scriptures, that he was buried, that he was raised on the third day in accordance with the scriptures, and that he appeared to Cephas, then to the twelve. Then he appeared to more than five hundred brethren at one time, most of whom are still alive, though some have fallen asleep. Then he appeared to James, then to all the apostles. Last of all, as to one untimely born, he appeared also to me" (1 Cor. 15:3–8). This is the Bible's first narrative of the resurrection. We note that it includes few details.

THE TRADITION PAUL KNEW

The first thing we need to force into our minds is that when Paul wrote these words, there were no such things as written Gospels. It would be ten to fifteen years before the first Gospel, Mark, would be written, twenty-five to thirty years before Matthew, thirty to thirty-five years before Luke, and thirty-five to forty years before John. This means that the accounts of Jesus' resurrection so familiar to us, as told by these Gospel writers, were by and large unknown to Paul and to Paul's readers. We have, through the years, tended to read Paul in the light of the Gospel stories and to blur significantly Paul's meanings in that process. Let me raise that reality to consciousness by making some observations.

Paul's resurrection account begins with the assertion that Jesus "died for our sins." In these words, future concepts such as ransom, vicarious suffering, and substitutionary atonement find their point of entry into the Christian story. In time, each of these concepts would be developed fully. The ransom idea came to involve a payment made by Jesus in some cases to the righteousness of God and in others to the devil who ruled the world. It would prove to be a crude but powerful image.

Jesus as the vicarious one would become a dominant definition in the Christian tradition, leaning especially, as we shall see later, on passages from 2 Isaiah.

Jesus as the substitute who was punished on my behalf would enjoy center stage in Christian history until the sadomasochistic elements of those theories were raised to consciousness.

The embryonic seeds for each of these understandings of Jesus are found, however, in Paul's primitive phrase that Jesus "died for our sins." That was his gift, out of his Jewish world, to the theological enterprise.

Next Paul says that "he was buried." It was a simple, straightforward statement. There is no legend or embroidery around this stark fact. Paul knew nothing of the traditions that would later develop around the figure of Joseph of Arimathea or Nicodemus or of the women who took spices to the tomb. Paul was concerned only to assert that the death of this Jesus was real and that his fate was the common fate of dead people in Jewish society. He was buried.

Next comes the Pauline assertion that these things occurred "according to the scriptures." "According to the scriptures" means that Paul, like all first-century learned Jewish men, was taught that the way to understand the present was to look for interpretive clues in the Hebrew sacred story of the past. This was the only way to guarantee that the God at work today is the same God who has been present in the past. This midrash process forced Jesus' followers to search the Scriptures in their attempt to understand his life, his death, and his resurrection. Such a search proved enormously rewarding, for these biblical references were easily located. The Psalms were filled with such phrases as "the Lord says to my lord: 'sit at my right hand'" (Ps. 110:1); "I shall not die, but I shall live, and recount the deeds of the Lord. The Lord has chastened me sorely, but he has not given me over to death" (Ps. 118:17, 18); "Therefore my heart is glad, and my soul rejoices; my body also dwells secure. For thou dost not give me up to Sheol, or let thy godly one see the Pit. Thou dost show me the path of life; in thy presence there is fullness of joy, in thy right hand are pleasures for evermore" (Ps. 16:9–11). Paul knew these Psalms well, and he and other first-generation Christians found the death and resurrection of Jesus prefigured in them and in many other places in the Hebrew Scriptures.

"The third day" was already in the Pauline formula. It, too, was a concept with deep history and significant meaning, to which full attention will be given in chapter 17. Suffice it to say now that this phrase appears to have little to do with chronological time but much to do with what the Jews thought of as eschatological or apocalyptic time.

Perhaps the most important thing to note in this Pauline passage is that in his formula the power of resurrection resided with God. God was the initiator, the actor in the drama of Jesus' life. Jesus was the recipient, the one acted upon. Paul never used anything but the passive verb to discuss the Easter event and he used that form thirty-seven times. For Paul, Jesus was raised by God. Jesus did not rise. It is a simple distinction to make, but it has overwhelmingly important consequences.

FROM THE GRAVE TO GOD'S RIGHT HAND

Our eyes have been shaped for so long by the Gospels that even when we are reading Paul's words, Gospel concepts dramatically distort our understanding of what Paul actually wrote. There is no sense at all in Paul of a physical resurrection of Jesus back into the life of this world. God did not, for this apostle, raise Jesus from the grave back to life on this earth. Rather, for Paul, God raised Jesus from death into God's presence; from the grave to God's right hand. Christ, for Paul, was the firstfruits of the final resurrection that would occur at the end of the age. It was not a "flesh and blood" body fit to inhabit this earth. It was rather a "spiritual body" designed for life in the kingdom of God. That is a vast difference. "Flesh and blood cannot inherit the kingdom of God," Paul asserted, "nor does the perishable inherit the imperishable" (1 Cor. 15:50). I do not know how Paul could have been any more specific.

Paul was not describing the resuscitation of a deceased body that would have to go through some process at some point to be removed once again from this earth. "The death he died he died to sin, once for all, but the life he lives he lives to God" (Rom. 6:10). Jesus lives in God! Jesus was resurrected from the grave to heaven, from death to God's eternal life. Paul's words must be heard apart from the distortions of the later Gospels. Paul placed his own exclamation point on this understanding of the Easter moment when he wrote, "Christ being raised from the dead will never die again; death no longer has dominion over him" (Rom. 6:9). Paul exhorted his readers who have "been raised with Christ" to "seek the things that are above where Christ is, seated at the right hand of God" (Col. 3:1).

We must keep in mind that Paul knew nothing of an event called the ascension that was separate or different from Jesus' resurrection. Paul's writings contain no hint of the two-stage process that would develop later, where resurrection brought Jesus from the grave back to life and ascension then took Jesus from earth to heaven. Paul's proclamation was that God had raised Jesus into God's very life. That was Easter for Paul. For Paul there were no empty tombs, no disappearance from the grave of the physical body, no physical resurrection, no physical appearances of a Christ who would eat fish, offer his wounds for inspection, or rise physically into the sky after an appropriate length of time. None of these ideas can be found in reading Paul. For Paul the body of Jesus who died was perishable, weak, physical. The Jesus who was raised was clothed by the raising God with a body fit for God's kingdom. It was imperishable, glorified, and spiritual.

We need to hear this clearly so as to counter the fear so rampant among literalizing Christians that without a physical body there is no Easter. Paul was the earliest author in what we now call the New Testament, and in his writings there was no resurrection of a physical body. Indeed Paul specifically denied that claim. Yet who would dare to suggest that for Paul the life of the risen Christ was not real? Who would argue that Paul's understanding of the Easter moment was weak, watered down, or inadequate to create a living faith? Who would venture to claim that there is in Paul an understanding of the living Christ insufficient to create new life, new being, victorious hope?

Did not Paul assert, the literalizers counter, that this risen Christ had appeared to certain witnesses? Indeed he did. But I would argue that if Paul's words are read apart from the distorting images of the Gospels, these witnesses were the recipients of revelatory visions of the living Christ exalted at God's right hand. Paul gave us the earliest official church chronicle of those who, like himself, stood ready to bear witness that the Lord lived, that the Lord had made himself visible to them, and that they had seen the Lord. Paul's list is fascinating in several ways. He asserted the primacy of Cephas (Peter) and somehow suggested that the vision went from Peter to the disciples. We shall examine this claim in more detail later, but here in the earliest New Testament account, we note that it is asserted.

Then Paul went on to refer to an appearance by Jesus to five hundred brethren at once, adding his comment that "most are still alive, though some have fallen asleep." Who were the five hundred brethren? What happened to this tradition? It was not picked up and described in any recognizable form in any of the later Gospels. There have been attempts to identify Luke's story of Pentecost with this Pauline reference, but no consensus has been reached.[1] It is possible that there was a common link between this note of an appearance to five hundred and Pentecost, though a considerable journey must be made before an event that has a risen body form can be identified with one that has a Holy Spirit form. This development is explored from another angle in chapter 7, which focuses on Luke's understanding of resurrection. It is enough now to acknowledge that Paul's reference to Jesus' appearance to five hundred people at once is found nowhere in the Gospel tradition.

The same is true of Paul's reference to James. This was surely the James identified in Gal. 1:19 as "the brother of the Lord," though there was no record in the Christian writings of any role of discipleship during Jesus' earthly life for anyone identified as a brother of Jesus, nor any appearance to James of the risen Lord, save for this single reference. The fact remains that James, the brother of Jesus, was a leader of the Christian church who exercised great authority (Gal. 2:1–10, 12; Acts 15:13; Acts 21:18). So the authority exercised demands some kind of explanation. Paul thus listed James as one who had seen Jesus.

Who are "the apostles"? Is this a repetitive reference to the twelve disciples? Is it a larger body? Is it a different group? Reginald Fuller argues that "James and all the apostles" must be understood to be parallel to "Cephas and the twelve" and represents a later appearance tradition connected with the church's mission-inaugurating function as it moved out of Aramaic-speaking Palestine into Greek-speaking Jewish communities in Phoenicia, Cyprus, and Antioch.[2] The first appearances were church-founding, and the second appearances were mission-inaugurating. The "twelve" were the "pillars"[3] and the "apostles" were the missionaries.

Then Paul inserted himself into the resurrection tradition. The essential thing to note about Paul's understanding of the appearance to him is that it was identical with every other appearance on his list. That is, it was not a physical, historical encounter but a revelatory manifestation of the living Christ from heaven, or from what the Jewish apocalyptic tradition called the eschatological future. That was a synonym for the heavenly kingdom of God, which would come at the end of time, when the eternal reign of God would begin. This was part of the same vision that included the New Jerusalem that was much more fully developed almost a half-century later in the Book of Revelation.

A VISION OF THE ULTIMATELY REAL

If there is still some question about what Paul meant by "the appearances of the risen Christ," it should finally be answered by looking at Paul's other claims to have seen the Lord. A reference in the Epistle to the Galatians is believed to be even earlier—some say as much as seven years earlier—than the First Epistle to the Corinthians. Here Paul said: "He who had set me apart before I was born, and had called me through his grace, *was pleased to reveal his Son to me,* in order that I might preach him among the Gentiles" (Gal. 1:15–16a).

Once more we must be reminded that Paul never knew the earthly Jesus. The God who "was pleased to reveal his Son to me" revealed the risen Christ from heaven. This was not a physical body recalled from the grave. The word for "reveal" in this text is *ōphthē,* the same word used in the Greek Septuagint translation of the Hebrew Scriptures to describe the appearances of God (theophanies) or angels of God (angelophanies). The Septuagint uses *ōphthē* to describe a theophany to Abraham: "Then the Lord appeared [*ōphthē*] to Abram, and said, 'To your descendants I will give this land'" (Gen. 12:7). What was the nature of a theophany? Was it really "physical"? What was the means of hearing God's voice speak? Was it audible to any ear? Was it capable of being recorded or objectified?

Ōphthē is also used in the Book of Exodus: "And the angel of the Lord appeared to him [Moses] in a flame of fire out of the midst of a bush" (Exod. 3:2). Knowing that this vision was put into writing perhaps three hundred years afterward, would anyone be willing to argue that Moses objectively saw the physical presence of a supernatural being at this particular moment in his life? Slightly later in the text of Exodus we read: "And God said to Moses, 'I am the Lord. I appeared to Abraham, to Isaac, and to Jacob, as God Almighty [El Shaddai], but by my name [Yahweh] I did not make myself known to them'" (Exod. 6:2–3). Once more "appeared" is an English translation of the Hebrew word, for which the Greek *ōphthē* was deemed adequate.

Ōphthē means to have one's eyes opened to see dimensions beyond the physical. It means to have a revelatory encounter with the holy. It relates to the nature of visions, but not so much subjective hallucinations as seeing into that which is ultimately real, into God or God's inbreaking future.

Luke used this same word when he had the disciples say Jesus "has appeared to Simon" (Luke 24:34). He used it again when Ananias went to see Saul of Tarsus after his Damascus road experience: "'Brother Saul, the Lord Jesus who appeared to you on the road by which you came, has sent me that you may regain your sight and be filled with the Holy Spirit'" (Acts 9:17). Luke used the same word in his version of Paul's sermon describing the original resurrection moment: "But God raised him from the dead; and for many days he appeared to those who came up with him from Galilee to Jerusalem, who are now his witnesses to the people" (Acts 13:30–31). Luke employed the word again in Paul's speech before Agrippa as Paul quoted the risen Christ: "'But rise and stand upon your feet; for I have appeared to you for this purpose, to appoint you to serve and to bear witness to the things in which you have seen me and to those in which I will appear to you'" (Acts 26:16). When Luke told the story of Paul's conversion (Acts 26:16), he said that those with him saw "no one." We shall return to the word *ōphthē* later in this volume. It will prove to be a powerful and provocative clue to the meaning of Easter.

The story of the Jesus' resurrection in this earliest written part of the New Testament reaches far beyond the contending voices that want to literalize the symbols that have been attached to this moment. It is certainly legitimate to say, as one archbishop has, that "belief in the resurrection is not an appendage to the Christian faith. It is the Christian faith."[4] But it is quite illegitimate, based on the biblical text itself, for anyone to say what another archbishop was quoted as saying: "I believe that those dead bones of Jesus got up and walked out of that tomb."[5] The first statement is the essential mark of the Christian story. The latter statement is a gross literalization made by those in fundamentalist or evangelical traditions who have not adequately searched the depths of the biblical text they claim to be championing and defending.

In closing this chapter I invite readers to listen to Paul apart from the later tradition of the Gospels. He is saying something quite different from what we have usually assumed he was saying:

> For they themselves report concerning us what a welcome we had among you, and how you turned to God from idols, to serve a living and true God, *and to wait for his Son from heaven whom he raised from the dead, Jesus* who delivers us from the wrath to come. (1 Thess. 1:9–10)

> Paul, a servant of Jesus Christ, called to be an apostle, set apart for the gospel of God . . . , the gospel concerning his Son, who was descended from David according to the flesh, and *designated Son of God in power according to the Spirit of holiness by his resurrection from the dead, Jesus Christ our Lord*, through whom we have received grace and apostleship. (Rom. 1:1–5)

And being found in human form he [Jesus] humbled himself and became obedient unto death, even death on a cross. Therefore God has highly exalted him and bestowed on him the name which is above every name, that at the name of Jesus every knee should bow, in heaven and on earth and under the earth, and every tongue confess that Jesus Christ is Lord, to the glory of God the Father. (Phil. 2:8–11)

For Paul, Jesus was the one exalted into God's realm, vindicated by God's action, and raised from death to God's right hand. Only later in Christian history, as we shall see, do legends of tombs that were empty, resuscitated bodies that were real, and ascensions that were cosmic appear in the Christian tradition.

Much had occurred to the Easter tradition before Paul wrote, as I shall try to demonstrate later. But what we need to embrace now is that much more occurred to the Easter tradition after Paul, and that enhanced tradition has in fact blinded us to much that Paul was saying. In our quest to determine as best we can what really occurred when Easter broke into human consciousness, there is no doubt that Paul is a crucial witness. Paul said that his "seeing of the risen Christ" was different from the others in no way except that his "seeing" was last. "He appeared to me" last of all. He made himself visible from heaven to me. There was no sense of an empty tomb for Paul. The seed that is planted—that is, the body—dies. God gives it a new body—a spiritual body—when God raises the dead to God's presence.

Chapter 5

Mark: The Kerygma Is Joined to the Sepulcher

Some fifteen years after Paul wrote 1 Corinthians and perhaps as long as twenty years after he wrote his letter to the Galatians, the first Gospel, known (in Greek) as *Kata Marcon*, made its debut. In those fifteen to twenty years, the Christian tradition surrounding that moment we call Easter had continued to be passed by word of mouth. Some have suggested that outlines of the passion narratives developed a liturgical use, and therefore a set form, earlier than that, and there is reason to think that this may have been so. However, we can discern between Paul and Mark the continuing development of the tradition and the enhancement of the details of the Easter story.

Mark was the first author to attach the passion narratives in written form to the story of the life of Jesus of Nazareth. When we read Paul, we find almost no biographical details about the life of the Jesus of history. Few people seemed to care about this in Paul's time. Paul was specifically not interested, he said, in the knowledge of Jesus from a human point of view (Col. 5:16). One reason for his lack of interest surely lay in the sense among primitive Christians that they lived at the end of history, that the dawn of God's eschatological kingdom was about to occur. What mattered was that Jesus had been exalted to heaven, from whence he would come again as the inaugurator of that new kingdom. But, as the years passed and the New Jerusalem did not descend out of the heavens, questions began to be asked not just about that postponement but also about the life of Jesus. By the time Mark wrote, those questions demanded answers, and part of Mark's motive for writing was to address such concerns as who Jesus was, whence his power came, the reasons for his crucifixion, and what constituted the basis of the claim that God had raised him from the dead. It is fair to say that the tradition of writing Gospels evolved in direct response to the need to address these issues.

THE RAW MATERIAL

The historical details on which the Gospel writers had to draw were scanty to say the least. The bare outlines of Jesus' life were about all they had. The major eyewitnesses were no longer living. The Christian community knew that Jesus hailed from Galilee. They knew that he had some connection with the movement started by John the Baptist. They knew that he journeyed from Galilee to Jerusalem at the end of his life. They knew that in Jerusalem he was crucified—probably during the celebration of the Passover. Finally, they knew that his disciples had had a powerful experience that led them to proclaim that God had raised Jesus from the dead. There was also the fading recollection of a teacher who had used memorable parables and whose reinterpretation of the Torah had brought him into serious conflict with the Jewish religious establishment.

Where there were blanks in the details of the portrait of Jesus' life his followers, most of whom at that time were Jews, simply searched the Hebrew Scriptures to find material that could be attached to Jesus' life and that would indicate that Jesus had in fact been validated, claimed, and inserted into the developing saga of God's relationship with God's special people. This is to say, Mark, the first Gospel, was Christian midrash at its best, and this Gospel set the style for all the other Gospels. In detail after detail the ancient narratives of the Hebrew people were simply retold with Jesus now portrayed as the new Abraham, the new Isaac, the new Moses, the new Joshua, the new Samuel, the new David, the new Solomon, the new Elijah, the new Elisha, the new Isaiah, the new Daniel, and so on and so on, as the midrash tradition unfolded. We need to understand that within the Jewish frame of reference no higher tribute could be paid to this Jesus than to embrace him in this tradition.

Before the writing of Mark only Paul had placed into the Christian written story some basic data about Jesus' life. This embryonic data served to give substance and the beginning of details to the ultimate Christian proclamation. Christ died, said Paul. He was buried. He was raised on the third day. He appeared to various validating witnesses, of whom Paul insisted he was one. It was inevitable that in time narrative details would develop around this core proclamation in Paul, and in time this came to be called the *kerygma* (i.e., the basic early proclamation of the Gospel story).

Because the kerygma turned on the experience of Easter, whatever that experience had been, it, above all else, had to be processed in order that others might be brought into its shared meaning. As this Easter experience made its human journey through time on the backs of human words, it was certain to grow and to become embellished. Before the first years of the eighth decade had passed, Mark put into written form the story of that tradition as it had evolved by that time in history. The early understanding of Easter was in fact the narrative through which he brought his story to an end.

MARK'S INVITATION TO BELIEVE

Mark's Easter narrative was remarkably brief considering that it described a moment that ultimately changed the world. Just 8 verses give Mark's account of that remarkable event, out of a total of 665 verses that make up this Gospel.[1] Approaching these verses today, we must understand that the original readers of Mark did not bring to that Gospel any knowledge, image, or pattern that was to appear later in other Gospel traditions. To read Mark for what Mark really said, we must clear our minds of the other versions. Mark cannot be read through the eyes of Matthew, Luke, or John, just as Paul has to be approached with no borrowed images from the Gospel tradition. As the first Gospel, Mark was also the only Gospel that the Christian church had for at least fifteen years and perhaps for as much as twenty years.

So, reading only Mark, we are able to examine the stage of development that the Easter tradition had achieved by the first years of the eighth decade. Mark's story of the resurrection presents us with a fascinating study that significantly challenges the common wisdom of those who call themselves traditional or conservative Christians and who, as such, are trapped inside the literal and physical images of a premodern world. A careful reading of the Bible in general, and Mark in particular, will simply not support those literal assumptions.

Mark's Gospel actually ends without any mention of the disciples' belief that Jesus had been raised from the dead. That is a literal fact. The only disciples to appear in Mark's account of Easter are women. Earlier Mark had informed us that the twelve forsook Jesus and fled, so they are not present. But in this account even the women do not believe. Instead they flee the tomb in confusion and disbelief. They say nothing to anyone because of their fear. That is the literal reading of Mark's present text.

Mark's resurrection account also contains no clearly identified supernatural agent called an angel. Mark has only a young man dressed in a white robe. When we picture an angel at the tomb, we are thinking of later stories, not of Mark. There might well be echoes of angelic figures here, but no claims of that were made. White robes were the traditional garb of those who inhabited the kingdom of God as well as the garments of liturgical functionaries.

In 2 Maccabees (3:26), a very popular book in Jewish circles during the century before the birth of Jesus, white robes are portrayed as the costume of supernatural beings. White robes are also the clothing of the redeemed in heaven after the end of the world in the apocalyptic Book of Revelation (7:9, 13). When Mark told the story that came to be known as the transfiguration, he indicated the transcendent heavenly character of Jesus by describing his robes as glistening white, beyond the capacity of earthly bleach to whiten. So there is a hint here of the vestments of the kingdom in Mark's description of the young man who made the resurrection announcement, but his supernatural identity, if actually claimed, was so understated as to cause the enhancement of this angelic status in later Gospels. We note in passing that Mark had just referred to another young man clad only in white linen cloth, who made a cameo appearance at Jesus' arrest (14:51). One cannot help but wonder if there was some connection.

We also observe that in Mark there are no guards at the tomb, no emergence of one from the grave, and no burial clothes left behind to prove that the body had been raised. Perhaps most important in this first Gospel, there was the stunning absence of the risen Lord. Mark's Gospel recorded no picture or vision of the risen Christ. Once the stone had sealed the tomb, in Mark's story, Jesus was never again seen by human eyes. The women who were visiting the tomb were told that Jesus had been raised, but that risen presence was simply not available to them. They therefore responded not with faith but with fear.

We need to make sure that we register the impact of Mark's portrait of Easter, so corrupted have our minds become by a resurrection collage created by blending all the Easter narratives. The empty tomb did not, when it first entered the Christian tradition in this Gospel, inspire faith. Neither did the first proclamation of the resurrection. I suspect that both of these facts arose out of an authentic memory that could not be denied. As the story stood in Mark's finished work, it issued an invitation to the reader to do what the women did not do—that is, to believe that Jesus had been raised and not to flee in confusion.

It is certainly fair to say that when Mark wrote, around the year 70 C.E., the promised-but-not-delivered future appearance of Jesus of which the messenger spoke still meant a revelatory manifestation out of God's eschatological future, and not a physical earthly resuscitation. At this time there were still no physical connotations connected with resurrection, no matter what the biblical literalists claim. Mark had, however, made two primary additions to the developing tradition. One was the picture of a vacated tomb, which was located in Jerusalem. The second addition was his suggestion that the power to rise dwelt in Jesus himself. "He has been raised" had become "He has risen." The story of Easter was expanding, and it was moving toward Jerusalem. Mark had not quite yet transferred the locale of the Easter experience to Jerusalem. He had located in Jerusalem only a symbol of that experience in his narrative about the emptiness of the Jerusalem tomb. His messenger was still saying that the disciples must go to Galilee to meet the risen Lord, for he was not yet risen in Jerusalem. The memory that it was in Galilee where whatever Easter was actually occurred was still affirmed even at this late date, some forty years after the crucifixion.

Edward Schillebeeckx, in his analysis of this text, sees two things that escape the casual reader.[2] First, he finds in this text the development of a Jerusalem Easter tradition that he suggests has liturgical connotations. Second, he finds Marcan redaction—that is, Mark's additions to and commentary on that developing Jerusalem tradition. The Marcan additions, he argues, are first the words of the messenger to the women to go tell the disciples and Peter that Jesus was going before them to Galilee and that he would meet the disciples there "as he told you." This was clearly redactional material because it referred back to something Mark had already written. In the story of the Last Supper Mark quoted Jesus as saying, "But after I am raised up I will go before you to Galilee" (Mark 14:28). Mark had simply added this note to his story of the tomb to tie the narrative into his earlier account. In the process of accomplishing this blending of traditions, he had made the messenger speak the very same words that he had Jesus speak earlier. To cover the clumsiness of this construction, he had to add the words "as he told you" to the messenger's statement.

The second redaction Schillebeeckx suggests is the response of the women to flee in astonishment and to say nothing to anyone "for they were afraid" (Mark 16:8). That was a strange response to portray forty years after the event. In my opinion, Mark's purpose here was to depict the women's response as identical with the twelve's at the time of the crucifixion. The twelve had fled in fear. I suspect they said nothing to anyone. In this way, two things were achieved. First, it preserved an authentic memory burned into the early church's mind in regard to the disciples' response. Second, by showing that the women responded exactly as the men had, Mark somehow pronounced that response to be inevitable and in some small way made the twelve look a bit better.

It is after this redactional material is removed that Schillebeeckx is able to analyze the Jerusalem tomb tradition in Mark's narrative. He argues that this tradition was not original but rather reflected a liturgical development during which apostolic belief in the resurrection came to be associated with visiting the holy sepulcher, where a religious ceremony took place. That ceremony might have been held annually at a place that came to be identified with the tomb of Jesus. Schillebeeckx suggests that an echo of a procession can be heard in the text, of pilgrims walking in the way of the cross with the final episode taking place at the proposed site of the burial. The young man dressed in white may be, Schillebeeckx surmises, a liturgical functionary who wore a white vestment to play his liturgical role in this drama. This, suggests Schillebeeckx, was something like a primitive version of what came to be called the stations of the cross. When the procession of pilgrims arrived at the place designated as the tomb of Jesus, a liturgy might have gone something like this:

Worship leader (dressed in white): Whom do you seek?

Women: We seek Jesus of Nazareth who was crucified.

Worship leader: He has risen. He is not here. See the place where they laid him.

That liturgy was developed in Jerusalem so that it could mark the holy places in the development of the Christian story. Its message was that those who sought Jesus in the tomb would always be left in the dark regardless of the tomb's contents. But the messenger at the tomb was in fact simply reciting the church's proclamation, its kerygma, not significantly different from Paul's recitation that he said he had received from others and passed on to his readers, "as of first importance" (1 Cor. 15:3).

We need to remember that a liturgical journey in the way of the cross that concludes with a visit to the tomb represents a later stage of development. It does not create faith; it expresses faith. It would never have developed had not the belief that God raised Jesus from the dead already been a reality. This narrative shows how drama, liturgy, and story telling developed around the last events in Jesus' life. It reveals the raw material on which legends would later be built—legends about burials and empty tombs, about great stones that were rolled away and supernatural angels, and even about appearances of the risen Christ in that garden at dawn on that first Easter. In Mark the seeds are there, but the legends have not yet been fully constructed.

Mark had taken the first steps toward objectifying the story of the resurrection, however, by giving it a Jerusalem setting. By putting the disciples and Peter into the messenger's announcement, he had begun to locate the disciples inside the Jerusalem tradition. They were not there yet; they in fact were still in Galilee in Mark's story, but their names were now at the tomb in Jerusalem. In time the legends would grow until the disciples themselves were transferred to Jerusalem and located where they could be portrayed as inspecting the tomb's emptiness and drawing resurrection conclusions. But that does not yet occur in Mark.

The cultic celebration, liturgically acted out in a procession at the supposed site of the tomb, was the strand of interpretive data that Mark incorporated into his Gospel. This celebration, I believe, became the mother of the legends that appeared in the later Gospels. Mark was the first of these Gospels, so we isolate him and freeze him for a moment in time so that we can see exactly what it was that he believed to have been the story of Easter in the year that he wrote his Gospel. The tradition had grown dramatically since Paul. Mark has also introduced us to a cultic liturgical celebration that appeared early in Christian history. This event has the capacity to take us back in time, to see some other possibilities. For now, however, all we must do is to notice, speculate, and file that note for future reference. How do you suppose such a liturgy developed at such a spot? We shall return to that question.

Chapter 6

Matthew: Polemics Enter
the Tradition

By the time Matthew's Gospel entered the developing stream of Christian tradition it was the early to middle 80s. More than a decade before, the city of Jerusalem had fallen to the Roman army. With the destruction of Jerusalem, the Jewish presence in the life of the Christian church had been diminished. Those Jewish people who believed that Jesus was the promised Messiah were under increasing pressure from the more conservative and orthodox Jewish religious authorities, who viewed Jewish Christians as a dagger aimed at Judaism's heart.

The Jews had lost their holy city. They had lost their sacred temple. Only one wall remained standing. At this wall the Jews wept, and it thus became known as the Wailing Wall. Many Jews had fled Jerusalem, so more and more Jews were dispersed into a Greek-speaking world, where the defining traditions of the Jewish people became syncretized and lapsed into disuse. Only the sacred Torah, the law, bound Jew to Jew and preserved any sense of their history and tradition. Jews therefore became stricter and increasingly conservative, literal, and fundamentalistic about the Torah. Jewish Christians were people who, by definition, relativized the claims of the law, for in Jesus they discovered not only a new thing but also a sense of overwhelming grace that seemed to minimize the rigid demands of the Torah. Jewish Christians did not adhere to the strictness of the law, nor did they ascribe an ultimate holiness to its demands. For these reasons, among others, hostility grew between the strict Jews, who clung to the literal words of the law as their only surviving symbol, and Jewish Christians who saw the law, in Paul's phrase, only as a schoolmaster that could lead people to Christ (Rom. 2:12).

In order to protect their fragile tradition from erosion, Jews began to attack Christian claims about Jesus. In rebuttal Jewish Christians began to defend their claims. Between 70 and 85 the polemical defenses of Jewish Christians against their Jewish attackers began to change the way the Christians told the stories of their faith, and these defenses came to be written down and incorporated into the developing Christian tradition.

BORROWING AND EXPANDING TO PROVE A POINT

The Gospel we call Matthew was written by a Jewish Christian during this time of increasing hostility. Its author was a Jewish scribe trained in the art of midrash and eager to defend Christian claims against Jewish attack. Mark's Gospel had left far too many unanswered questions to be of great use in this battle, so the author of Matthew (whom I shall call by this name despite the fact that its authorship has never been certain) rewrote Mark to suit his own purposes. He did his revision using the time-honored method of midrash. It is possible that he modeled this midrashic rewriting after the chronicler of old who had rewritten the Hebrew Books of the Kings to suit his own purposes.[1]

Matthew seems to have been unaware of the underlying liturgical observations connected with Mark's story of Easter. Perhaps with the destruction of the temple the connection between Jewish worship traditions and Christian interpretations of these traditions had been considerably weakened. As more and more Jews became Greek-speaking citizens of a hellenized world, and as their lives came into closer contact with Gentiles, Jewish liturgical services lapsed in both usage and importance. Once deemphasized, these formerly strict observances were misunderstood not only by the Gentiles but by the now hellenized Jews. It was not a large step for these traditions to move from being misunderstood to being ignored.

For Matthew the Jerusalem tomb story was not a liturgical reenactment of a founding moment. The tomb story was the way in which the reality of the resurrection had actually dawned. Mark had his messenger deliver the resurrection message to the women visitors to the tomb, only to have the women disobey the instructions to go tell the disciples and Peter to go to Galilee and that there the risen Christ would meet them. In Mark the women said nothing to anyone. They fled in fear with a kind of trembling astonishment. It was easy for the enemies of the Christian movement to ridicule so weak a conclusion to so inadequate a narrative. So Matthew rewrote Mark to be more effective in the polemic that engulfed the Christian community in the ninth decade.

First, Matthew adapted the text to heighten the power of the miraculous. Mark's young man dressed in white became quite clearly a supernatural "angel of the Lord." His appearance (i.e., his face) was "like lightning." He descended in an earthquake. The guards were struck dumb, or unconscious, in fear. The angel removed the large stone from the mouth of the tomb and sat on it in a sign of triumph. Many echoes of the Jewish past are found in this passage. Indeed in almost every place that Matthew changed Mark, there is a midrashic detail and a midrashic rewriting.

To prepare his readers for his new version, Matthew told the story of the chief priests and Pharisees going to Pilate to ask that a guard of soldiers be placed at the tomb. They called Jesus "an impostor" and cited his threat to rise three days after his death to justify their request. The stated fear was that the disciples of Jesus would steal his body and claim that he had risen from the dead. This "last fraud will be worse than the first," they asserted. These words clearly constituted the emotional tone and even the vocabulary flowing at that time in the polemic between Jews and Jewish Christians.

But Matthew, as a Jewish scribe trained in the tradition of midrash, had found in the Hebrew Scriptures another hero who long ago had dealt with a similar situation, and he borrowed freely from that earlier narrative in order to retell his story. In the Book of Joshua (spelled Jesus in the Greek translation of the Old Testament, from which Matthew quoted whenever he quoted the Hebrew Scriptures), the hero Joshua/Jesus placed a guard of soldiers at a cave into which he had imprisoned five captured kings. To keep them from escaping, Joshua also sealed the mouth of that cave with a large stone. This narrative was read in the Jewish lectionary as the second lesson in the liturgy for the third Sabbath of Nisan,[2] which came shortly after Passover and was therefore quite familiar to the Jewish people, including Jewish Christians. Matthew borrowed the cave, the guards, and the stone and wrote them into the narrative of his drama at the tomb of Jesus.

In the story of another Jewish hero of the past, other details emerged. A young Jewish man named Daniel had suffered and yet had made his way to glory. He, too, was put into a deathlike tomb, a den of lions. That "tomb" had also been closed by placing a great stone over its entrance, and it had been sealed by the king's signet so that nothing inside the den might be changed (Dan. 6:17). It was this kind of security that Matthew said the chief priests and Pharisees sought to bring to the sealing of Jesus in his tomb. Yet Daniel had emerged from his sealed den of lions alive. Matthew saw in this earlier story a prefiguring of Jesus' emergence from his tomb alive, so he also wrote these nuances into his narrative.

The Book of Daniel also provided Matthew with his description of the angel. When Daniel was in mourning, said that earlier story, an angel appeared to him whose "face was like lightning" and whose garments were "glittering white" and who, when he appeared, caused Daniel's guards to be "overcome with great trembling" (Dan. 10:2–9). That was the effect the angelic presence had on the one who was God's chosen vessel, so Matthew used this narrative to form his developing story. This was not the last time that Daniel would shape Matthew's story of the resurrection, as we shall see.

One further note needs to be added that also contributes to the nonoriginality of Matthew's tale. The activity of the chief priests—going to Pilate, securing the guards, and placing them on duty at the tomb—took place on the Sabbath, in clear violation of the rules of the Sabbath. Matthew was so eager to establish his anti-Jewish polemical themes that he was insensitive to the traditions of the Jews, which his narrative itself was assailing.

Matthew took the response of the women in Mark and turned it sharply in a new direction. First, in Matthew's account, the angelic announcement was changed. Mark had the messenger say, "He has risen, he is not here." Matthew reversed that message: "He is not here for he has risen." It was a subtle and yet powerful change. The literalizing influences had taken hold. The body had disappeared because Jesus had risen. The action had now fully shifted from God to Jesus. What had occurred in the Easter experience was no longer a revelation from God's eschatological future, accomplished by God's power in raising Jesus into God's presence. It had now become Jesus' action in fulfillment of his own prediction about himself.

The women still responded in fear, but the trembling that Mark said accompanied this announcement was turned by Matthew into a sign of the ecstasy of great joy. In direct opposition to Mark's account, Matthew had the women rush to comply with the angelic demand to tell the disciples. But they did not get out of the garden before they confronted the risen Christ himself. This was the first account in written Christian history where the appearance of the risen Christ was described. Keep in mind that this element of the Easter story did not come until the middle years of the ninth decade of the Christian era.

Jesus spoke to the women with the word "Hail!" It was the same word Matthew had used to convey the greeting of Judas Iscariot at the time of Jesus' arrest. The women "came up and took hold of his feet and worshiped him" (Matt. 28:9). In the ancient Hebrew story of Elisha, the Shunammite woman took hold of the man of God's feet before he raised her son from death (2 Kings 4:27ff). In Matthew's story the supernatural angelic messenger had now faded into being Jesus himself. The words Matthew had Jesus speak in this episode were identical with those spoken by the messenger. He first calmed the women's fears and then directed them to "go and tell my brethren to go to Galilee, and there they will see me" (Matt. 28:10).

There are two interesting twists in Matthew's narrative. In Mark the messenger directed the women to "tell my disciples and Peter." Matthew changed that to "tell my brethren." It was a summons to the whole community to go to Galilee. Second, even though Matthew had stretched the tomb story enormously by adding to it an appearance of Jesus, he nonetheless still affirmed the fact that the disciples had to return to Galilee if they wished to see the risen Lord.

From Matthew forward, the empty tomb tradition and the appearance traditions were merged, which would force the locale of the resurrection more and more into Jerusalem. Then Matthew closed his account with the story of the soldiers who had been posted to guard the grave. The addition gives us a new insight into the level of intensity that marked the dispute between Jewish Christians and Jews. This time, however, we see that polemic from the Christian side. The soldiers, we are told, reported to the chief priest. They were bribed to lie. "Tell people, 'His disciples came by night and stole him away while we were asleep'" (Matt. 28:13). "Impostor" and "fraud" (27:63, 64) were the Jewish words in this polemic. "Acceptors of bribes and liars" were the Christian words. This story had been spread among the Jews to this day, Matthew concluded (28:15).

The late-developing Jerusalem tradition had now been literalized. The action had been shifted from God to Jesus. The emptiness of the tomb had become the sign of the truth of the resurrection over which Jews and Christians traded barbed insults in their attacks against or in defense of their understanding of Easter—that moment when the Christian faith was born. The narrative had journeyed a great distance from its ecstatic proclamation. Now even the late-developing narrative details were caught up in the dynamic of argument, attack, and defense.

In Mark's Gospel there was a promise of an appearance to the disciples and Peter in Galilee. Matthew was not content to let that appearance go undescribed. Though Jesus invited "my brethren" to this event, Matthew followed Mark's direction that the Galilean appearance would be just to the disciples. Even Peter was no longer singled out. Since no tradition existed to provide the details of this appearance, Matthew once again employed the method of midrash. Back to the Book of Daniel he went, to the portrait of a heavenly figure clothed with both divine and earthly authority whose dominion was everlasting (Daniel 12).

Using this image called the Son of man, Matthew portrayed Jesus as appearing from heaven to the eleven on a mountaintop in Galilee. To this particular mountain, Matthew said, Jesus had directed the disciples, although Matthew did not state when Jesus gave that direction. Matthew had an affinity for mountains, as he reveals in his portrait of Jesus as the new Moses, giving the new law from the new Mount Sinai in what we call the Sermon on the Mount. Now the risen Jesus makes an appearance on a mountain. He had in Matthew's mind quite clearly come to that mountain out of heaven. He had not like a mortal climbed up the mountain from its base. The disciples, like the women in the garden, worshiped him. "All authority in heaven and on earth has been given to me," Jesus said (Matt. 28:18).

Those words present a very different image of the risen Jesus from the resuscitated body that spoke to the women outside the tomb in Matthew's earlier vignette. Here Jesus was the exalted one who was raised by God into heaven. There is in Matthew no sense of an ascension as a separate action, which makes Matthew's fairly clumsy narration of a garden appearance by Jesus to the women ring with little or no authenticity.

But now Matthew had Jesus commission his followers to their task of making disciples of all nations. It was a theme that came close to Matthew's heart as he had presented Jesus as the son of Abraham through whom all the nations of the world would be blessed. To this commission Matthew then added the baptismal formula. The disciples were to baptize "in the name of the Father and of the Son and of the Holy Spirit." This formula could not possibly have come from the lips of Jesus, for it represented a theological development that did not occur until well after Jesus' earthly life was concluded; but it was abroad by this time, as a similar reference in the First Epistle of Peter (1:2) reveals. It was a formula destined to play a crucial role in the development of Christian creeds and theology for the next four hundred years. Michael Goulder maintains that Matthew's Gospel was written to transform the Hebrew worship cycle by adding Christian readings. This particular passage, he suggests, was to be read on Easter eve when the catechumens were waiting to be baptized. "What could be more suitable," Goulder asks, "than that the authority of the risen Jesus should be cited for the occasion?"[3] A church procedure could thus be justified with a word from the Lord.

Matthew now brought his story to an end. At the beginning of his story Matthew had the angel tell Joseph that Mary's child would be Emmanuel, which means "God with us." He now ends his story having Jesus make that claim for himself, when Jesus says that he is what Emmanuel means: "Lo, I am with you always, to the close of the age" (Matt. 28:20). The Jewish Messiah of Matthew had become the Cosmic Christ of the whole world.

WHAT MATTHEW'S CHANGES HAVE WROUGHT

We see the narrative of Easter take quantitative leaps in Matthew. The exalted Jesus, reigning in God's eternal future, who appeared from that future to certain witnesses as the firstfruits of the kingdom of God, was now a semiphysical being inside history who could speak to women who grasped his feet in worship. The story of Easter was changing its content, becoming more vivid, more concrete, and more miraculous. That would not have appeared as a problem at that time in history. In a later age, however, these very literalized details would become that which repelled many from the cause of Christ. These same details would also become for some fundamentalist Christians the litmus test for true believers, who would insist on the literalness of aspects of the Easter story that in fact developed very late.

On a British Broadcasting Corporation television program in the early 1990s, I watched a reporter interrogate clergy in an Easter program. Her primary question was, "Was the tomb empty?" The answer the clergy gave, either yes or no, would determine for this reporter, and presumably for her audience, whether or not these clergy were Christians. This television program provoked a spirited debate in the United Kingdom. Many believed that Easter could be real or true only if the body of Jesus had been physically resuscitated and therefore only if the tomb was actually empty. This was a sad exercise in biblical ignorance, as I hope this analysis thus far has shown. Whatever Easter was and is, it had to be and has to be more than the narrative about a body that walked out of a tomb almost two thousand years ago.

We must press on to see how the details continue to develop before seeking to understand how early Christians envisioned this risen Christ. Only then can we begin a journey back in time to the point of origin as we raise the speculative but necessary question: How was it that people came to believe that a crucified man had conquered death? What really happened to change despairing men and women into courageous witnesses who believed that Jesus lived and that they had seen the Lord? What was there about this Jesus that forced open the very definition of God among Jewish men and women, so that Jesus could be seen inside that definition? As we watch the Easter tradition grow through its early history, these questions become more and more compelling.

Matthew had expanded the story of Easter dramatically, but he had not come near the limits to which that story would be taken. We must now move on to the next phase of its development.

Chapter 7

Luke: The Turn Toward Gentile Understandings

By the time the Gospel we call Luke had entered the world of Christian writings, some thirty years had passed since Paul's description of the original tradition of Easter in 1 Corinthians. Perhaps as many as forty years had passed since Paul's claim to have seen Jesus had been written to the Galatians. It had been as many as twenty years since Mark, the first Gospel, had made its debut. The rapid pace of change already noted in Matthew's Gospel appears only to have accelerated by the time of Luke. Christianity's transition away from being a Jewish movement had continued. From its Palestinian center, to the Jews of the dispersion, to the world of Gentiles—this was the route the church had followed. Before Luke's story was complete, the gentile direction was not only established, it was in full control.

We need to be aware that the same person who wrote the Gospel of Luke also authored the Book of Acts. His story began with the family of Jesus going up from Galilee to Judea to be enrolled on the orders of Caesar Augustus. Although this author told of a birth in Bethlehem, David's town just south of Jerusalem, he quickly moved both Jesus and his family to Jerusalem for the liturgy of presentation and purification (Luke 2:22). Jerusalem drew this author rather dramatically. From Galilee to Jerusalem he moved the twelve-year-old boy Jesus early in his story. From Galilee to Jerusalem he had the adult Jesus go at the time of the Passover. From Jerusalem to the nations of the world, he believed, the message of Jesus must be proclaimed. His second volume, officially called the Acts of the Apostles, was not complete until the Gospel had moved from Jerusalem, the capital of the Jewish world, to Rome, the capital of the entire world. Inevitably this dominant emphasis would affect the way this author told the story of Christianity's originating moment.

BRIDGING THE GENTILE AND JEWISH WORLDS

Who was Luke? He was either the first and only Gentile to write what came to be known as Christian Scripture, or he was a thoroughly hellenized Jew. If he was Gentile, then we must acknowledge that he was one who had been drawn deeply into the orbit of Judaism in his search for authenticity in worship. If he was a hellenized Jew, he was one who had moved far beyond his roots into a world that was primarily Gentile. My best guess is that he was a gentile proselyte, one of those people who frequented Jewish synagogues looking for something that would fill the empty places where once the gods of the Olympus had dwelt.[1] Gentiles were drawn to Jewish synagogues in such numbers that the synagogues had to make provisions for them. The oneness of God and the ethical demands required by this God, expressed in such documents as the Ten Commandments, were the centers of attraction for the Gentiles. It was to this group of gentile worshipers that Paul seems to have exerted the strongest appeal as he journeyed to the synagogues of the Mediterranean world. It was on the backs of these gentile proselytes that Christianity finally leaped the barrier of Judaism and became a Western institution, profoundly shaping the life of a gentile world.

This meant that for at least the first one or two generations of gentile Christians there was still a deep connection with things Jewish. Certainly the author of Luke's Gospel appears to have been significantly familiar with parts of the Jewish heritage such as the stories of the Red Sea crossing, the wilderness wandering, and messianic expectations. He also had a significant familiarity with such biblical figures as Moses, Elijah, David, Solomon, Isaiah, Micah, and Daniel. He was not as adept as Matthew in the tradition of Jewish midrash, but he did know how to search the Hebrew Scriptures for clues with which he could clarify for his readers the new ways in which the old story was being told.

Luke also revealed a view of the world that had significantly escaped the boundaries of Judaism. When he wanted to tell of Jesus' genealogy, his ancestral line went back to Adam, the father of the whole human race, in contradistinction to Matthew, who only went back to Abraham, the father of the Jews. Luke alone included in his story the parable of the good Samaritan, which struck a blow at the most emotional prejudice in the life of the Jewish people. Luke wrote the story of Peter's willingness to set aside the kosher dietary laws in the service of a universal vision that Peter himself was made to articulate in these words: "Truly I perceive that God shows no partiality, but in every nation any one who fears him and does what is right is acceptable to him" (Acts 10:34, 35). That was a very different image of Peter from the one drawn by Paul in the Epistle to the Galatians (chaps. 1 and 2). But years had passed between the writing of Galatians and the writing of the Book of Acts, and the gentile presence was not only established in the church, it had become dominant. Luke was the first author to write out of that gentile dominance, and he wrote with a clear bias toward it.

When we consider Luke's account of Easter, we discover that quantitative leaps have occurred in the tradition. The images that rise out of Jewish mythology, anthropology, and apocalyptic visions present in Paul and Mark and, to a lesser degree, Matthew, have been replaced in Luke by what Edward Schillebeeckx calls the "rapture model" image, or what Reginald Fuller calls the "divine man" image (or the *theios anēr*). This was an image that Gentiles would understand, Schillebeeckx states, because it was popular in Roman mythology.[2] In this model, when a pious or heroic person died, all of his or her earthly remains would disappear totally, because that person was believed to have been snatched up to heaven. Luke emphasized the contrast with David, who was still in his grave, in the Book of Acts (2:29). From heaven this now divine life would regularly materialize, especially to those carrying out the earthly work of the departed one. When the heroic figure materialized, he or she would be recognizably human.

Mythical stories about Romulus, the founder of Rome, employed this divine man model. In this Roman story the glorified Romulus revealed to the people of Rome that Caesar was "lord of the world." According to Schillebeeckx, Luke borrowed this image but applied it to Jesus of Nazareth in order to make a counterclaim to the people of the Roman Empire. The lord of the world was not Caesar, Luke was saying. The lord of the empire was Jesus of Nazareth, who was also the Christ who had been taken up to God.[3] In the service of this image Luke had to recast the resurrection tradition. It would never be the same after Luke had finished his work.

HOW LUKE CHANGED THE STORY

First, Luke dramatically transformed the story of the empty tomb. In Mark the women found the stone rolled away but didn't bother to check the tomb any further. In Luke, by contrast, they entered the tomb, explored it, and vouched for its emptiness. For Luke that emptiness was itself a proof of resurrection. Then, in perplexity and wonder, the women saw not one but two men in dazzling apparel, who interpreted what the women had already discovered. The angelic question was also different, as it assumed resurrection: "Why do you seek the living among the dead?" (Luke 24:5).

Second, Luke denied the Galilean location for any part of the Easter drama. To rid himself of that tradition, Luke changed the message of the angel in Mark and the message of Jesus himself in Matthew, which directed the disciples to Galilee. It now became an angelic reminder that while Jesus was in Galilee he had told them that resurrection would transpire.

Third, in that angelic announcement Luke introduced one of his dominant theological themes—that of divine necessity. The Son of man "must" be delivered, the angel said. It was a note that would be sounded again and again in Luke's drama.

The fourth change was in the behavior of the women. All four Gospels disagree with one another in their lists of women who shared in this experience. More important, however, Luke's women returned immediately to the disciples to give them the message. The disciples were still in Jerusalem in Luke's Gospel. They would shortly be drawn into the narrative of the empty tomb. In no other Gospel thus far had the disciples been more than a name spoken at the site of the empty tomb. Now they were actors in the drama. The story of the empty tomb no longer had either the form or feeling of a liturgy. It had become an essential part of the objective, literal historical event called Easter. It took some sixty years to make this journey from the crucifixion of Jesus to the literalness of the empty tomb as the proof of his resurrection, but in Luke that journey was now complete.

In Luke the eleven appear to be an augmented group. The women went to tell the eleven "and all the rest." Luke had constantly expanded the core group, most notably in his Pentecost story (Acts 2), but hints of this are also found earlier in his text (Luke 8:10; 19:9–11). Perhaps this was his way of presaging a church that was far more inclusive than eleven Jewish males suggested it was destined to be.

After an initial expression of doubt and disbelief, the narrative describes the journey to the tomb by Peter and John. Peter and the tomb were thus merged. There has been some dispute over whether or not this part of Luke's text was a later redaction to bring Luke into harmony with the Fourth Gospel. The Revised Standard text, for example, omitted the verse (24:12) about Peter's visit to the tomb, relegating it to a footnote. However, there is a reference to this verse in the next episode, and that does appear to be an original and authentic part of Luke's Gospel, so I see no reason to suggest that this detail was a later editorial addition. Peter's visit to the tomb made the details of the miracle even more literal. The tomb was empty. The grave clothes were present. The tomb had now become not the sign but the proof of the resurrection.

Then Luke proceeded to tell a story repeated nowhere else in the Bible. It is an elegant gem of a story, but it also served to enhance the physicality of the resurrection in a strange way, and it involved the "rapture model," or divine man concept, of resurrection that Luke had adopted. In this story, the risen Christ walked unrecognized with Cleopas and a companion on the road to Emmaus. Jesus talked with them about the Scriptures as they wrestled with their grief and with the pain of Jesus' execution. Jesus opened the Scriptures to show them that the grief and pain were steps on the pathway to glory, necessary to the divine plan. Finally they ate together, and in the breaking of bread Jesus was recognized as the risen Lord, after which he disappeared. Cleopas and his companion rushed back to Jerusalem to tell the disciples, only to be informed that the risen Christ had also appeared to Peter.

Speculation as to the identity of Cleopas has exercised many minds. The tendency of the majority has been to identify him with Clopas in John 19:25 and to suggest that he was the son of Joseph's brother and the father of Symeon, who became the head of the church in Jerusalem after the death of James. Although that has been the popular speculation, it can never be more than that.

In its earliest form this story was reminiscent of a popular theme in folklore and story telling in which someone entertains a supernatural being under the guise of entertaining someone else. This genre of stories is referred to in the Epistle of the Hebrews, where the readers were exhorted to welcome strangers for in that way "some have entertained angels unawares" (Heb. 13:2). It was also similar to the Genesis account of Abraham receiving and serving divine messengers, who came in a human form to tell the aged patriarch that he and his wife, Sarah, would have a son. Later these divine messengers went to warn Lot to flee from the doomed city of Sodom (Gen. 18:1–9; 19:1–3).

When Lucan theological themes are removed from the dialogue of the Emmaus road narrative, the core of the story seems to be fourfold: The risen one appeared as a traveler incognito. He encountered disciples who might have been included in Paul's phrase "all the apostles" (1 Cor. 15:3–5). He manifested his identity in a common meal. He vanished. The earthly Jesus walked with his disciples, taught his disciples, shared a common meal with his disciples, and when he died vanished from their sight. These memories of earthly experiences were simply read into the divine man, or rapture, model of the risen Christ.

There are, however, two notes in this account of the Emmaus story that ring with authenticity. One is the mood of Cleopas and his companion early in their journey. This seems to be an accurate reflection of the postcrucifixion but pre-Easter mind of the disciples: "We had hoped he would be the one who would redeem Israel." That hope had come crashing down in the act of the crucifixion. The second note in this account that seems authentic is his allusion to a liturgical experience of some long standing—namely, the Eucharist. By the time Luke's Gospel was written, the church's common meal was apparently in some unique sense thought to be the meeting place between the believer and the Lord of life.

Beyond that, Luke used this narrative to portray Christ himself as the one who opened the Scriptures, including Moses (i.e., the Torah), the prophets, and the Psalms so that all were seen to point to Jesus as the crucified and risen one. This was unquestionably a major preoccupation in the first generation or two of Christians. This midrash tradition combined easily with Luke's sense of the divine necessity of the events that led to Jesus' cross. The story of the suffering savior, Luke asserted, was not written in the stars but in the Scriptures. It was, in Luke's mind, equally inescapable. Luke was giving substance to the earlier words of Paul, whose confession of faith in the lordship of Jesus resided in the conviction that these things had occurred "according to the Scriptures."

When Luke brought this episode back to Jerusalem, he asserted, with no narrative details whatsoever, the primacy of Peter by having the eleven tell the Emmaus twosome that the Lord was alive and had appeared to Peter, even before they could blurt out the details of their experience. We need to note that in this Emmaus episode Luke was admitting that the first experience of the risen Christ came to those who had fled Jerusalem following the death of Jesus, that it was connected with the breaking of bread, that it was prepared for by the reinterpretation of Scripture, and that it necessitated their return to Jerusalem to share the good news. In these incidents Luke had, in my opinion, captured an authentic memory, but he did so inside a nonauthentic narrative. He revealed, I believe, the actual movement, the historical order of events in the lives of the disciples, and he did so in a proper sequence. In order to protect the tradition of the centrality of Jerusalem, however, he placed this story in the wrong location. We will return to this suggestion a bit later. For now, Luke succeeds in leaving us to wonder how an insignificant name like Cleopas, not mentioned in any other Gospel yet written,[4] could have played so central a role in the drama of Christianity's birth. How that came to be is forever lost inside the developing Christian tradition.

Luke now had the group of disciples back in Jerusalem, where both Peter's story and the Emmaus story were being discussed among them. The time appeared to be the evening of the first day of the week, and thus the scene was set for Luke to give his version of that moment described so many years earlier by Paul—after Jesus appeared to Cephas he then appeared "to the disciples." This appearance, however, was dramatically different from any experience that had yet been claimed in the writings of any Christians. Even Matthew's account of the appearance of the risen Christ on a mountaintop in Galilee—a Christ who claimed in that episode that "all authority in heaven and earth" had been given him and who commissioned the disciples to a worldwide ministry of teaching and baptism with the promise of an eternal Emmanuel presence— did not come close to what Luke was now prepared to relate. Matthew's appearance was clearly of the glorified Christ out of heaven. Luke was now presenting us with the appearance of a resuscitated physical but not-yet-ascended Jesus, who had escaped the bonds of death in the tomb. The only hint of this image prior to this moment in Christian writings was when the angelic messenger faded into being the risen Christ and repeated the angel's message to the women in Matthew's account of the empty tomb. Luke took that image and heightened it dramatically.

Lying behind this narrative of Luke's was his division of Jesus' exaltation into two separate actions, separated by time. For Luke there was first the resurrection of Jesus from the grave. Much later there was the ascension of Jesus into heaven. Between those two actions Luke located the appearances, all of which had the quality of the divine man, or rapture, model. In this process of splitting the Easter event into two separate actions, Luke had also changed the language of resurrection for all time. The action that brought Jesus from the grave back to life was now attributed to Jesus himself, not to God. Jesus now did his own rising. God did not raise him. The emptiness of the tomb was no longer a sign that Jesus was reigning in heaven by the action of God. The empty tomb was now a sign that the deceased person had come out of the tomb and was a walking, talking, and eating person who was back in life as one who had been resuscitated.

Since this was the way Luke had chosen to portray resurrection, he was forced to develop a narrative to account for Jesus' final departure from this earth. The story of the ascension, which is found only in Luke, therefore became a necessity. It was in this story that the original passive voice of the resurrection (Jesus was raised by God) came to find its permanent place of lodging in the Christian tradition. Jesus rose from the grave, according to Luke. The active verb form was now resurrection language. But he was raised by God into heaven. The passive verb form became the language of the ascension, although Luke's account of it still contains the hint that Jesus himself was the source even of the ascension.

But as the disciples discussed with one another these eye-opening Easter Day experiences, Jesus suddenly materialized in their midst. This was not an uncommon event in the tradition of the rapture model, which dominated Luke's understanding of resurrection. In a note quite reminiscent of the story of Jesus walking on the water in Galilee, the disciples were startled and believed that they were seeing a ghost. It seemed that even the Emmaus account and Peter's account of seeing the risen Lord had not yet fully prepared them for this event. Jesus responded to their fear and astonishment by inviting them to touch him and handle him. He suggested that a ghost would not have flesh and bones as they saw that he had. Pressing this physical imagery, Jesus asked them for food, and they gave him a piece of broiled fish, which he ate.

Then Jesus became once again the mouthpiece of Luke's theological understanding that Jesus' life was the fulfillment of Scripture, the living-out of a sense of inevitability that had been written into God's eternal plan. Phrases such as "It was necessary that" and "the Scripture must be fulfilled" were employed again and again. Jesus then commissioned the disciples, as Matthew's risen Christ had done in Galilee, but it was a divine commission given in Luke's theological words. Repentance and forgiveness were to be preached in Jesus' name to all nations. These disciples were to be his witnesses. They were, however, to remain in Jerusalem until they were clothed with power from on high. Matthew had the risen Christ promise to be with them always. Luke understood that eternal presence of Jesus to be the Holy Spirit, who had by this time emerged in Luke as an entity distinct from the spirit of Jesus. That Spirit would be poured on them later in still another narrative that we have come to call Pentecost. Luke had to remove the physical presence of this resurrected Jesus, which he had himself in large measure created, before that universal life-giving Spirit could come to abide with them forever. So the disciples were to wait in expectation in the city of Jerusalem until that promise was delivered.

One wonders if there was not an echo here of another memory. After Jesus' death the disciples fled the city in fear. Perhaps now they were being given a second chance to redeem themselves. On both occasions Jesus was separated from them. This time, however, he ordered them to do what they had not done before, that is, to remain in the city until they were clothed with power from on high. Before departing, Jesus blessed them. We recall that Luke began his story with the vision to Zechariah, the father of John the Baptist, in the temple, where, because of his muteness, he could not bless the people. The one to whom Zechariah's son pointed was now, Luke asserted, to give that blessing of the high priest. It was not given from an earthly temple but rather as Jesus prepared to enter the very temple of God in heaven. The disciples, we are told, went back to the temple in Jerusalem to wait until that temple could be claimed forever as the center from which all the nations of the earth would finally be blessed. In the light of this, perhaps the story of Jesus cleansing the temple so that it could be a house of prayer for all people was in fact a postresurrection occurrence and part of the disciples' Easter proclamation that was read back into Jesus' life.

Luke related the story of Jesus' ascension in full physical detail in chapter 1 of his second volume, the Book of Acts. Luke's view of resurrection as a resuscitation compelled him somehow to get this very physical Jesus off his stage to make way for the Spirit-driven mission of the church, which would carry the message of this Jesus to the center of the known world. Just as Luke's understanding of the resurrected one was crudely physical, so was his understanding of Jesus' ascension. Luke was clearly influenced by the story of Elijah being carried up to God. Midrash was still at work, but whereas Elijah needed a fiery chariot, Jesus ascended on his own. As Jesus' body rose physically into the clouds, the two angels that had adorned the tomb in Luke's resurrection story made a second appearance to interpret the meaning of the ascension: "Why do you seek the living among the dead?" they inquired at the tomb. "Why do you stand here gazing into heaven?" was their question now. Jesus had ascended to his heavenly throne. He would come again in a similar manner presumably at the end of time. Between these two moments in time the mission of the church, under the guidance of the Spirit, was to be carried out. These disciples were not to spend their time speculating about when the kingdom was to come. They were to wait for the Spirit and then to take Jesus' message to the world. That early sense of the imminent second coming of Jesus had clearly begun to fade by the time Luke wrote.

WHAT LUKE MADE OF THE SPIRIT AND PENTECOST

Luke's story of the coming of the Spirit was also patterned after biblical images. Within the story are echoes of the wind of God giving life to the dead bones in the valley in Ezekiel's dream (Ezekiel 37). It has the fire of Elijah that he regularly called down from heaven, but in this story that fire does not destroy but purifies, purges, cleanses, and empowers the recipients for ministry. It has the image of the tower of Babel told in reverse as languages are restored in a symbol of human unity. This narrative also has echoes of the Jewish festival of Tabernacles in which all the nations of the world must come to Jerusalem to acknowledge the Son of man at the end of time when the kingdom is established.

I file one further caveat for future reference. Luke seems to have been aware that there were two events divided in time by a not-insignificant number of days. One event was the crucifixion, which was associated with the Jewish festival of Passover. The other event was the proclamation of the resurrection of Jesus in the city of Jerusalem, which occurred sometime later. By placing the story of the coming of the Holy Spirit some fifty days after the story of the resurrection, Luke seems to have been cognizant that originally it was a two-stage process.

By identifying the outpouring of the Holy Spirit with the Jewish feast of Pentecost, Luke locked that part of his narrative into a Jewish celebration different from Passover. If Luke was indeed a Gentile, he would not have been terribly aware of the differences in various Jewish festivals. He certainly was not aware of the difference between the presentation of Jesus in the temple and the purifying of Mary, which he fused into a single episode (Luke 2).

The gift of the Spirit was thought by Christians to come through the glorified, exalted Lord. In the earliest Christian tradition that glorification and exaltation into heaven was the essence of what was meant by the resurrection. All of it was God's action to vindicate Jesus and his life by raising Jesus from death to God's right hand in heaven. When the spirit of this Jesus was thought of as the power by which believers celebrated his resurrected presence among them, then that spirit was thought to be Jesus' final gift. In Matthew the Spirit had been pictured as an abiding presence that remained when Christ was exalted to heaven. Now in Luke the Spirit was a new gift of God, who would come to inaugurate the mission. The disciples were to wait in anticipation of that gift. Jerusalem was the designated waiting place, for that city was where the mission of the Christ was to be launched into the world. The clear memory of Luke and of the early church was that the mission of the church was launched in Jerusalem sometime after the crucifixion. Luke had separated the resurrection, the appearances, the ascension, and the gift of the Spirit, and he had spread them out over fifty days. There may also have been a memory that the mission was launched during a regular Jewish festival, so he chose the Jewish festival of Pentecost and transformed it forever for Christians into a celebration of the birthday of the church.

The content of Luke's Pentecostal story, however, does not fit the Jewish festival of Pentecost very comfortably. Pentecost knew nothing of the nations of the world being gathered in Jerusalem to receive the gift of the Spirit or of being bound together into a holy fellowship that transcended every known barrier. Did Luke choose the wrong festival? Did he rightly guess that significant time had lapsed between crucifixion and mission? The need to account for that time may have motivated him to do what no one had yet done: to separate the resurrection from the ascension as if they were two different events and to insert the appearances into that time frame.

I want to propose another possibility. Perhaps what was actually separated in time was not the resurrection from the ascension. Early testimony indeed revealed that these were but two different words used interchangeably to describe one action. Perhaps what was separated by a significant length of time was crucifixion from resurrection. Perhaps there were other explanations for the three-day, or first-day-of-the-week, Easter tradition. Perhaps what Luke interpreted as the beginning of the Christian mission in Jerusalem was the moment when the disciples returned to Jerusalem from Galilee to proclaim Christ resurrected, ascended, and at God's right hand, a conviction that arose out of a Galilean experience. Perhaps the transforming power of the testimony of these resurrected disciples was what caused people to assert that they were grasped by the Spirit of God, and that in fact inaugurated the mission of Christ to all nations, as Matthew recalled, and regardless of what language they spoke, as Luke suggested.

We keep these possibilities in mind as we continue to scrutinize the developing tradition of Easter in the Christian Scriptures.

Chapter 8

John: Sometimes Primitive, Sometimes Highly Developed

The most difficult of all the Gospels to date accurately is the fourth Gospel, known as John. It is a book that appears to have been written over a number of years, perhaps even in layers. In many ways it reflects an early and authentic tradition. In other ways it reflects a long-developing tradition. Many of its theological discourses reveal a level of sophistication that could only have taken place in a time well past that of Mark, Matthew, and Luke. At the same time, some of its specific details point to the acute memory of an eyewitness and challenge the prevailing point of view expressed in the synoptic Gospels.

That is certainly true when we begin to evaluate the Johannine version of the resurrection. This Gospel includes crude, late-developing physical descriptions of the resurrected body that rank it with Luke, and even beyond Luke, in its ability to literalize the Easter story. Yet this Gospel, in contrast to Luke, refused to separate the resurrection from the outpouring of the Holy Spirit. The risen Christ breathed on the disciples in his first resurrected appearance on Easter Day, said this writer, and they received the Holy Spirit (John 20:22). It is also clear that resurrection and ascension had not been completely separated from each other in the tradition that

John records, although the fissure can certainly be seen. In the fourth Gospel, as in Matthew, the risen but not-yet-ascended Lord was seen by none but the women in the garden. In John, however, the viewing was by but a single woman, Mary Magdalene. In Matthew the group of women grasped the risen Jesus' feet in worship. In John's story Jesus told Mary Magdalene not to cling to him because he had not yet "ascended to the Father"; "but," he continued, "go to my brethren and say to them, 'I am ascending to my Father and your Father, to my God and your God'" (John 20:17). The story of Jesus' ascension was not told in John, but it was assumed, because that evening when Jesus appeared to the disciples, he had already become the ascended, glorified Lord, who was now making himself manifest to the disciples. John's narrative united the three dimensions of resurrection, ascension, and the gift of the Spirit in a way that reflected a tradition more original and more primitive than the one we met in Luke.

When John told the stories of the risen Jesus' actual appearances, however, they were tales of one who walked through secured doors and at the same time offered his wounded body for physical inspection. In another episode John may even have been responding to a tradition, known among the Jews, that a gardener named Judah had actually removed Jesus' body.[1]

Whereas the synoptic Gospels tended to place the motifs of doubt and disbelief in their portrayals of Peter, the fourth Gospel, while not sparing Peter, created a new narrative featuring Thomas as the unbeliever.

Most biblical scholars agree that the earliest strata of New Testament tradition never designated Jesus as "God." Indeed in the primitive tradition God was the source of the action and Jesus was the one acted upon. The story of Thomas represents rather late material. John had introduced this identity between the Father and the Son in his prologue. Throughout his text he declared it quite blatantly by using the holy name of God, "I am," revealed to Moses at the burning bush, as the way in which Jesus spoke about himself. *I am* the resurrection, *I am* the bread of life, *I am* the door, *I am* the vine, and when you lift up the Son of man, then you will realize that *I am*.[2] These are but a few of those claims. In this Gospel the hints of a primitive strand of resurrection material were woven in and around late-developing theological and legendary material, perhaps reflecting in the Easter story the same layering that others have noted in the balance of the fourth Gospel.

Reading through that Johannine account of Easter, we observe the following details. The setting in chapter 20 is Jerusalem, not Galilee. John joined Luke in claiming primacy for the holy city. A major part of that Jerusalem tradition was centered on the tomb, again agreeing with Luke. The burial of Jesus was treated in a far more elaborate form in the Gospel of John than in any of the synoptic Gospels, which means that the tomb was clearly important. John also located the resurrection on the first day of the week. That location was denied in Mark, debated in Matthew, but established in Luke. In John's story only Mary Magdalene came to the tomb. Finding it empty, she assumed not resurrection but robbery of the grave, whether by chance or design. Mary Magdalene quickly took this news to Peter and "the disciple whom Jesus loved," thus allowing the fourth Gospel to include yet another story about the one it regarded as mentor and hero.

At this point in John's Gospel many scholars note the conflation of two Easter narratives.[3] The first involved the whole drama of Mary Magdalene, and the second involved Peter and John at the tomb. These scholars argue persuasively that these two narratives were originally separate but then came together later in Christian history. The later tradition linked the two stories by having Mary Magdalene report to the disciples and then return to the tomb.

In any event, in this narrative two disciples went to the tomb. Luke had been the first to combine the disciples and the tomb. John continued that link, and with it the physical nature of the resurrection continued to expand. Peter and John noted the grave clothes lying in the tomb as if the risen body had simply come out of them. The head napkin was rolled up by itself at a place where the head ought to have been. The direct contrast to the details of

Lazarus are obvious (2 John). The "other" disciple (i.e., John) then entered the tomb, and he was given credit by this author for being the first to see and to believe. Peter may have been the first to arrive, for Peter's leadership was too deeply set in the memory of the church for that idea to be challenged, but the Johannine community from which the individuals emerged who authored the gospel, the Epistles, and the Book of Revelation, all of which bear John's name, gave their beloved mentor the honor of being first in faith, though that faith seems never to have moved from the beloved disciple to anyone else, as the rest of the Gospel makes clear.

THE JOHANNINE COMMUNITY'S UNIQUE ASSERTIONS

In place after place the fourth Gospel elevated the man it called the beloved disciple, whose authority was claimed to give this Gospel its power. In this tradition the beloved disciple was clearly John Zebedee. It is quite probable that only because of this book's association with John Zebedee was a new Gospel able to achieve authority so quickly. Mark, who was said to have served as Peter's interpreter and whose Gospel was thought by the early church to lean on Peter's authority, achieved its power as a direct result of that claim. Both Matthew and Luke validated that claim by using Mark in their writings. Now, in the tenth decade of the Christian era, this fourth Gospel came out of the shadows and challenged the Petrine authority of the synoptic tradition at a number of places.

Jesus became the Son of God at baptism by the descent of the Spirit, said Mark. Jesus became God's Son through the Spirit at conception, said Matthew and Luke. Not so, said John. He was the very Logos of God, preexistent since the dawn of time but enfleshed in history in Jesus of Nazareth. John's Gospel seems to imply that natural birth and being the enfleshed Word of God were not incompatible, and thus this Gospel called Jesus the son of Joseph with no sense of contradiction (John 1:45). Beyond that, this Gospel denied the Bethlehem birth tradition in favor of Nazareth (John 1:46) and stated that the duration of Jesus' public ministry was three years, not one as Matthew, Mark, and Luke had asserted.[4] John maintained that the Last Supper was not the Passover but rather a Kibburah meal on the day before the Passover and that the crucifixion itself occurred on the day the Passover lamb was slaughtered (John 19:14). John also moved the cleansing of the temple in Jerusalem into the early phase of Jesus' public ministry (John 2:14ff), instead of making of it the major event of Jesus' ministry on the day after his Palm Sunday journey, where it was placed in each of the synoptic Gospels.

When this Gospel portrayed John as the first believer, even while acknowledging Peter as the first entrant into the tomb of Jesus, it supplied the final coup de grace for the Johannine tradition. In the same vein this school of thought also portrayed John alone of the twelve as present at the foot of the cross. This Gospel had Jesus commit his mother to John, as the nearest of kin, and it rehabilitated Peter only in the final chapter, even though that chapter is now thought by most scholars to be a later appendage but still from the community shaped primarily by John Zebedee and perhaps even from the same author as the rest of the Gospel.

So with a sense of fascination as to how his mind was working, we watch this author develop the details of the resurrection story. After Peter and the beloved disciple left the scene, the original Mary Magdalene story was once more picked up. Mary returned to the tomb, still alone. She was weeping. She was acting as the chief mourner. She, too, stooped to look into the tomb, but this time she saw not grave clothes, as the disciples had seen, but two angelic figures sitting where the head and feet of the body ought to have been. A conversation ensued: "Woman, why are you weeping?" Mary displayed none of the fear shown by the women at the tomb in the other narratives. Mary answered: "Because they have taken away my Lord, and I do not know where they have laid him."

Note the shift from verse 2: "the Lord" has become "my Lord"; "we do not know where they have laid him" has become "I do not know where they have laid him." The personal possessive element has been considerably heightened. Mary then turned, and this time she saw Jesus but did not recognize him. Jesus renewed the conversation, using the same words the angels had used, which scholars believe points to the fact that angelophanies simply developed into Christophanies in the tradition.[5] "Woman, why are you weeping? Whom do you seek?" Thinking him to be the gardener, Mary replied: "Sir, if you have carried him away, tell me where you have laid him, and I will take him away." This is a remarkable line, seldom noticed but perhaps revealing something significant whose memory had been all but suppressed by this time in the Christian movement, but not forgotten in the Johannine school.

Mary Magdalene in this Gospel was first presented as the sole woman at the tomb. Next she was presented as the chief mourner. Then she was portrayed as laying a claim to the body—an action appropriate in the customs of Jewish people only for the nearest of kin. Was John hinting that the romantic liaison between Jesus and Mary Magdalene, whispered about through the centuries, was in fact real? Was he portraying Mary as Jesus' wife and now his widow? It makes for a fascinating and, I believe, life-affirming speculation, powerfully and innocently lifting women into the account of the resurrection.[6]

Jesus spoke her name: "Mary!" She turned, "Rabboni." It was an endearing diminutive form of address, heightening the sense of a bond of affection. This rich story moved on. The reason Mary could not hold him was stated: "I have not yet ascended to the Father." The process of the glorification of Jesus was temporarily interrupted to provide the readers with this poignant insight. Mary was then sent away to bear her second message of the day to Jesus' brethren. The message was "I am ascending."

In these words we again discover the primacy of ascension language, glorification language, exaltation language over the language that speaks of the resurrection as a resuscitation to life on this earth. When one enters the biblical texts deeply, surprises often await. These surprises are particularly noteworthy if the reader of the texts has made a commitment to a literalistic viewpoint, which the actual texts of the Bible will not support.

The next scene is set on Easter evening. The disciples were gathered. "The fear of the Jews," said the text, had caused them to shut the doors. But this did not constitute a barrier to the ascended Lord and his glorified body. He stood miraculously in the midst of the room. He spoke a word of peace. He demonstrated his continuity with Jesus of Nazareth by showing them the crucifixion wounds. In what must be the classic understatement of the ages, the text declared: "Then were the disciples glad when they saw the Lord" (John 20:20). Once again, Jesus spoke the word "Shalom" (peace). He empowered the disciples to be apostles, sent by him, as he was sent by the Father. Then he breathed on them with the breath of God, the divine wind, the *ruach,* and they received the Holy Spirit.

COVERING THE DISTANCE OF THE YEARS

John's language moved back and forth. Sometimes it reflected the primitive tradition of glorification, and other times it supported the physical, corporeal, earthly presence of Jesus. But John was not through. Thomas, called "the Twin," was now moved to center stage. Somehow he had not been present at the first Easter. This may reflect a memory that when Easter first dawned, the disciples were still scattered, and only a few of them had come together; but it also reflects the situation of the Christians of John's time, who had now come into the church. They, too, had not been present at the first Easter. Their link with this Easter reality was through words from the mouth of a faithful witness. Indeed, far more than we seem to recognize, that is still the link.

Between the writing of the fourth Gospel and the first awareness of Easter's meaning, there was a gap, perhaps as long as seventy years, in which the word of mouth of a faithful witness was the tenuous and only link. Thomas stood as a representative of those removed by decades from Christianity's foundational events, as indeed he stands for you and for me. The other disciples told Thomas of their experience, but he was not satisfied. He wanted evidence, empirical data, and an infallible proof text or an authoritative proclamation. Without that, asserted Thomas, "I will not believe" (John 20:25).

In this narrative Jesus confronted the disbelief incarnated in the person of Thomas. Their encounter came after "eight days," according to the text. The scene is almost identical with the previous

93

week's appearance. The disciples were once again gathered. Once more the doors were shut. Once more the presence of the ascended Lord was not bound by any barrier. He was in their midst again, pronouncing the shalom of God, "Peace be with you." Then Thomas was brought to the center of attention and invited to touch and to feel: "Do not be faithless, Thomas, but believing." Thomas replied with the ultimate affirmation. He saw the great "I am" in the ascended Jesus: "My Lord and my God" are the words John put into Thomas's mouth. Then, speaking to those to whom John's Gospel was written and to generations yet unborn, Jesus said: "Blessed are those who have not seen and yet believe" (John 20:29).

The work was over. A summary statement was added. It said that Jesus did many other signs with his disciples that were not included here. These are described for you so that you may believe that Jesus is Messiah, Christ, Son of God, and that, believing, you might have the gift of abundant life that earlier in the Gospel had been claimed by Jesus as his to give (John 10:10).

We prepare to close the text but, alas, there is an appendix, Johannine in character but clearly not part of the original text, though nonetheless apparently authentic. In chapter 21 the scene shifts to Galilee, where we find affirmed again memories of that primary Galilean moment of Easter, to which so many of the earliest sources pointed. The setting is strange. The disciples were at home; at least seven of them were together. They were picking up the pieces of their lives. The mood was certainly not the mood of those who had already encountered the risen Christ. The mood was much more reflective of the days after the execution of their master but before the meaning of Easter had dawned.

Peter and the others decided to return to their pre-Jesus style of life as fishermen on the Sea of Galilee. In that setting they once again confront the risen Jesus as dawn breaks across the lake. Jesus stood on the shore. The disciples still at sea did not recognize him. Jesus inquired, probably cupping his hands to project his voice across the water, "Children, have you any fish?"

Strangely enough, Luke has given us a similar version of this story in his Gospel, but there it occurred in the Galilean phase of

Jesus' early ministry. This makes it even more surprising that this episode has been tacked onto John's story of resurrection in Galilee and made to seem quite secondary to the location of the resurrection in Jerusalem.

Yet the themes in this passage were all church-life themes. Peter was first rehabilitated. After he recognized the Lord, he swam to shore and three times professed his love and loyalty. The defection of Peter was too deep, too real, too genuine not to be addressed, especially since Peter clearly had been the figure of authority in the church from the time of Easter until his death. Perhaps in this fragment resides the earliest vestigial narrative remains of Paul's assertion in 1 Corinthians that Jesus appeared first to Peter. Surely the threefold reconciliation that would follow the threefold denial must have come in the first postresurrection encounter and not several encounters later, as John's order would now suggest. The primacy of this experience also seems to be warranted by Peter's failure to recognize Jesus. If he had seen the risen Christ before, in Jerusalem, his response later in Galilee would be strange indeed.

Two traditions, once separate, also seem to underlie the construction of this episode. One was a fishing story. The other was a meal story. Both center on Peter, and in both there are some clear connections between this narrative and Matthew's story of Jesus walking on the water (Matt. 14:28–33), to which we will return when we focus directly on Peter.

John's epilogue closed on an interesting note that once more played on the relationship between Peter and John Zebedee. Clearly both men were dead when this account was written. Peter's death was foretold (John 21:18ff), and then it was explained that Jesus did not promise that John would be alive when he returned (John 21:22). The expectation of the near return of the ascended Lord of heaven had begun to fade, and with it Christianity was evolving into something the earliest Christians never anticipated. Christianity was becoming an institutional force in history, a body with a mission to proclaim Jesus and forgiveness to all the world. Luke made that transition very clear in the writing of the Book of Acts.

By the time the finished product of the fourth Gospel was available, the first century of the Christian Era was at an end. Some seventy years had passed since the events of the crucifixion and some one hundred years since the birth of Jesus. We have allowed the books that form the New Testament to speak for themselves. We have tried to walk through these accounts as they were written, locating in them some of the ways they told their story in terms of the events of that ancient century. I suspect it is a picture quite different from the one held in the mind of the average churchgoer who celebrates Easter each year listening to but a fragment of the tradition being read as the Gospel for the day. I have sought to enlist the Gospels themselves as allies in my attempt to get beneath and beyond the words to the experience those words seek to describe.

If that experience was of an event inside history, then it had to have been located in time. Every day that takes us farther away from that time helps to make that event a fading, even powerless, moment. But if that Easter moment did not constitute an experience that could be known by people who in fact lived in time and history, then no reality could be attributed to it. But can a transcendent, timeless, eternal moment be grasped by those who live in time and history? Can something be real and yet not occur in history? That is the query that I believe Christians who are devoted to their sacred story must be willing to ask. That is a possibility, the truth of which modern Christians, including those who continue to literalize the crucial moment in their faith story, must be willing to embrace.

Chapter 9

A New Starting Point

We have now traveled in this journey on the highway of words from the heart of the Christian story to the time when the biblical story was complete. We began with a warning of the limitations in all words. Words are the symbols of communication used by a subjective people who seek to make sense out of and to incorporate into their being the objective and external experiences of their lives. Objective events occur, but objectivity never endures. The moment the present fades into the past, objective reality becomes subjective memory. The species *Homo sapiens* has always sought to counter this weak hold we have on objective reality. We have tried to freeze the past into vignettes that we can enter and through which we can touch something called our roots in order to determine that they are deep, stable, and unchanging.

A primary function of every religious liturgy is to achieve just that kind of union with a timeless, eternal truth. So, in the dawning years of the twenty-first century, Jews celebrate the Passover, which marks the defining moment of history in the worship of these people of history. In the event marked by the liturgy of the Passover, some thirty-five hundred years ago this tribe stepped out of slavery and into freedom. Only by remembering who they were will they survive and live into the future as a community of shared faith and values.

Likewise Christians gather in worship each week to step liturgically into the defining history of another captured, frozen moment: "For on the night in which he was betrayed, he took bread, and when he had given thanks, he broke it and gave it to them and said, Take eat, this is my body which is given for you. Do this for the remembrance of me."

Other tribes of ancient people had oral historians, whose task it was to commit to memory their people's spoken histories, to guard it from erosion, distortion, forgetfulness, or error, so that the terrifying specter of living only in a transitory, subjective world could be ameliorated. Alex Haley brought this ancient role to life in *Roots*, his powerful novel about the dawn of slavery. The book became an epic beyond the power even of *Uncle Tom's Cabin* in the human struggle for racial justice.

In our contemporary world we have dedicated enormous energy to developing the technology that will enable us to freeze moments of history in their objective purity. Instant replay is a secular form of a liturgy. Like all liturgies, its purpose is to freeze objectivity so that we will not lose contact with it. Television, film, tape recorders, photographs—all become the tools of our obsession as we seek to stop the constant flux beneath our feet, to capture, relate to, and use objective reality to create a new security. It is a passionate human quest that will never succeed.

United States President John F. Kennedy was assassinated in Dallas, Texas, on November 22, 1963. He was attended, as are all heads of state, by a full panoply of recording technology and experts. Every public moment of his life was on film. Every word he spoke in his office was recorded.[1] So it was that on the television screens of the world millions of people were able to see hundreds of times the film of that Dallas parade and its aftermath. Even today, decades later, it is riveted to our conscious minds. Yet, despite this, its reality and what actually occurred in Dallas on that day are still debated as vigorously as in the days immediately following the event.

Subjectivity is not escapable; rather objectivity is itself a carefully cultivated human myth. It is a myth to which we cling with the tenacity of one who hangs by his or her fingernails over the bottomless pit of subjectivity. This does not mean there is no objective reality. It does mean that none of us will ever possess it. Perhaps that is what we really mean when we say that we must walk by faith. Time is an ever-moving stream. We are creatures of time. Every step we take in life gives us a new perspective, and from that new perspective everything is different. Theology is a mental exercise engaged in by people who have two feet. It is always moving, never static, always changing, never fixed, and certainty and security can never be its goals. Integrity and honesty, not objectivity and certainty, are the highest virtues to which the theological enterprise can aspire.

From this perspective, all human claims to possess objectivity, certainty, or infallibility are revealed as nothing but the weak and pitiable pleas of frantically insecure people who seek to live in an illusion because reality has proved to be too difficult. Papal infallibility and biblical inerrancy are the two ecclesiastical versions of this human idolatry. Both papal infallibility and biblical inerrancy require widespread and unchallenged ignorance to sustain their claims to power. Both are doomed as viable alternatives for the long-range future of anyone.

THE FINITE SEEKS TO DESCRIBE THE INFINITE

What I seek in this study is to separate the moment of Easter from its subjective interpretation. I seek to affirm the reality of that moment without claiming that any interpretation of that moment possesses objectivity. I have to use subjective, time-limited, distorting words. I have nothing else to use. It is the proper function of words to serve us as vehicles to point us beyond the limits of this world. I want us to open eyes and minds to that transcendent, eternal truth which surrounds us but which can be experienced only as it enters our subjective, transitory world. That is finally all that revelation is. To enter the essence of Easter we must admit the subjectivity of all revelation even as we affirm the objective reality of the source of revelation.

If we locate the narratives of Easter in an objective moment, we will doom Easter to extinction. Attempts to capture that moment in theological words or liturgical symbols only lead to the tyranny of the creeds or the hostile, oppressive actions of those who call themselves true believers, who act as if they alone possess something called the true faith. They amuse themselves by playing an irrelevant ecclesiastical game called "Let's Pretend." Let's pretend that we possess the objective truth of God in our inerrant Scriptures or in our infallible pronouncements or in our unbroken apostolic traditions.

If, however, Easter and resurrection are aspects of a human experience, timeless but always subjective, breaking through our barriers now and again in mind-altering, consciousness-raising revelations, then we can use the words of our forebears in faith to journey toward the experience in which their lives were changed. We travel in the hope that we might at some time or some place in the subjectivity of our experience touch that reality that they also seem to have touched.

Perhaps we need to be reminded that our ultimate goal is not objectivity, certainty, or rational truth. It is rather life, wholeness, heightened consciousness, and an expanded sense of transcendence. Our goal is to escape limits, to transcend barriers, to stand in our finitude while participating in infinity. That is why we pause around a moment called Easter, or resurrection, when some of these things seem to have occurred. We take the symbols and the words of those who attempted to capture that moment and try to let them carry us beyond themselves into the experience these words sought to interpret.

We have now journeyed through what I would call the foundational words, the interpreting tradition, and the earliest witnesses. Our conclusion is a simple one. The words cannot be objective because they are too often contradictory. In certain places the words used to speak of Easter are legendary, exaggerated, and, on occasion, even untrue. These words have been bent and shaped in the service of an agenda that will probably be lost to us forever. If our goal has been to examine sacred sources that purport to tell us about the objective truth of our foundational moment, then we have failed. Indeed that failure was 100 percent predictable. That task was doomed. Allow me to drive home this point in a quick summary.

THE IMPOSSIBILITY OF CONSISTENCY

According to the literal biblical texts of the Gospels, who went to the tomb at dawn on the first day of the week?

Since Paul did not seem to know anything about the tradition of an empty tomb visited by women, he said nothing about any woman going to any tomb. Mark named Mary Magdalene, Mary the mother of James, and Salome as his Easter Day tomb visitors. Matthew named only "Mary Magdalene and the other Mary." Luke said that Mary Magdalene, the other Mary, Joanna, and some other women went. Since both Matthew and Luke had Mark's words in front of them as they wrote, they had to have known about the woman named Salome, but both chose to drop her. It is probable that neither writer had any idea who Salome was, nor did anyone else they asked know about her; so Matthew simply omitted her, and Luke covered himself with a catch-all category "some other women." John said it was Mary Magdalene alone who went to the tomb.

This bit of contradictory data is not terribly significant, but it does reveal at the very beginning of our inquiry a lack of objective reliability in the texts that purport to capture for us in words the most critical moment of our faith story. It also relativizes at once any claim that might be offered under the banner of biblical inerrancy, but that is only the beginning of the contradictions.

What did the women find at the tomb? Since Paul knew no tomb tradition, his voice was silent. Mark said they found a young man dressed in white sitting inside the tomb. Matthew said they found an angel of the Lord, who had descended from heaven in an earthquake and rolled the stone away. He greeted the women from atop the now-removed stone. Mark's "dressed in white" became in Matthew an appearance "like lightning," and his raiment was "white as snow." It is clear that homiletic hyperbole was at work.

Luke, having Mark and possibly Matthew before him, reconciled their conflict. One angel inside the tomb and one perched on the stone make two angels, Luke concluded, so his narrative said that the women confronted two angels—both dazzling. John seems to have gone back and forth on the issue of angels. In John only one angel spoke. Mary saw two angels, but not until she looked the second time into the tomb. On Mary Magdalene's first visit to the tomb, she found nothing save the tomb's emptiness. That vision provided her with no hope, no dream of resurrection. It meant only that some hostile group identified as "they" had taken away the Lord. Only on Mary's second visit, after reporting the tomb's emptiness to "Peter and the other disciple," who came and investigated for themselves, did Mary confront the angelic messengers. A conversation ensued, and John depicted a kind of surreal fading as the angels were replaced by Jesus himself, who asked the angel's question in identical words.

One could argue that through the years the record grew from Mark's young man dressed in white, to Matthew's dazzling angel of the Lord, to Luke's two angels, to John's two angels who fade into being Jesus himself. One wonders where objectivity is in this migratory narrative that picks up legendary details as it wanders through time.

Did the women see the risen Lord in the garden on that first day of the week? Mark said no, Matthew said yes, Luke said no, John said not at first, but Mary Magdalene did on a subsequent visit. Since I believe that miraculous, startling details were always being added and seldom if ever repressed, I would read this data to say that originally the visit of the women to the sepulcher was not connected to either a resurrection proclamation or experience but was something quite different. I will return to that thought a bit later.

Where did the risen Christ make himself known as alive to his disciples? Surely a moment that profound and life-changing would be recalled with accuracy in the memory of the early church. But, alas, the written record reveals no such certainty.

Paul does not locate any appearance of Jesus in either time or space, except to claim that the appearance of Jesus to Paul (Saul) was "last of all." It is also amazing to realize that Paul seems to know nothing of his own conversion experience on the road to Damascus. Those details were created for him by Luke some twenty-five years after Paul's death. If 2 Corinthians (12:1–10) contains Paul's autobiographical account of his resurrection experience, as some scholars maintain, we need to note that it is presented as a timeless, spaceless vision, an irrational, nonobjective, unmeasurable, out-of-the-body experience. If this connection can be established, then we have in this account the earliest first-person narrative of how Easter looked to a first-century subject. It defied all of the later attempts to objectify the empty tomb or to make physical the resurrected body.

Mark also related no resurrection appearances, but he did indicate that such a meeting would take place and that it would be in Galilee, for it was to Galilee that the messenger directed the women to send the disciples. Matthew, after a clumsy pause in the garden with the women clinging to Jesus' feet, related only a single account of the appearance of the risen Christ to his disciples. It took place, he said, in Galilee on top of a mountain, and its content was that of a commissioning, a piece of data that surely cannot be original. Scattered people must be regathered before they are commissioned to a specific task. The location in Matthew may be accurate, but the content of the episode is highly developed and reflects a much later theological frame of reference than that of the immediate post-Easter period. However, it puts Matthew clearly in the Galilean camp.

Luke specifically denied the Galilean tradition. That denial began, as we noted earlier, in the message of the angelic duo that Luke placed at the tomb. Luke continued his active suppression of the Galilean tradition in the final conversation Jesus had with his disciples prior to his ascension into heaven, as told in the Book of Acts. "He charged them not to depart from Jerusalem, but to wait for the promise of the Father, which, he said, 'you heard from me, for John baptized with water, but before many days you shall be baptized with the Holy Spirit'" (Acts 1:4–5). Luke insisted that every resurrection appearance took place either in Jerusalem or its immediate environment, since the village of Emmaus appears to have been in the vicinity of Jerusalem, toward Bethany. These texts reveal that within at most two generations of the original apostles, the Christian community could not agree on where the foundational moment for that community's life had taken place. Where is reality? Objectivity? Truth?

The fourth Gospel does not help. John located the first experiences of resurrection to the disciples in Jerusalem in a secured room, perhaps the upper room in which the Last Supper was shared. He used this setting twice, separated by one week's time, to achieve his Thomas absent–Thomas present narrative. Then an epilogue was appended suggesting that much later other resurrection appearances took place in Galilee by a lake to which the disciples had repaired to put their lives together after their experience with Jesus. Objectivity and history fade and details sink into a shroud of darkness and mystery over where the resurrection experience actually belongs.

When did the risen Lord appear? How accurate is that "third day" which rings throughout history in the Christian creeds? Starting with the sacred texts of the New Testament as evidence, our answer has to be not very accurate at all, as I shall seek to demonstrate in chapter 17. For now we must only observe that the resurrection texts themselves do not agree even on that answer. Did resurrection appearances stop at the end of forty days, as Luke suggested, or did they continue long enough to include the conversion of Paul, as he claimed? If Paul is included in the primary list, then, according to most historians, that would extend the time of resurrection appearances to a period ranging from one year to six years.

How are the events we now call resurrection, ascension, and Pentecost related in the Gospel texts? Which is primary? Historically, in the liturgical life of the church, the resurrection is thought to be the primary and most powerful event, and Easter, therefore, the major observance. Ascension has been relegated to a Thursday observance in the liturgical year, and Pentecost now falls, at least in the Northern Hemisphere, in the late spring or early summer.

Since the ascension is hard to envision in a space age and since the Holy Spirit is difficult to envision at any time, both of these celebrations have failed to develop a consistent history. In the Northern Hemisphere the observance of Jesus' resurrection comes, not by accident, at the time when the warm mother earth, impregnated with the seeds of the previous fall and fertilized with the heavenly rains that ancient people thought to be the divine semen, begins to send forth the shoots of new life, connecting these symbols of nature's rebirth and resurrection in the human psyche to shape and determine the content of this celebration. The word *Easter* itself is a pagan word that simply means "spring." The resurrection of Jesus is now marked by eggs, bunnies (highly prolific rodents), spring flowers, new fashions, and parades in celebration of the rites of spring. However, is any of that historically or biblically accurate? For now it is important only to note that the Gospels themselves do not agree on the order, and the church has in fact followed Luke's order, which no other Gospel affirms.

THE SHALLOWNESS OF "OBJECTIVE" MEASUREMENTS

In this journey through the New Testament I have sought to let the story of Easter be heard as each writer recorded it. When we embrace all of their versions in our minds at one time, we discover that all we have in the Bible about Easter is an inconsistent, contradictory, mutually exclusive witness. I have traced this development slowly from Paul writing in the sixth decade to the fourth Gospel's appearance as a completed work in the tenth decade. I have allowed the Scriptures themselves to obliterate the traditional ecclesiastical claims that the Christian faith rests on objective history, physical reality, infallible authority, or inerrancy.

I have raised the fears, and I suspect the anger, of those who, not understanding, have vested their faith in a literalness that finally is not trustworthy. In their minds the faith by which they live must either deny this study or it will die. They are correct. A literal view of the resurrection narratives of the New Testament is not sustainable. The oldest way human beings deal with a message that they find unacceptable is to attack the messenger. That will be done in fundamentalist reviews of this book, from fundamentalist pulpits, and in conservative evangelical classrooms. The exposure of the inadequacy of their understanding of Christianity, however, has not come at my hands. I am merely the communicator. The exposure has come from Roman Catholic, Protestant, and Jewish scholars alike who, by engaging the sources of our faith story, have revealed the literal inadequacy of those sources to carry the weight Christians have generally assigned to those texts.

One conclusion looms as obvious. Institutionalized religion in general and institutionalized Christianity in particular is in serious trouble. That has been the assessment of society for several decades now. The structures of the church seek to meet the challenge by narrowing their focus, which has the effect only of increasing the heat but not the light. It also creates a momentary illusion—a temporary blip on the EKG chart of church history—that suggests that all is still well. It will not last. A Christianity that seeks to literalize its story is doomed, but most Christians seem to believe that a Christianity that has no literal point of reference is also doomed. I hope to counter that persuasion in what follows as I now turn to examine other ways of looking at Easter.

For me "Jesus is Lord." Jesus is my way to enter the experience of God, and the story of Easter is the story of that point of entry. Easter, for me, is eternal, subjective, mythological, nonhistorical, and nonphysical. Yet Easter is also something real for me. How can something real be nonphysical, nonhistorical? The usual contrasting words *spiritual* and *physical, historical* and *nonhistorical, objective* and *subjective* are, in my opinion, far too empty and shallow to bear the freight I wish them to carry.

It is my intention now to reverse the process so far employed in this book and to begin a journey backward in time. By exploring, shedding details here, and taking up others there, I will attempt to enter the mystery of Easter that lies seventy years before John and twenty years before Paul. In that place I hope that both I and my readers can find the living Lord who will compel our worship. This reconstruction will not be adequate. It will not remove all questions. It will, however, free the imagination to roam in new directions and it will cite clues that can evoke new possibilities.

I explore this territory as a believing Christian who will not literalize the details of my faith story. I also do it as one who yearns for the church to be alive, vibrant, reformed, not defensive to uphold the indefensible, but once again able to see itself as the community through which God can be known and Jesus can be acknowledged and worshiped as:

> *God of God, Light of Light,*
> *very God of very God, begotten not made,*
> *being of one substance with the Father*
> *by whom all things were made.*[2]

Is this an impossible, audacious, even arrogant dream? Probably. But I invite you to read on.

Part Three

Interpretive Images

Chapter 10

The Primitive Interpretive
Images

No idea ever emerges in a vacuum, nor is it ever interpreted outside its moment of history. That which we Christians call the Easter moment was an experience that certain first-century people had in some form with the life of a first-century Jewish man named Jesus of Nazareth. A description of that actual experience was written nowhere. We have only stories, symbols, and folklore that interpret the experience and describe the effects of the Easter moment. Jesus was crucified. He died. He was buried. Then the conviction grew that God had raised him in some way from the dead. Beyond these basic assertions, which were made with enormous power, every other detail is debated even in the Bible itself.

Without presuming at this point in my story to assess either the truth or the accuracy of the Easter claim, I do want to look at the meaning of resurrection, or life after death, in Jewish society so that we might understand the images and concepts by which the experience, whatever it was, came to be understood.

THE JEWISH VIEW OF LIFE AFTER DEATH

Life after death was not a popular concept among Jewish people until very late in their national life. The great change came between the years 350 B.C.E. and 50 C.E. Life after death still had a novel ring to it at the dawn of the common era and was therefore much disputed. The poles of this dispute were established by the Pharisees, who affirmed life after death, and the Sadducees, who did not. Certainly the weight of biblical evidence at that time was on the side of the Sadducees. The creation story was quite specific. When the human family was banished from the garden, the Lord God said: "In the sweat of your face you shall eat bread till you return to the ground, for out of it you were taken; you are dust, and to dust you shall return" (Gen. 3:19). There is nothing very eternal about that, we must admit.

In the creation event God's *nephesh*, "breath," had vitalized the human being. This was no creature with an immortal soul; it was rather a creature with an animated body. The most ancient Hebrew tradition suggested that when one died, God's breath had simply returned to its source and the body then disappeared into the dust of the ground.

The first text in the Hebrew Scriptures that seems to assert some form of survival beyond death is found in 1 Samuel, where King Saul is said to have paid a visit to the witch of Endor (1 Sam. 28:3–25). Saul asked the witch to help him consult with Samuel, the deceased prophet. Saul's reign is dated toward the end of the eleventh century, but the Book of Samuel that contains this narrative was probably not written until some fifty to one hundred years later. Placing a date on this concept of life after death is therefore not easy, but it does appear to be quite early. In this passage Samuel was in some way called back into life. He was portrayed as recognizable, capable of remembering the past and seeing the future, and possessing some ability to return to the earth when summoned by the medium.

This account presents an unusual and rare Jewish image. Archaeological evidence from Hebrew graves of the ninth and eighth centuries B.C.E. attests that some concept of survival after death existed among these people. At least they buried their dead with plates, bowls, jewelry, and weapons of warfare.[1] But this kind of cultic practice seems to have belonged to the more primitive Hebrew world and was vigorously opposed by the more progressive Yahwist religious tradition that originated with Moses. Indeed such beliefs and customs were forbidden even when Saul asked the help of the witch of Endor, as the text in Samuel clearly reveals. The prophet Isaiah spoke for this prohibition when he wrote, "And when they say to you, 'Consult the medium and the wizards who chirp and mutter,' should not a people consult their God? Should they consult the dead on behalf of the living?" (Isa. 8:19).

By the seventh century, however, these vague references to life after death began to coalesce around the presumed existence of a region that came to be called Sheol. Sheol was a land of shadows, dust, and darkness. It was also thought to be a place beyond the scope of the God Yahweh. Sheol was a common abode of the dead. There was no desire for Sheol among the people, no reward in it, no return from it. Sheol in fact served no real purpose. When people gave a location for Sheol, it tended to be in the center of the earth. Its primary purpose was to give some personification to death itself. Sheol was like a bottomless pit that devoured life after the analogy of a ravenous monster (Isa. 5:14) who was never satisfied (Heb. 2:5; Prov. 27:20).

When the Jewish people went into exile in the early years of the sixth century, however, their concept of the omnipresence of God had to expand. Like most ancient people, they conceived of God as being within the borders of their nation only and concerned only about the affairs of their tribe. During Judah's captivity in the land of Babylon, that idea had either to die or to grow. It grew. So then the postexilic psalmist could write of a universal deity, "Whither shall I go from thy Spirit? Or whither shall I flee from thy presence? If I ascend to heaven, thou art there! If I make my bed in Sheol, thou art there! If I take the wings of the morning and dwell in the uttermost parts of the sea, even there thy hand will lead me, and thy right hand shall hold me" (Ps. 139:7–10).

After the exile even Sheol was no longer apart from the grasp of God, and that was a change of some significance. By the time that the postexilic Book of Proverbs was being put together, fire and Sheol were at least being talked about in the same breath (Prov. 30:16), but since this text is in one of the appendixes to Proverbs, it is therefore quite difficult to date.

These early references contain no hint of such later afterlife themes as justice, reward, and punishment, one reason being that such themes require a clear concept of an individual consciousness. There was no clear concept of the individual in Jewish society at this time. The basic unit of society was the tribe, not the individual. The judgment of God, justice, reward, and punishment was meted out on the entire people, not on the individual person. This was the perennial message of the prophets. Israel was defeated or exiled because the nation was not faithful. Sometimes in the chronicle of Israel's national history one offending act would result in a whole family's or clan's execution lest the entire nation suffer ill (Josh. 7:16ff).

Individualism emerged as a viable concept in Israel only in the seventh century B.C.E., but it did not become a dominant idea until after the exile. It can be seen, however, in such texts as "the fathers shall not be put to death for the children, nor shall the children be put to death for the fathers; every man shall be put to death for his own sin" (Deut. 24:16). A similar emerging idea can be found in Jeremiah (31:29) and Ezekiel (18:2, 30), the authors of which all lived and wrote in the late preexile or early exile period of Jewish history.

No great idea ever develops in a straight line, however, and the concept of life after death certainly had no uniform step-by-step development in Jewish history. Frequently an experience from a minor episode in the life of one generation would be latched onto by the next generation to build a new consensus. Perhaps because bones demonstrably lasted longer after death than did the softer body tissues, the Jews attached particular importance to bones. When Ezekiel wanted to portray a living future for his prostrate and exiled nation, he spoke of the wind, or *ruach,* of God blowing over the valley of dry bones until they revived in a kind of nation-state resurrection. That vision helped to solidify the link between the breath of a person and the ruach of God, and it also planted an image that would some day blossom into the notion of bodily resurrection.

There was one other minority report in the Hebrew writings that was destined to have wide influence. Three people in Jewish history were said to have had mysterious endings to their lives. The first person was Enoch, who was identified as the father of Methuselah and about whom the sacred text said, "Enoch walked with God; and he was not, for God took him" (Gen. 5:24). The second person was Moses, who was said to have died and been buried by God, "but no man knows the place of his burial to this day" (Deut. 34:6). The third person was Elijah, about whom it was written that as he and Elisha talked, "behold a chariot of fire and horses of fire separated the two of them. And Elijah went up by a whirlwind into heaven" (2 Kings 2:11).

What these three episodes were originally written to convey is hard to say at this point, but what these three lives begin to mean in Jewish folklore is easy to chronicle. Here was scriptural evidence that a very few extraordinary people might live lives so righteous, so holy, and so pleasing to God that somehow they would be invited to enter the realm of God without going through the pathway of death. It was a minor idea at the beginning of its mention in each of the episodes in the biblical text. But this idea exercised enormous authority when Jewish apocalyptic literature became quite dominant in the two centuries before the birth of Jesus. Enoch was the name attached to a very popular piece of first-century B.C.E. Jewish apocalyptic literature that did much to shape Jewish images of life after death. Elijah and Moses were portrayed, at least in the synoptic Gospels, as capable of appearing out of heaven in illuminating visions, which seem to me to shape the later Christian narratives of Jesus' post-Easter appearances. So I file these three figures here almost by title, with the pledge to return to them later in more detail.

THE CONCEPT OF JUSTICE ENTERS THE IDEA
OF LIFE AFTER DEATH

Jewish history after the exile proved to be quite painful. Migrations to return to the homeland began in the latter years of the sixth century and continued well into the fourth century. Never, however, did the Jews really reestablish their independent national life for any great number of years. The Persians, Medes, Macedonians, and Romans all exercised authority and power over this victimized people. There was only a brief period of years when anything like independence was achieved, under the leadership of the Maccabees, who became known as the Hasmonians. Many efforts were made to repress the religious life of the Jewish people. I shall discuss that repression in more detail later.

For my purposes now, let me simply state that these persecutions created martyrs, and martyrs fed the imaginations and fantasies of the people. Above all, martyrs faithful to God, faithful to the worship life of the Jews who were executed by the enemies of the Jews, and therefore by the enemies of God, began to force the issue of justice into the Jewish concept of life after death. If a courageous, God-fearing Jewish lad was required by his enemies to profane the name of God or else lose his life, and he, choosing to be faithful, gave up his life, was there no recourse for justice? Could God somewhere balance the scales of evil? This became a burning issue in a nation seemingly always under some other nation's domination. Apocalyptic writings about the end of the world, the final judgment, and restitution for the righteous proliferated to address these concerns. So it was through this bitter history that postdeath reward for those who were faithful to God began to be very popular.

This same painful history also created a widespread messianic expectation. There would arise a new Moses or a new David or a new Elijah, who would restore Jewish fortunes, defeat Jewish enemies, and inaugurate the kingdom of God. We meet many of these ideas in the Gospel narratives as they came to be attached to the story of Jesus of Nazareth. In this section of this book I want to analyze the primary images through which Jesus was interpreted. I need to state first that few of these images were quite as separate as I think some scholars now try to imagine. I present them in a somewhat separate and distinct way with the knowledge that they tended to run together significantly.

THE IMAGE OF PROPHET/MARTYR

Edward Schillebeeckx seeks to identify the first post-Easter image attached to Jesus of Nazareth under the title prophet/martyr.[2] He finds the background echoes for this image in the Aramaic-speaking, primitive Jewish Christians who believed that Jesus had been killed by the Sadducean elements of the temple priesthood—those who most overtly cooperated with the foreign powers and therefore those who most compromised the integrity of the Jewish religion. The theme behind this primitive explanation, according to Schillebeeckx, is that "Jerusalem," a synonym for the religious establishment, historically had been "the killer of the prophets." Schillebeeckx isolates certain texts that he attributes to the "Q community,"[3] and therefore to the most primitive strand of written Christian materials, to support his case. Matthew had Jesus declare woe to those religious leaders who build monuments for the prophets of antiquity while they scourge, kill, and crucify the prophets of today (Matt. 23:29–36), a verse that Luke also included but couched in a bit more moderate language and with the word *crucify* removed (Luke 17:47–51).

Matthew further quoted Jesus as saying, "O Jerusalem, Jerusalem, killing the prophets and stoning those who are sent to you! How often would I have gathered your children together as a hen gathers her brood under her wings, and you would not!" (Matt. 23:37). This was repeated almost verbatim in Luke (13:34). The Gospels also portrayed Jesus as self-consciously in the prophetic tradition that would not perish outside Jerusalem (Luke 13:33). If one wished to challenge the religious leadership of the Jewish people, it had to be done in Jerusalem. Jerusalem was the proper place, and, as the narrative unfolded, it became clear that the feast of the Passover was the proper time.

There was a long history behind this idea. The destruction of the Northern Kingdom of Israel at the hands of the Assyrians in 721 B.C.E. served as the fulfillment of the prophetic warning. From Elijah forward, the prophets had warned this nation of the danger connected with apostasy but to no avail. The leaders of Israel, both king and priests, had banished Amos and refused to listen to Hosea, and consequently the history of this nation, said the prophets, was punctuated with the suffering they deserved. That was the prophetic interpretation of most Jewish history. But the prophet always stood outside the religious establishment of the Jews. A prophet was raised up to speak by the direct call of God, not by the authenticating power of the official priesthood. So throughout Jewish history there was always a tension, and sometimes even a war, between the temple priesthood and the prophetic voices.

This ancient tension, Schillebeeckx argues, influenced the most primitive interpretation of the life, death, and resurrection of Jesus. Jesus was the righteous prophet who challenged the official priesthood. His death was facilitated by that priesthood, but God vindicated him by raising him into God's presence. Jesus' message was validated by proclaiming that God was on the side of the prophet and not on the side of the priesthood, a revolutionary concept from the priesthood's perspective. Jesus' being raised by God indicated that Jesus was right and that the religious leaders were wrong. It would be easy, therefore, to understand why the official temple authorities were not impressed by these Christian claims.

Schillebeeckx finds this theme over and over again in the sermons attributed to Peter in the Book of Acts. These sermons were created, he maintains, in the primitive Aramaic-speaking Jewish community of Christians, and Peter was a part of that community:

> "Men of Israel, . . . Jesus of Nazareth, a man attested to
> you by God with mighty works and wonders and signs
> which God did through him in your midst, . . . this Jesus
> . . . you crucified and killed by the hands of lawless men.
> But God raised him up." (Acts 2:22–24)

> "Be it known to you all, and to all the people of Israel, that
> by the name of Jesus of Nazareth whom you crucified,
> whom God raised from the dead . . . " (Acts 4:10)

> "The God of our Fathers raised Jesus whom you killed by
> hanging him on a tree. God exalted him at his right hand
> as Leader and Savior." (Acts 5:30–31)

"They put him to death by hanging him on a tree; but
God raised him on the third day and made him manifest."
(Acts 10:39b–40)

Schillebeeckx detects the most primitive strand of early Christian thinking in these texts not only because they portray Jesus as prophet, martyr, and hero, whose righteousness won for him God's vindication in the face of his victimization by the religious leaders, but also because they contain no salvific element. That idea had not yet emerged. That is to say, Jesus' death and his having been raised did not yet affect anyone else. God raised Jesus simply to right the scales of justice. That is the most ancient note to be found in the New Testament. That action reflected an experience with little interpretation. For that reason it could arguably be said to be the first and most primitive strand of explanation attached to the power of Easter.

The second primitive note that Schillebeeckx sees in these isolated texts was one that we noted as we walked through the biblical data. In these texts Jesus was the passive subject of God's resurrecting action, which meant that the resurrection was seen not as a resurrection back into life but as an exaltation of Jesus into God and God's heaven by God's divine action.

Locating these ideas among the Jewish Christians of Palestine as part of the most primitive strand of Christian development is more important to me than ascribing them to the Q document. My commitment to the existence of a Q document has been shaken significantly by Michael Goulder's brilliant analysis of that theory in his commentaries on both Luke and Matthew. Goulder asserts that Q is nothing but Matthew doing midrash on Mark and its claim to being primitive is not the ability to date it early but the recognition that the author of Matthew may himself have been a scribe who was part of a struggling community of Jewish Christians. However, the dependence of the author of this Gospel on the Greek translations of the Hebrew Scriptures raises some questions for me about that premise, though it does not invalidate it. In any event, I present this idea to show how the experience of Jesus, crucified and raised, was thought to have found its first expression inside the symbols operative in first-century Jewish circles.

Schillebeeckx goes on to argue that the prophet/martyr theme did not live in isolation very long before other major Jewish themes embraced it, expanding this primitive explanation both dramatically and theologically. First, an element of divine necessity was added. Jesus' death was said to be by divine plan, not by accident or by the action of a lone prophet. This view of Jesus' death was one pace beyond the conflict with the Jewish religious leaders, for a divine purpose had been added.

It was not long after this that Jesus' death was given a theological explanation. This explanation hints that the development of a catechism for teaching purposes had been inaugurated. One can see the catechetical method developing in a question-and-answer form. How could Jesus be crucified and not be accursed, as Deuteronomy says is God's judgment on anyone who is executed (Deut. 27:23)? If Jesus suffered for a purpose, if he died to live out the will of God for him, then his death had to have meaning that needed to be examined and understood. At this crossroads, salvation, eschatology, apocalypticism, and vicarious action begin to come together, and each in its turn would affect the way Jesus was proclaimed. Each in its turn would also shape the others until all became dimensions of the many-sided spectacle we call Easter.

Moving beyond the prophet/martyr image, we will seek to understand how the other images grew and expanded until Jesus in fact was covered with the hopes present in the Jewish past. The most important question to keep in mind is, What happened that caused first-century Jewish people to employ these images to explain what they believed they had experienced? Why did they begin to see Jesus in terms of the atoning sacrifice, the suffering servant, and the Son of man? What facet of the Easter narrative is illuminated by each image? As we bring them into focus one by one, objectivity vanishes and the need to understand the history and background of each image grows, for each image has helped to shape the story of the resurrection.

Chapter 11

The Atoning Sacrifice—The Image
of the Book of Hebrews

Nestled near the back of the New Testament is a book the King James Bible called the Epistle of Paul to the Hebrews. That title is inaccurate on two counts. First, it was not written by Paul. Its style, language, vocabulary, and content are so totally un-Pauline that no biblical scholar in the world today attributes this work to the great missionary apostle.

Second, this book is not an epistle. An epistle is a letter written by someone who is not present to his or her audience—living somewhere else. This work does not assume distance. It is, rather, cast in the form of a sermon or a treatise. It was probably written originally to be spoken by the writer. It was composed in Greek and appears to be addressed to a group of Greek-speaking Hebrews who, in all probability, had come from outlying parts of the empire to their spiritual home on a pilgrimage to Jerusalem. That means that the audience to whom this homily was addressed was Jewish people who had become Christians.

Like so many of the first generation of Christians, these people expected the imminent return of Jesus from heaven, to which they believed he had been exalted. Since his return was to be accomplished in Jerusalem, Jewish Christians would periodically journey to this holy city to await their Lord's return. In Jerusalem they might stay in a monasticlike setting, providing for one another out of their common provisions. A monastery guest house would be a familiar context for such activity. Indeed it may have been the head of that monastic community who wrote and delivered the oration to his resident pilgrims that came to be called the Book of Hebrews. At the very least, monasticlike terms such as *brothers* and *beloved* give monastic overtones to this piece of literature.

Regardless of whether or not this particular reconstruction is accurate, the Book of Hebrews reflects an early stage in Christian development. It presents us with a picture of Christianity before it escaped its Jewish womb or leaped its Jewish barrier and became primarily a gentile movement. This may point to the possibility, as some have argued, that this work is pre-Pauline. Some commentators place it as early as the fifth decade of the Christian era, though that is clearly a minority point of view. If it is post-Pauline, or a product of the seventh or eighth decade, as others have suggested, it may nonetheless be the work of that part of Christianity which had not been significantly touched by either Paul or the gentile movement.

I am increasingly convinced that this work was completed before the fall of Jerusalem in 70 C.E. I suggest this date because doctrinally the Book of Hebrews offers a point of view that reflects a very primitive Christianity. The elaborate theological systems at work even in the Gospels have not yet been formulated in this book. In Hebrews, for example, Jesus is referred to as a son of God, not the Son of God (Heb. 1:2). In Hebrews Jesus is one who is perfected by his suffering and death (Heb. 5:9). Jesus is not the preexistent perfect one. In the Book of Hebrews there is not one single reference to that view of the resurrection that includes a return to life on earth from the tomb. Rather, this work draws the resurrection image of Jesus' having been exalted by God at the moment of his death to God's right hand in heaven (Heb. 2:9; 4:14).

The Book of Hebrews is one more prime example in the Christian Scriptures of the style of Jewish writing called midrash. The first Christians, drawing from their Jewish roots, were simply composing a new chapter in an ongoing, unfolding, consistent religious drama. The earlier and the more Jewish the writing, the more midrash appears to be in operation.

The Epistle to the Hebrews was written by a Jewish Christian to present Jesus within the traditional Jewish frame of reference to other Jewish Christians. Its starting point was Psalm 110. If it was indeed a sermon, Psalm 110 was its text. This psalm was one of Israel's enthronement psalms celebrating the assumption of power by a priest king—perhaps someone like Ezra. Early Christians thought this psalm presaged the enthronement into heaven of the priest king Jesus of Nazareth, and so it became very popular in Christian circles. In the Gospel of Mark, Jesus was quoted applying this same psalm to himself. Matthew and Luke repeated that Marcan thought, which indicates that early Christians did not read this psalm except as a pointer to Jesus.

So by entering the Book of Hebrews we find another doorway into primitive Christianity, and through its words we can entertain a picture of Jesus as he was seen in Christian theology near the dawn of the Christian era.

WHAT JESUS MEANT TO THE WRITER OF HEBREWS

The writer of Hebrews gives no evidence of ever having known the Jesus of history. He had heard the story of Jesus' life and death. He had heard the claim that somehow Jesus' death was not final, that death could not contain him. This author was a Jew steeped in the experience, the history, and the Scriptures of his people.

He knew, for example, about the Jewish tradition of the Day of the Atonement. He had probably participated in it countless times. It was part of his annual liturgical life. In that liturgy a priest purified himself with ceremonial cleansing activities before entering the Holy of Holies, the most sacred part of the temple, to offer to God a perfect sacrifice. Entry into this sacred sanctuary occurred only once a year. The sacrificial animal was itself scrutinized. It had to be a perfect specimen. There could be no scars, no broken bones, no blemishes. A ceremonially purified priest would take a demonstrably perfect animal into the Holy of Holies to offer it to God for the sins of the people—corporate and individual.

The Jews had in their religious folklore a theory called the treasury of merit. Both sins and virtues in this theory accumulated and were stored in a divine treasury, just as money today is placed into a savings account. The accounts on this divine treasury were kept by the Lord, who required that the books be balanced from time to time on both individual and corporate levels. Disaster or sickness or military defeat was seen as a way to balance people's accounts, for these were the payment in the coin of divine punishment for their sins. But any excess virtue that existed could also be used to balance excess sins. A particularly virtuous Israelite could enable God to forgive the sins of many and therefore spare them punishment. The perfect sacrifice made by the purified priest was understood after this analogy. That sacrifice created a treasury of merit. It brought atonement and redemption and balanced the scales by which God related to God's people. In this manner the sacrificial animal could take away the sins of the people.

When first-century Jews sought to understand Jesus, the analogy of the Day of Atonement was employed but with an interesting twist. First, Jesus himself came to be understood as the perfect sacrifice. He took the place of the lamb. He became, in the words of our liturgy, the Lamb of God. His sinlessness was described after the analogy of the sacrificial animal. His was a perfect body—young, mature, no scars or broken bones. To this was added the element of his moral perfection, achieved by a human being with free choice. The story of Abraham offering his son Isaac as commanded by God in the Book of Genesis was then understood midrashically as a story designed to foreshadow the Father God who would also sacrifice his only son, Jesus, to build the infinite treasury of merit that would redeem people for God for all ages. It was in this manner that the phrase "Jesus died for our sins" entered the Christian vocabulary. Jesus took upon himself the weight of our misdeeds and balanced the books forever with the perfect offering of his sinless life. The treasury of merit was filled with an infinite supply of virtue. When one came to Jesus, one had his merit to cover all of one's own shortcomings. As the bloody hymns of the nineteenth century put it, we are "washed in his blood" and "cleansed by his blood."

But Jesus was also seen as the perfect and purified priest in this midrash tradition. By the pureness of his own life, not just by ceremonial purification, he was able to offer the perfect sacrifice of himself. He did not need the lavabo;[1] he did not need to be cleansed. His innocent suffering purged all life of sin, including his own. The sacrificial animal was replaced by the crucified Christ, but he was also the purified priest who offered himself. By his suffering and death Jesus brought atonement and redemption.

Since Jesus was not of the authentic priestly line, however, a valid claim to priesthood had to be developed for him by the early Jewish Christians. Psalm 110 provided the author of Hebrews the clue to enable him to do just that, for it referred to the strange, enigmatic priest whose name was Melchizedek (v. 4). In the Book of Genesis (14:18ff), where the story of Melchizedek was recorded, he was identified as king of Salem and a priest of God Most High. In that story also Melchizedek blessed Abraham, and Abraham gave to Melchizedek a tenth of everything in return.

Regardless of the original meaning of that narrative, which to modern critics looks very much like an extortion payoff, the midrash tradition developed Melchizedek as a priest forever without beginning or end, to whom even the Jewish people had paid homage. Building on the reference in Psalm 110, which he quoted (Heb. 5:6), the author of Hebrews interpreted Jesus as the perfect priest after the order of Melchizedek. As the priest, Jesus was qualified to enter the Holy of Holies and to offer himself as the perfect sacrifice. The author of Hebrews interpreted Melchizedek's name to mean "king of righteousness." He interpreted his designation king of Salem (Shalom) from which Jerusalem takes its name to mean king of peace. He described Melchizedek as being without father or mother or genealogy, without beginning or end, but resembling the Son of God, a priest forever. Because Abraham had given offerings to Melchizedek and because Abraham was the great-grandfather of Levi, who was the patriarch of the line of Israel's legitimate priesthood, Levi was said by the author of Hebrews to have paid tithes to Melchizedek, since when Abraham paid the tithes to Melchizedek Levi was carried in Abraham's seed. So this author argued that a priest like Melchizedek was an eternal priest, coming out of nothing, answerable only to God, and therefore superior to the Levitical priesthood.

The Levitical priests could not attain perfection. They had to repeat their purification rites to enable them to enter the Holy of Holies. They had to repeat their sacrifices also, ever seeking atonement and ever building up anew the treasury of merit. But a priest after the order of Melchizedek, one who was affirmed not by legal ascent or apostolic succession but by an indestructible and pure life, could offer himself as both priest and victim and thereby could be the agent for bringing about an eternal redemption, a once-for-all-time atonement, filling up forever the treasury of merit upon which all depended, with the infinite merit of his perfect life.

This was the understanding of the life of Jesus as found in the Book of Hebrews. When this Jewish understanding is grasped by modern people, to whom this way of thinking is so strange, then the first step to understanding this book has been taken. The interpretive midrash of this author, however, did not stop there.

The Jews also believed that heaven replicated things on earth but in a grander, more glorious way. The temple on earth was a temple made with hands. There was in heaven, however, just beyond the sky, a temple not made with hands. The Holy of Holies in the earthly temple was thought to be a replica of the throne of God in heaven. The sacrificed animal offered in the Holy of Holies rose to God through the smoke and fragrance of the fire and from the spices used in the preparation of the sacrifice combined with the incense, and the cooking meat. In Hebrew history a pillar of fire by night and a pillar of cloud by day were believed to have kept the Hebrew people connected with God during their exodus from slavery in Egypt (Exod. 13:21). The fire and smoke of the sacrificed animals kept that vital connection intact.

When Jesus, the great high priest with a perfect life, offered himself as the sacrificial animal, he entered through his sacrificial death into the heavenly place by way of the pillar of cloud. In the smoke of the sacrifice the cloud connected earth and heaven, and by this pillar, this smoke, Jesus was carried up to heaven, enthroned at God's right hand, thereby becoming ready and available for all eternity to intercede for those who acknowledged him as Lord. So Jews who acknowledged Jesus as Lord had no further need for sacrifices. They had no further need for atonement. Jesus had made the perfect sacrifice, he had offered himself. God had exalted him, seated him on a heavenly throne, and appointed him a Son who had been made perfect forever (Heb. 7:27–28). In the words of this treatise, Christ

> has entered once for all into the Holy Place, taking not the blood of goats and calves but his own blood, thus securing an eternal redemption. (9:12)

> For Christ has entered, not into a sanctuary made with hands, a copy of the true one, but into heaven itself, now to appear in the presence of God on our behalf. (9:24)

> Since then we have a great high priest who has passed through the heavens, Jesus, the Son of God, let us hold fast our confession. . . . Let us then with confidence draw near to the throne of grace, that we may receive mercy and find grace to help in time of need. (4:14–16)

This was the witness and the understanding laid out by this Jewish Christian homily.

So here we have an early Christian writer who did not know the Jesus of the Gospels but who had shared in a powerful experience of Jesus in a community of Jewish Christians. Within the scope of his frame of reference, he sought to make sense out of that experience. The Book of Hebrews contains no concept of a risen Jesus appearing to various people as the resurrected Lord—none whatsoever. That tradition, we have previously noted, is also not found in either Paul or Mark. It was developed by Matthew, Luke, and John in the ninth and tenth decades of the Christian era. Yet the Book of Hebrews powerfully conveys the uniqueness and the goodness of Jesus' life, the inappropriateness of Jesus' execution, and the affirmation that God reversed the human verdict on Jesus' life by exalting him to the right hand of the heavenly throne of grace.

There is in these ancient words a tremendous sense that by elevating Jesus into the meaning of God, God had placed into the divine life one who knew human weakness, human frailty, and human temptation. There was a strengthening sense that all people could now come before God through the intercession of a great high priest who not only empathized but also understood, because he had shared our humanity and he had been victimized by our sin.

The symbols are Jewish, the understandings are first century. The images of heaven are from a pre-Copernican world. Literalize them and they die. Recognize them for what they were and they become doorways through which we are still invited into an experience of transcendence that is somehow associated with Jesus of Nazareth. This was the only understanding of Jesus the writer of Hebrews seems to have had. He knew nothing of the virgin birth, though he talked about Jesus having neither father nor mother nor genealogy, like Melchizedek (Heb. 7:3). By so doing, he may have opened the door for someone's later imagination to develop a miraculous birth tradition. He had no concept of resurrection as resuscitation or as a physical reality. Empty tombs and appearance stories would have been nonsensical to him. He had no concept of physical ascension. Jesus went to God as the smoke of the sacrificed victim rose to heaven.

What this author did have was a sense of Jesus as exalted, ever present, perfected, freeing all who called on him from the bondage of sin. Borrowing one final midrashic detail from the Old Testament, this author portrayed Jesus as offering to the people the "rest" that had been promised to the people of God as they wandered in the wilderness. The "rest" was originally to be gained upon entrance from the wilderness to the holy soil of their homeland. But because of their sinfulness in the wilderness, the Jews of the exodus were forbidden to enter into God's rest. All who left Egypt died before they crossed the Jordan River (Heb. 3:11). Even Joshua, who led the people into the promised land, still did not give them the rest they had yearned to receive. The psalmist, said the Book of Hebrews, long after the time of Joshua still yearned to enter God's rest (Heb. 4:1–11) (Ps. 95:11).

Rest, as biblical writers of the Hebrew tradition used this word, was defined in the Sabbath Day tradition. God rested when God's work was completed on the seventh day. It was therefore into God's completed work that God had promised access to the Jewish people. When this author pictured Christ as the high priest at God's right hand in the heavenly place, the rest that God promised was finally achieved. Through this great high priest and the treasury of his merit, the promise of God, the eternal Sabbath, could finally be entered. In a Gospel written, I believe, some years later, this idea was further developed and put onto the lips of the historical Jesus when he said, "Come to me, all who labor and are heavy laden, and I will give you *rest*" (Matt. 11:28). And a moment later the promise was made that in him "you will find *rest* for your souls" (Matt. 11:29).

I relate in this chapter one early description of how Jesus was understood. It is, strangely enough, one that is not generally known even by Christians. It is quite different from the familiar descriptions of Easter found in the Gospels. Perhaps it is earlier than all of them. It is certainly older than any but Mark. In many ways it is more primitive, more symbolic, less miraculous, less supernatural, maybe even more original, but it is equally real. I invite you to examine this image, to stand with an open mind before this witness until you can begin to comprehend the incomprehensible, for no matter what words we use to describe Easter, it is only a faith affirmation that finally stands alone before us, beckoning us to enter its meaning. When that affirmation is reduced to words, it says something like this:

Jesus lives.
Death cannot contain him.
God loves.
Death cannot limit this love.
We are not alone.
In the vastness of this universe we have been valued and
embraced.

I invite my readers to look at Jesus through the lens of the Book of Hebrews. It will move you beyond just believing in the resurrection into living the resurrection. For only when we live the resurrection will we finally know the experience of resurrection. It is not finally the explaining image that is important. It is rather the experience that drove the earliest Christians to search for an explanation.

Chapter 12

The Suffering Servant—
The Image of 2 Isaiah

"You are the Christ." These are words from Mark, the earliest Gospel (8:29). They were attributed to Peter and were spoken, Mark said, in the town of Caesarea Philippi in the earlier part of Jesus' public ministry sometime before his triumphal arrival in Jerusalem. I suspect that this placement in the text is inaccurate.

The application of the title "Christ" to Jesus of Nazareth surely did not come until after the experience of Easter. If any of the disciples understood Jesus as the Christ on any level at this point in their lives, then the rest of their behavior recorded in the Gospels was nonsensical. Surely one who was thought by his followers to be the Christ would not have been betrayed, denied, or forsaken by his followers.

This reality was acknowledged by the writer of Mark because he went on to show how badly Peter misunderstood the Christ-title he had just used, for Peter was almost immediately called satanic by Jesus when he did not seem to realize that being the Christ and walking a path of suffering that would lead to crucifixion could not be separated. It is interesting to me that Mark placed this confession by Peter of the Christ-nature of Jesus right after Mark had told his readers about the progressive healing of the blind man from Bethsaida. In Mark's narrative, the blind man was taken gradually from no sight, to partial sight, to full sight.

The fourth Gospel later informs us that Peter was from Bethsaida (John 1:44). Perhaps this simple healing story was not so simple after all. Perhaps it traced Peter's experience as he made the journey from sight to insight in his attempt to understand the meaning of the one he knew as Jesus of Nazareth. In any event, this was the first time in Mark's Gospel that the word *Christ* was used, save for Mark's opening sentence in which he informed his readers that he was about to relate to them the Gospel of Jesus Christ, the Son of God.

In Mark, Peter's confession is brief and straightforward: "You are the Christ." By the time Matthew wrote his story, some fifteen to twenty years later, this Petrine confession had been embellished to read, "You are the Christ, the Son of the living God" (Matt. 16:16), and Peter's failure to grasp what his affirmation meant is deemphasized. Prior to the rebuke, Matthew actually had Jesus bless Peter. Jesus told Peter that flesh and blood could not have revealed this insight to him and extolled Peter as the rock upon which the church would be built. He was given the keys to the kingdom as well as the promise that whatever he bound or loosed on earth would be bound or loosed in heaven. Matthew's changes to this episode reveal all the more clearly that it was a postresurrection memory in which Peter stood at the very center of the Christian community's life. Peter's confession had simply been read back into the life of the historical Jesus by the interpreting Christian community.

The way Luke treated this Marcan text is also revelatory. In Luke, Peter's confession is not the simple "You are the Christ." Here Peter said, "You are the Christ of God" (Luke 9:20). Luke then omitted altogether Jesus' rebuke of Peter's misunderstanding of what that confession meant. Jesus enjoined secrecy on all the disciples in regard to this revelation. He commanded them to tell no one, and then he began to speak of his suffering, rejection, execution, and resurrection. In the mind of each Gospel writer the designation of Jesus as the Christ was a designation that associated who he was with suffering. Luke spelled this out quite specifically, for he had Jesus immediately talk about self-denial and the taking up of the cross daily as the means of following him.

That was an interesting phrase to place into the rhetoric of the historical Jesus before his crucifixion. If his point was not made well enough by now, Luke went on to quote Jesus as saying, "For whoever would save his life will lose it; and whoever loses his life for my sake, he will save it. For what does it profit a man if he gains the whole world and loses or forfeits himself? For whoever is ashamed of me and of my words, of him will the Son of man be ashamed when he comes in his glory and the glory of the Father and of the holy angels. But I tell you truly, there are some standing here who will not taste death before they see the kingdom of God" (Luke 9:24–27).

CONNECTING CHRIST WITH SUFFERING

Examining Peter's Christ-confession at Caesarea Philippi and the way it was presented by each Gospel writer enables us to see immediately that the Gospels are not biographies meant to be read as linear history. They are midrashic interpretations. Midrash is a way to incorporate timelessness into a sacred narrative. As Luke's text reveals, the early Christians were trying to deal with the need to remove from Jesus the sense of shame connected with the fact that he had been executed. On this battle line the enemies of Christianity had launched a determined attack. The Christian defense was to apply a word rich in Jewish history and mythology to Jesus of Nazareth. It was a title that connected Jesus with suffering: "Jesus, you are the Christ."

From where did the word *Christ* emerge? What did it originally mean? How did suffering enter that word? How did its meaning change through history? Christ is our English translation of the Greek word *christos*, which means "messiah," "savior," or "redeemer." But Christos is an attempt to put the Hebrew word *mashiach* into Greek. Mashiach originally simply meant God's anointed one. In Israel's early history only the king was anointed and so only the king was called God's anointed one, or God's

Christ. The king was praised as a "man after God's own heart" (Isa. 13:14), a person endowed with God's own strength (Isa. 2:10; Ps. 21:3). In time this royal tradition was incorporated into the religious life of Israel, and the king came to be seen as the center of God's activity (2 Sam. 7:4–17) and the kingly anointed one came to be thought of and called "Son of God." This was especially true in the southern kingdom of Judah, where the holy city of Jerusalem, the royal house of David, and the temple were the visible symbols of God's presence among the Jewish people. The Jewish king came to be described in such phrases as "You are my Son, today have I begotten you" (Ps. 2:7) or "The king will call God 'Father'" (Ps. 89:26), and God will acknowledge the king as his "firstborn" son (Ps. 89:27). God's promise to David was "I will be his father and he shall be my son" (2 Sam. 7:14).

To call Judah's king the Son of God was not to imply that the king was divine or that the king had achieved moral perfection. Nothing in Jewish literature suggests that. David was portrayed as an adulterer who caused Uriah, the cuckolded husband of David's illicit lover Bathsheba, to be put to death (2 Sam. 11:1–27). Solomon was pictured as allowing religious syncretism to invade Jewish worship by building chapels to foreign deities to keep his many foreign wives happy (1 Kings 11:1–8). King Manasseh was said to have been so wicked that the only good thing he ever did was to utter a prayer (2 Chron. 33:1–13). Kings in Judah were not dehumanized; they were not thought of as semidivine figures; but they were anointed, hence the title mashiach.

The Jewish understanding of Yahweh, their tribal deity, expanded during Israel's history until Israel's God was thought of as the King of the universe, who ruled the whole world from a heavenly throne. This of course meant that Israel's view of God transcended the boundaries of Israel's territory. They began to dream that someday Israel's realm, over which God would rule, would be extended to include the whole earth. The Divine will would be done on earth as it was in heaven, and when that day arrived, Israel's king would be universally recognized as the earthly representative of God. Grandeur filled their dreams.

But in the early years of the sixth century before the common era, tragedy befell the little principality of Judah, and that tragedy was to shape Jewish history significantly. The Babylonians conquered Jerusalem. The people were herded together and marched into captivity.

The Jewish nation appeared to be at the end of its identifiable history. Judah's only future hope lay in the restoration of its monarchy, which in time came to be thought of as beyond the scope of history so it was located by the Jews in the fantasy of their mythology.

Some part of this fantasy, among the Jews, envisioned the mashiach as a new political leader who would arise in the distant future and would be a victorious military figure. By the might of this figure's arm, and aided by the power of God fighting at his side, this mythical hero would restore the kingdom of the Jews. These dreams created a nationalistic ego-boost for a defeated, downtrodden people and consequently became quite popular.

Late in the sixth century, Cyrus, the king of the Persians, emerged to challenge the Babylonians for hegemony in world politics. The Jewish people applied the term *mashiach* even to Cyrus, thinking he was the agent through whom God would act to restore the Jewish nation (Isa. 45:1). Popular Judaism anticipated and prayed for God's coming—in the person of the great king, the expected messiah, the newly anointed one who would right the wrongs of history.

There was, however, a minority, but far more realistic, view of the coming mashiach that existed among these exiled Jewish people. This nation had known no real greatness since the reign of Solomon some three hundred years prior. Certainly an exiled people with no homeland find it quite difficult to dream of future conquests. It was out of this context of powerlessness and defeat that a new view of messiah, or mashiach, as the righteous victim began to emerge in Jewish fantasy. It was not a popular view. It was more the counterpoint view of a remnant. It became even less popular when the exiled people were finally freed and could begin the journey home.

Their freedom to return to their homeland fanned the fantasies of most of the exiled people. They dreamed of restoring their institutions, rebuilding their temple and city walls, reestablishing the Davidic throne, and reinstituting all of their sacred traditions. Since these were the children, grandchildren, and, in some cases, even the great-grandchildren of the defeated Jews from some sixty years earlier, there were no realistic memories against which to measure their fantasies. The only Jerusalem they knew, the only temple they could envision, and the only dynasty they could imagine were the ones described to them around the campfires of Babylon by their now-deceased parents and grandparents. The Jews of the exile possessed only word pictures shaped by the loneliness and fear of the storytellers. In the imaginations of the listeners these pictures were significantly embellished and modified upward as they passed from one generation to the next. In such an environment, a view of the coming one as the suffering victim could not flourish. Rather, a renewed triumphalism was the order of the day.

But when this caravan of exiled people finally arrived in their homeland, their dreams and fantasies for Judah died a violent and cruel death. They looked around at their sacred soil and saw only devastation. Their homeland was a waste place. Their holy city was an abandoned pile of rubble. Their temple was a field of weeds and stones. There was no hint of greatness, no symbol of power, nothing by which to be impressed. Undaunted, some set about the monumental task of clearing and rebuilding. Illusions die slowly. Yet there was at least this other minority Jewish response, and that portrait was brought to a new luster through the creative pen of an unknown prophet whose work of art came to be attached to the scroll of the prophet Isaiah. For this reason alone it is called 2 Isaiah, and today it constitutes chapters 40 through 55 of that book.

This writer knew instinctively that Israel would never again rise to world dominance. He knew that no vocation as God's chosen people could be sustained if it was based on the illusion of a future greatness or world power. The desolated vision that greeted those returning from exile brought immediate death to both their dreams and their illusions. Slowly but surely, a new conclusion forced its way into Israel's reality. If Israel was to be great again, it would need to be a different kind of greatness. The yearned-for ideal king, the victorious mashiach, the Christ, had to be redefined in a radically different way. This anonymous prophet set about to do just that.

God's mashiach would not belong to Israel alone, he wrote. This hoped-for messiah would break the bands of nationalism. The one for whom Israel yearned would also be a light to the Gentiles, one who would bring justice to the world. This ideal ruler, rising out of weakness rather than strength, would be able to express God's tenderness for all humankind. The messianic task would no longer be to lead Israel to greatness but rather to liberate all people from whatever bondage possessed them. As one who knew suffering, this figure would comfort all sufferers—the thirsty would be guided to water, the blind to sight, the prisoners freed, the poor would hear the good news of God's love. This messiah would bring wholeness to human life.

Second Isaiah, I am confident, saw this as a new vocation for God's chosen people. If the whole nation could not accept this vocation, then it must be the task of a remnant of God's people. If not a remnant, then perhaps one solitary child of Israel might live out this role. It was a startling concept, a powerful portrait of the way God's purpose of calling the world into the divine presence might be accomplished through weakness rather than through strength. Gone from this portrait was any semblance of worldly and earthly grandeur. Those qualities, understood by this writer in a totally different way from his contemporaries, would never again be part of Israel's self-definition. They were now a defeated, broken nation. God's purposes were either at an end or they must be achieved through weakness. There were no other alternatives.

So this nameless prophet wrote that the servant would accomplish the divine purpose not by power and might but by meekness. The servant would be self-effacing and would not resist hostility or draw back from maltreatment. The face of the servant would be set only on the vocation, now understood in dramatically different categories. Before hostility the servant would not flinch. Through the pathway of affliction the divine purpose would be achieved. Even if the servant met a violent death in living out this vocation, even if the servant was slain as a criminal, the purposes of God would still be achieved. Through suffering and death, rather than through victory and glory, the reign of God would be seen.

So it was that messiah and weakness, messiah and suffering, came to be merged. Second Isaiah said it in powerful poetry. The servant was "despised," "rejected," a person of "sorrows," one "acquainted with grief" (Isa. 53:3). A vicarious note was sounded when this ancient writer suggested that the servant was the one who would be "wounded for our transgressions," the one whose "stripes" would bring healing to the world (Isa. 53:5).

Needless to say, this idea never won majority approval. Whenever the fortunes of the Jewish people took an upward turn, the far more satisfying fantasies of restored glory would reappear. When the Maccabean revolution achieved independence for the Jews in that brief window between the Macedonian Empire and the Roman Empire, the dreams of yesterday's grandeur became strong, and the idea of the messiah as a victorious military leader was once again popular. But such moments were short-lived, and soon these hopes would be dashed on the hard rocks of reality. Israel was not ever to be more than a pointer to God, a pointer that had to be seen amid weakness, suffering, and defeat. But at least someone had dared to suggest that the messiah, mashiach, Christ might be imagined among Jewish people in such terms as weakness, powerlessness, defeat, and death. The concept was filed away and all but forgotten for several hundred years until another figure arose in Jewish history and people tried to make sense out of what they had experienced in the life of one called Jesus of Nazareth.

HOW JESUS WAS SEEN TO FIT THE ROLE

He was crucified. Jewish law declared that one who "has committed a crime and he is put to death, and you hang him on a tree, his body shall not remain all night upon the tree, but you shall bury him the same day, for a hanged man is accursed by God; you shall not defile your land which the Lord your God gives you for an inheritance" (Deut. 21:22ff). Jesus, the crucified one, the one hanged on a tree, was therefore accursed in the eyes of the Torah, the law. But that conclusion did not fit other parts of his life. How could a life marked by such love be accursed? How could one who drove them beyond the boundaries of their prejudices to love the Samaritans, to embrace the lepers, to turn the other cheek, to pray for their enemies be accursed? How could one who taught that God was bread for the hungry, water for the thirsty, caring for the lost, life for the dying be accursed by God? How could one who forgave his persecutors, prayed for his executioners, reached out to love those who rejected him be evil and be accursed by God? How could one who lived God's love, proclaimed the inbreaking of God's realm, and likened God to a father who welcomed the prodigal son be worthy of death and thus be accursed by God?

There was a radical, jarring disjunction between this man's life and this man's fate. They could not understand why he had died. It was not fair. He was charged with blasphemy. God must have been offended by him. He was dead. He must have been something other than what they had experienced him to be. For the righteousness they saw, the love they knew, the forgiveness and the caring they received—all of these had not been rewarded. He was dead, hanged upon a tree, accursed of God.

Then, like all devout Jews, some of them began to search the Scriptures in order to understand. That search brought them face to face with the portrait of a suffering mashiach in the writings of one named Isaiah. Here they found a messiah who achieved God's purposes through weakness, not power. For these discouraged disciples it was as if a light had begun to dawn. Perhaps Jesus could be messiah and still die. Perhaps the Scriptures did include the image of a mashiach who suffered. In that biblical narrative they discovered that the one who bore the abuse of others for the sake of righteousness was called God's son. He was also called God's Christ. God would be at the side of such a figure. If that person was defeated or killed, God would vindicate the servant by raising that figure into the life of God.

Suddenly these disciples had an image from their sacred writings by which they could now understand their experience with Jesus of Nazareth. They began to tell his story after the analogy of the servant in 2 Isaiah. We find these notes time and again in the Gospels themselves so the connection between the Jesus of history and the servant of Isaiah had to develop prior to the writing of the Gospels. It makes us powerfully aware that only because Jesus was Jewish did this portrait out of Jewish folklore get applied to him. When Luke had Simeon refer to Jesus as a "light to lighten the Gentiles" (2:32) he was leaning on the words of Isaiah 49 said to the servant, "I will give you as a light to the nations."

When the story of Jesus' adult life was told, a figure named John the Baptist was interpreted as his forerunner. John was a voice crying in the wilderness, "Prepare the way of the Lord." Those words were lifted directly from Isaiah 40 (v. 3). If one takes out the punctuation of the first sentence of Mark's Gospel, punctuation that was not original to the text, then that verse reads: "The beginning of the Gospel of Jesus Christ as it is written in the Book of Isaiah." Professor Dale Miller has argued that that is the proper reading of Mark, who was convinced that the story of Jesus actually began with the servant passages of Isaiah.[1]

The Gospel writers chose to narrate Jesus' baptism with words from 2 Isaiah: "Behold my servant, whom I uphold, my chosen, in whom my soul delights; I have put my Spirit upon him" (Isa. 42:1; Mark 1:10; Matt. 3:17; Luke 3:22). The only way Isaiah's servant could accomplish his purpose was to suffer indignity, rejection, and death. Jesus, the servant, was now seen in this same pattern by the early church.

When Jesus inaugurated his public ministry in his hometown of Nazareth, he was pictured as doing so by reading from the Book of Isaiah (Luke 4:18, 19). When he had finished reading, the identification the early Christians were making between Jesus and the servant figure was stated publicly. "This day," Jesus was reported to have said when he returned the scroll of Isaiah to the officials of the synagogue, "this scripture has been fulfilled in your hearing" (Luke 4:21).

According to Luke (5:20ff), on another occasion Jesus startled the crowd by saying to the paralytic man, "Your sins are forgiven you." But the servant in 2 Isaiah said, "I am he who blots out your transgressions for my own sake, and I will not remember your sins" (43:25). When Jesus began his inevitable journey to Jerusalem, Luke said he "set his face." In 2 Isaiah the servant said, "Therefore I have set my face like a flint" (50:7) as he walked the path of suffering and death.

Prior to the story of the Palm Sunday entry into Jerusalem, Luke had Jesus say to his disciples, "Behold, we are going up to Jerusalem and everything that is written of the Son of man by the prophets will be accomplished" (18:31). The primary writing of the prophets to which Luke was referring was 2 Isaiah and his picture of the servant who brought life by suffering and dying.

When the story of the crucifixion was told, the details were supplied by the interpretive portrait of Isaiah's servant figure. According to Luke, Jesus said at the Last Supper, "This scripture must be fulfilled in me, 'And he was reckoned with transgressors.'" He was quoting Isa. 53:12, which says, "Yet he bore the sins of many and made intercession for the transgressors." Finally, after Jesus' death, Luke told the story of two disciples on the road to Emmaus who did not see Jesus as risen until he "opened to us the scriptures" (Luke 24:32). "'Was it not necessary,'" Luke portrayed Jesus as saying, "'that the Christ should suffer these things and enter into his glory?' And beginning with Moses and all the prophets he interpreted to them in all the scriptures the things concerning himself" (Luke 24:26, 27).

No, the Jesus of history did not say and do these things. What we have in the Gospel story of Jesus is a midrashic interpretation of his life and death based upon an ancient biblical image. His disciples finally came to see his death, not as his due, not as God's punishment, not as the cause for him to be accursed by God, but rather as the means by which they recognized Jesus as God's suffering servant—the innocent anointed one, or the Christ who was to suffer the pain and humiliation of that mythical figure whose vocation it was to bear the sins of the world. They made sense of his death by seeing him after the analogy of the mashiach, the Christ, who suffered. Only when they saw this could Peter have said of Jesus, "You are the Christ," and only on the far side of the cross could Peter understand that to be the Christ meant to suffer, to die, and to have God alone vindicate your life. So the title "Christ," interpreted as the servant who died, was applied to Jesus and became part of the church's creed. Jesus—the crucified one— you are the Christ, the Son of the Living God.

Did these early Christians create the story of God raising Jesus back to life so that Jesus could be given what they believed he really deserved? Was this the way that defeat, rejection, and the death on the cross were simply transformed into victory, vindication, and the life of Easter? Is Easter just one more human wish fulfillment, one more Hollywood happy ending, one more myth that attempts to proclaim that God is fair, that life is fair, that finally we will all, like Jesus, get what we deserve? Many people today make such a claim, but I am not persuaded by their analysis.

Jesus really died. He was taken violently from their lives. His absence was darkness. It was painful. In their minds a dead Jesus could not be the Christ, the mashiach, so the disciples returned to their lives as Galilean fishermen and began to live into the meaning of Jesus' absence—his death. His life was at that moment on its way to being nothing other than the life of a tragic hero. That would have been his fate had not a tiny crack appeared in the darkness of his absence when someone began to suggest that the way he died was exactly like the way he lived. He gave his life to others and for others. He loved wastefully and selflessly. In that living and dying this dawning insight suggested that Jesus revealed the meaning of God. God is not victory, their point of view stated. God is the presence of transcendent meaning in the midst of human defeat. God is not eternal life. God is the presence of an indestructible meaning in the face of very real death. God is not the promise of infinite reward. God is the meaning that is present in the face of fate, tragedy, and undeserved pain. God cannot be seen in Jesus' miraculous escape from death at Easter until God is first seen in the crucified one who gives life as he dies, who offers forgiveness as he is victimized, who shows love as he is hated.

Christ is the victim, Christ is the one who suffers, Christ is the name of the suffering servant who dies.

Easter did not change the fact that Jesus had died. What Easter did was to open the eyes of the disciples so that they could see into the heart of God. There they could begin to perceive the deepest truth of the Christian story; namely, that it is in dying that we live; it is in loving that we discover love; it is in giving that we are opened to receive. In some such manner on the far side of the cross this insight dawned and only then did the Caesarea Philippi confession become possible. That narrative then must be read as an Easter story. "Jesus said to his disciples, 'Who do you say that I am?' Peter answered, 'You are the Christ.'" And Jesus said yes and began to teach them that to be the Christ he must give his life away. He must suffer, be rejected, and be killed. He warned the disciples that if they could not see the Christ as one who suffers, is rejected, and is put to death, then they would not be able to see him raised.

Did Easter reverse the verdict of death? No, I do not think so. What Easter did was to lift death into the meaning of God by asserting that that is what happened to Jesus. Does this mean that the resurrection of Jesus did not really happen, that Easter is a hoax? No, I do not think so. I think Easter is real, but it is not an event that takes place inside human history. It is ultimately the revelation of who God is, seen through the lens of Jesus by those of us who do live inside history. Easter becomes for us a timeless invitation to enter the meaning of God by living for others, expecting no reward, loving wastefully no matter what the cost. When we do that, we are Easter people and resurrection becomes real. Then we, too, will grope for appropriate words to give form to what we know is true as men and women of the twentieth century. God is real. Jesus is our doorway into God. Death cannot contain those of us who live out of God's love. When you and I stand here, when we see Jesus as the servant Christ, Easter will dawn anew for us, and we will know that it is real. So we use the symbol Christ, with its suffering righteous content as one more way to comprehend just how it was that God was met in Jesus.

Chapter 13

The Son of Man—The Image
of the Book of Daniel

The creed of the Christian church that most scholars believe to be the earliest is either "Come Lord Jesus" or "Jesus is Lord." In the first version, "Come Lord Jesus," the creed is a prayer. In the second version, "Jesus is Lord," the creed is an affirmation. In these early creeds not even the title "Christ" had yet been attached to the name of Jesus.

This original creed grew out of the experience that in time Christians came to call the resurrection. One does not call a dead man Lord or pray for a dead man to come unless one is mentally unbalanced. Something had to have happened to transform the crucified Jesus into the one called Lord or else these creeds would never have developed. So these creeds drive us to seek the nature of the reality that caused early Christians not just to proclaim that Jesus is Lord but also to pray for his second coming. They force us to ask, Where was this Jesus dwelling from whence they yearned for him to come? How did he get there? What did his being there mean to those who called him Lord? These are now our questions.

In what many scholars believe to be Paul's first epistle, 1 Thessalonians, a work dated in the early 50s, the apostle wrote these words: "For the Lord himself will descend from heaven with a cry of command, with the archangel's call, and with the sound of the trumpet of God. And the dead in Christ will rise first; then we who are alive, who are left, shall be caught up together with them in the clouds to meet the Lord in the air; and so we shall always be with the Lord" (4:16–17).

The imagery of the Lord coming through the air on the clouds of heaven comes out of a Jewish tradition known as apocalypticism, a concept I hope to clarify in this chapter. Paul's letter to the Thessalonians, written a bare twenty years after the end of our Lord's earthly life, reflected this apocalyptic strand of biblical tradition, which quite clearly supplied the vocabulary for and shaped the content of the early Christians' interpretation of their experience.

With the apocalyptic literature to guide me, I want to roam now into another early understanding of Easter that was recorded in the Bible.

Easter began with the ecstatic cry, "Jesus lives! Death cannot contain him!" It evolved into a primitive creed, "Jesus is Lord" or "Come Lord Jesus." In time, those ecstatic cries and those primitive creeds were wrapped into narrative details. We need to understand that progression in thought: First there was the experience. Second there was the ecstatic cry or proclamation that rose out of the experience. Third there was the creedal affirmation that gave form to the proclamation. Fourth there was the explanation that sought to convey to others the reality of the experience. Finally there was a narrative that turned the experience into a rational episode. When any experience finally reaches the narrative phase, details are always given as to who was involved, where they were when the experience occurred, what they did, and how they responded.

It is the narrative phase of the developing tradition of Easter that we have primarily in the Gospels of Matthew, Mark, Luke, and John.

But the narratives, please remember, were five steps removed from the reality of the original experience. The primary value of the narratives, in our effort to reconstruct the events of Easter, comes from those residual clues still present in the stories. Those clues point us to primitive understandings that will illumine the ultimate moment that made the narratives necessary. These understandings also force us to recognize that every word of every Gospel was written in a post-Easter context. If we want to understand how the early church viewed Easter, therefore, we do not look just at the resurrection narratives. We look rather at the whole work. We look at the words attributed to Jesus, and we ask questions.

For example, could the historical Jesus have actually said, "I am the resurrection and the life" prior to his crucifixion? What could such words possibly have meant to his hearers? Before the Eucharist became a part of the church's liturgy, could the Jesus of history have said, "I am the bread of life. He who eats my flesh and drinks my blood has eternal life, and I will raise him up at the last day"? What on earth would that have meant to people who had not yet lived with the practice of eucharistic worship?

When we leave the Gospels for a moment and step back into the epistles, which were written fifteen to thirty years earlier, we have not only stepped back in time but we have also stepped from the level of narrative to the level of explanation. Once we get beyond the narratives, the contradictory details of the Gospels are missing. But we become immediately aware that concepts rising out of the previous religious history of the one doing the explaining are now appearing before us. It is with those concepts that I am concerned in this section of this book. It was on this level that Jesus was seen and explained in terms of the sacrificial lamb from the liturgical observance of the Day of the Atonement, and as the *mashiach* who was identified with the suffering servant of 2 Isaiah.

In this chapter I want to press yet another image that rose in this period of the pre-narrative development of Christian explanation. It was the image of Jesus understood under the symbol "the Son of man." This symbol had a long Jewish history, but it also took on a distinctively Christian definition in the first century of the Christian era.

THE ORIGINS OF THE SON OF MAN SYMBOL

"Son of man," like other Jewish images, had been defined in Jewish history long before it was applied to Jesus of Nazareth. It was a dominant concept in apocalyptic writing.

"Son of man" occurs more than seventy-five times in the New Testament. Sometimes these instances seem to mean little more than another name for Jesus, which the Gospel writers employed when he was talking about himself: "Foxes have holes, and the birds of the air their nests; but the Son of man has nowhere to lay his head" (Matt. 8:20); "The Son of man will be delivered into the hands of men, and they will kill him; and when he is killed, after three days he will rise" (Mark 9:31); "We are going up to Jerusalem, and everything that is written of the Son of man by the prophets will be accomplished" (Luke 19:31).

This last text from Luke asserts a connection between the title "Son of man" and a particular definition from the writings of the prophets. In this instance the use of the phrase is something more than merely a self-designation. That it does imply more becomes even clearer when we examine those places where the "Son of man" title on Jesus' lips seems to refer to another figure—perhaps supernatural, perhaps heavenly in origin, with overtones of the final day of judgment. Take, for example, Mark 13:24–27: "But in those days, after that tribulation, the sun will be darkened, and the moon will not give its light, and the stars will be falling from heaven, and the powers in the heavens will be shaken. And then they will see the Son of man coming in clouds with great power and glory. And then he will send out the angels, and gather his elect from the four winds, from the ends of the earth to the ends of heaven."

Or Mark 14:62: "Again the high priest asked him, 'Are you the Christ, the Son of the Blessed?' And Jesus said, 'I am; and you will see the Son of man seated at the right hand of Power, and coming with the clouds of heaven.'"

Or Matt. 16:27: "For the Son of man is to come with his angels in the glory of his Father, and he will repay every man for what he has done."

Or Matt. 25:31, 32: "When the Son of man comes in his glory, and all the angels with him, then he will sit on his glorious throne. Before him will be gathered all the nations, and he will separate them one from another as a shepherd separates the sheep from the goats."

147

Or Luke 21:36: "But watch at all times, praying that you may have strength to escape all these things that will take place, and to stand before the Son of man."

Or John 6:61, 62: "But Jesus, knowing in himself that his disciples murmured at it, said to them, 'Do you take offense at this? Then what if you were to see the Son of man ascending where he was before?'"

Many other texts could be cited, but these illustrations from each of the four Gospels are sufficient to indicate that the title "Son of man" had content, definition, and meaning that the Gospel writers and their audiences must have understood in common or the phrase could not have been used without extensive explanation.

"Son of man" seemed to be a title associated with the day of judgment. It appeared to have a supernatural context. This figure was intimately related to God—so much so that he came in the glory of the Father. He was superior to angels, he traveled on the clouds, and he may well have been thought of as a preexistent heavenly being.

Once again these words, placed in the Gospels on the lips of the Jesus of history, present literalism with some severe problems. If Jesus really understood himself this way, could he have undergone the doubt and the fear revealed in the story of the garden of Gethsemane? If the disciples had understood him to be the Son of man in the supernatural sense, as these texts reveal, why would there have been anxiety and fear at the time of the crucifixion? Why would his own disciples have betrayed him, denied him, forsaken him, and fled from him? If the disciples knew Jesus as the Son of man, why would they have locked the doors after the crucifixion for fear of the Jews? Why would they have returned to their livelihood in Galilee after his execution? If one reads the Gospels as biographies, these become incomprehensible questions and nonsensical observations. The Gospels were not, however, biographies; they were proclamations of the meaning of Jesus as the bringer of salvation. They were written in the light of whatever Easter was. They were attempts to interpret Jesus' power in terms of the religious history of the Jewish people. It was not until the first Christians had gone deeply into the task of interpreting Jesus that they began to write books about him, called Gospels.

At some point after Jesus' death they came to believe that Jesus was to be identified with the title "Son of man." What drove them to that conclusion, and what did that conclusion mean? As we confront these questions and begin to delve into them, we find that those mysterious and dark years between the end of Jesus' life and the beginning of the written tradition about this Jesus can be broached and even illumined.

The phrase "son of man" first entered the Hebrew vocabulary in the writings of Ezekiel in the early years of the sixth century B.C.E. In that work the phrase seems to have been nothing more than the name by which God addressed the prophet: "And he said to me, 'Son of man, stand upon your feet, and I will speak with you'" (Ezek. 2:1); "And he said to me, 'Son of man, eat this scroll that I give you and fill your stomach with it'" (Ezek. 3:3); "And you, O son of man, take a sharp sword" (Ezek. 5:1).

It next appeared in the Psalms, most of which were written during the exile or afterward. In three of the four instances in the Psalms, son of man meant either humankind in the collective— "What is man that thou art mindful of him, and the son of man that thou dost care for him?" (Ps. 8:4); or it meant humankind understood as a particular human being—"Put not your trust in princes, in a son of man, in whom there is no help" (Ps. 146:3).

But in the fourth instance, found in Ps. 80:14–17, some new data seem to have been gathering around the phrase. Here the psalmist wrote: "Turn again, O God of Hosts! Look down from heaven, and see; have regard for this vine [a popular symbol for Israel], the stock which thy right hand planted. They have burned it with fire, they have cut it down; may they perish at the rebuke of thy countenance! But let thy hand be upon the man of thy right hand, the son of man whom thou hast made strong for thyself!" Here a note of judgment was added, and the son of man was a figure in intimate relationship with God.

Ezekiel was the prophet carried into exile by the Babylonians along with his fellow Jews in 596 B.C.E. The Jews were allowed to return to their homeland in various waves over a period of two centuries. Second Isaiah was in one wave in the late sixth century. A second wave was led by Zerubbabel and Joshua in the early years of the fifth century and was recorded in the writings of Zechariah and Haggai and mentioned in Ezra. A third journey was led by Nehemiah near the end of the fifth century.

These returning exiles struggled with varying degrees of success to rebuild their nation, their temple, and their city wall, but they were forced to endure one national humiliation after another. With their defeat by the Babylonians and through the exile, they had lost the symbol of their national life. In time they came to believe that no longer would the voice of prophecy be heard in their land. That voice was replaced by the scribes and the Torah. Obeying the law became the central mark of Jewish life. Moses, the presumed author of the Torah, came to be regarded as the principal source of Jewish authority. God's message was heard in the interpretations of the sacred text. The prophets began to be subordinated to Moses.

People began to talk of the increasingly important image of Moses as the divine prodigy, akin to God, and even as one assumed into divinity. They made much of the story that said Moses had talked so intimately with God that God's radiance caused Moses' face to shine with transfigured glory (Exod. 34:29). Moses' death was also shrouded in mystery. The biblical text said that no one knew the place where Moses was buried, so people began to suggest that he had not died at all, that he had been assumed bodily into heaven.

As I previously mentioned and promised to discuss further, there were two other figures in Hebrew history whose deaths were surrounded by mystery. Elijah, who was said to have been taken bodily into heaven in a fiery chariot in the sight of his disciple Elisha; and Enoch, a minor character in the Book of Genesis who was the father of Methuselah. The sacred text said, "Enoch walked with God; and he was not, for God took him" (Gen. 5:24).

In the postexilic Hebrew folklore these three figures came to be envisioned as living in God's presence. The hoped-for and yet-to-come messiah was often pictured in terms of one of these figures. When the image of Moses was dominant, the coming messiah would be the great teacher of righteousness. He would lead his people through the wilderness of their present history into the promised land, which, as history turned increasingly grim for the Jews, was pictured as existing beyond history in the realm of God. Before the end of the world would come, the folklore suggested that Elijah would return from his heavenly dwelling to prepare the world for this eventuality. He would be the forerunner of this final event in world history when the vindicating God would right the wrongs that his people had suffered, and he would usher in God's eternal reign.

In the years between 200 B.C.E. and 135 C.E., the plight and fate of the Jews was perhaps the most severe in their history until the rise of Adolf Hitler. They were first a conquered province of the Macedonian Empire. After the death of Alexander the Great the empire was divided among his generals. Palestine became a territory caught between two of these generals—Ptolemy, who seized Egypt, and Seleucid, who seized Babylon, Iran, and Syria. Ptolemy won Palestine in the battle of Ipsus in 301 B.C.E., and for the next century the Jews were dominated by Egypt. But during this time the battlefield between these two parts of the empire encompassed the land of the Jews. There was much intrigue and little peace.

Because of the hellenizing influences of the Macedonian world, Greek language and Greek culture dominated both sides of this struggle. Indeed Alexandria in Egypt in this period rather than Jerusalem became the symbol of world Jewry. So many Greek-speaking Jews lived all over the empire that in Alexandria in the third century B.C.E. the Hebrew Bible was translated into the Greek language, in a form we call the Septuagint.

In the early years of the second century (198 B.C.E.), Palestine was wrenched from the Egyptians for good and became part of the Seleucid Empire. Yet it was still an uneasy peace, and strife persisted. The army of Rome blocked the western expansion of the Seleucid Empire, and the Seleucids refused to invade Egypt. So they signed a peace treaty with Ptolemy V and sealed the treaty by giving in marriage the daughter of the Seleucid king, Antiochus III, to Ptolemy V of Egypt. Her name was Cleopatra. But within all that military and political activity, peace descended on Palestine.

Most of the Jews, however, preferred the Egyptian overlords and were not pleased to be under the Macedonian-Syrian rule. The

Seleucid emperor decided to deal with this recalcitrant population by enforcing with particular eagerness the Grecianization of the citizens of his realm. Only by establishing Greek culture, Greek language, and Greek religion in the conquered provinces did he believe he could achieve peace and stability throughout the empire. The tiny land of the Jews proved to be the most resistant to these plans. When Antiochus IV, known as Epiphanes, came to the throne in 175 B.C.E., the battle reached white-heat intensity.

It was during this struggle that the form of writing known as apocalypticism made its appearance in Jewish history. Apocalyptic literature was designed to encourage the Jews to be faithful in this time of overwhelming oppression. It promised vindication at the end of time for the victims of persecution, as well as "heavenly rewards" for those who died without sacrificing their religious beliefs. It was literature designed to encourage those who could find no hope in the moving events of their human history.

Antiochus Epiphanes IV was the cruelest king the Jews could imagine. He moved with dispatch to destroy Jewish worship. He violated Jewish customs, removed Jewish holy places, tore down Jewish symbols, and executed those Jews who resisted. He went so far as to appoint a nonpracticing Jew to be high priest, and he set up in the Holy of Holies, in the Jewish temple, a statue of Zeus, the Greek deity. So cruel and hostile were these symbols to the devout Jews of this period, and so powerless to resist did they feel, that adaptation or death seemed to be the only choices.

It was in this painful and often tragic environment that apocalyptic writing flourished. The two major apocalyptic works written during this period were the Book of Daniel, named for a minor prophet who lived during the time of the exile, and the Book of Enoch, named for the one whose righteousness had won him exaltation into heaven. Scholars debate which came first and, therefore, which one influenced the other. Most scholars tend to say that Enoch was a later development of Daniel's writing, but both use the figure and image of the son of man.

It must be said now that "son of man" may not be the best translation of this phrase. In Aramaic the phrase is *bar enas,* and it means literally "one in human likeness." But when that phrase is translated into Hebrew it becomes *ben adam,* which simply means "a man" or "a human being." Both *bar enas* and *ben adam* are translated into Greek with the words *ho huis tou anthropou,* and from that Greek phrase we get "son of man" in English.

In the Book of Daniel, where this figure emerged with a new meaning, the content is complex. The prophet had a vision in which four beasts came up out of the sea. The first three beasts were recognized as a lion, a bear, and a leopard. The fourth beast, however, was so grotesque as to be unrecognizable. These beasts, which represented the succession of dominant powers under which Israel had suffered, pointed to their present history (the era of the most grotesque beast), where oppression was the most severe.

The scene of Daniel's vision then shifted to thrones being set up and one known as the Ancient of Days taking his seat, accompanied by signs of supernatural power and glory. Then the record books were opened. The day of judgment, the day of the Lord, had begun. In that judgment the sentence was pronounced and the grotesque beast was slain.

Then in this vision there came one like a "son of man" or "one in human likeness," being borne on the clouds of heaven into the presence of the Ancient of Days. In apocalyptic literature, clouds were thought to be the means of transportation between earth and heaven. We have previously met this idea in the discussion of the Epistle to the Hebrews. To this figure was given dominion, glory, and kingdom. All people, all nations, and all languages were to serve him. His throne would last forever; it would never pass away.

Daniel asked that his vision be interpreted and he was told that the "son of man" was a symbol for the saints of the most high God, those who had endured the persecution and who had remained faithful. To them would be given the ultimate gift. They would live in God's kingdom, under God's rule forever. The son of man—the one in human likeness—was Israel, or the faithful, godly remnant of Israel. It was another metaphor for the suffering servant, the remnant of Israel who would accomplish the messianic purpose we met in 2 Isaiah.

Like the servant of Isaiah, the "son of man" soon became a personal title the common folk assigned to the expected messiah, and to that messianic image was thus added the element of heavenly exaltation. By the time of the writing of the Book of Enoch, this identification had already occurred. Enoch used references to suggest that the son of man would remove the mighty from their seats and the strong from their thrones (1 Enoch 46).

Indeed in Enoch the son of man began to be considered not just a human figure who, by means of exaltation, had become a heavenly being; Enoch also suggested that the son of man was a preexistent heavenly being, whom God had appointed to an earthly destiny that had to be accomplished before the son of man could return to his heavenly existence. The son of man was thought of as existing first with God then entering human history to vindicate God and God's elect. This was not far removed from the prologue to the fourth Gospel: "In the beginning was the Word, and the Word was with God, and the Word became flesh and dwelt among us." In his human form this preexistent son of man came to be viewed as the suffering servant, and in this manner the two images merged. Son of man before incarnation, suffering servant while on earth, and at death exaltation back to the throne of God.

A book entitled the Wisdom of Solomon, probably written sometime during the fifty years before the birth of Jesus, brought these two images together dramatically: "If the righteous man is God's son, he will help him, and will deliver him from the hand of his adversaries. Let us test him with insult and torture, that we may find out how gentle he is, and make trial of his forbearance. Let us condemn him to a shameful death, for according to what he says, he will be protected" (Wisd. of Sol. 2:17ff). This author went on to say, "But the souls of the righteous are in the hand of God" (3:1). "God tested them and found them worthy of himself; like a sacrificial burnt offering he accepted them. They will govern nations and rule over people" (3:6).

The tradition of messianic expectation continued to grow. The new Moses, the new Elijah, the new Solomon—all were visions of the hoped-for messiah. They dreamed of a messiah who would reproduce the miracles of the exodus. He would provide bread in the wilderness. He would restore the twelve tribes of Israel. Instead of parting the waters of the Jordan River, he would stand in the waters of the Jordan and part the heavens so that God's Spirit could come upon him. He would expel demons and perform exorcisms. People would question his origins. They would wonder by whose authority he was acting. Was his spirit the spirit of God or of Beelzebub? When his earthly role was finished, he would return to God's right hand and prepare for the end of history when he would come again on the clouds of heaven, clothed with God's authority to judge the nations of the world, to separate, if you will, the sheep from the goats.

The signs that would indicate to the faithful Jews that this second coming was near included the outbreak of new prophetic activity. All would become prophets. The old men would dream dreams, and the young men would have visions, and God's Spirit would be poured out on all flesh.

These images entered Jewish life and literature in the second century before Christ, and they remained strong, even dominant, until the early part of the second century of the common era. They were shaped by the Maccabean revolution that in fact broke the power of Antiochus Epiphanes IV and allowed the Jews a moment of relative freedom under the Hasmonean dynasty, set up by the Maccabees. But then Rome conquered Palestine, and religious oppression once more descended, until Rome all but destroyed the Jewish nation in 70 C.E. and finally destroyed it in 135.

THE CHRISTIAN APPLICATION OF MANY IMAGES

Needless to say, it was in this Roman period with Caesar Augustus on the throne and his agents Herod in Galilee and Pontius Pilate in Judea that one named Jesus of Nazareth was born, lived, and died and became the center of the experience that created for certain Jews the moment we call Easter. Inevitably, the Jews interpreted it in terms of the images available in their religious history, including the images of their messianic expectations. These images in turn shaped the content of their memory. When they called him Son of man, they were relating him to the one who in their mythology stood at the right hand of the Ancient of Days to be the final agent of God's judgment of this world and the one who would inaugurate God's kingdom. As the Son of man they saw him clothed with heavenly power and dominion. Under each symbol was the conviction that Jesus was the messiah, the anointed one, the Son of God who had been lifted from his earthly life into God, and, once there, he became cloaked on one side with the myths of preexistence and on the other side with the image of the final judge who comes at the end of history.

All we have done thus far is to begin to discern how the experience of Easter was interpreted under the symbols of the religious tradition of the Jewish people. None of these symbolic interpretations can capture for us either the reality or the objectivity of the experience itself. We are still left with questions: What caused these disciples to employ these symbols in order to make sense out of that life?

Experience demands interpretation. We have sought to understand the content of that interpretation. But interpretation cannot create experience. So we are back to the Easter moment.

Perhaps Mark was right. All we can do is stand before the empty tomb and hear the resurrection message and decide for ourselves how we will live in relation to that proclamation. Perhaps Paul was correct. All we can do is proclaim this truth in ecstatic utterances that do not lend themselves to narration. Perhaps Luke, writing in Acts, was accurate in insisting that we must await power from on high before we begin to live the life of resurrection.

What we cannot finally deny is that Easter dawned and that a community of people became convinced that Jesus was alive in a new way and that the grave of death could not contain the meaning of his life. Furthermore we cannot deny that because of their conviction their lives were dramatically and qualitatively different, and that they were able to pass that difference on for two thousand years so that you and I can now be part of the community that lives in this conviction. So here I stand, a citizen of the twentieth century, called, I believe, to live as a part of the people of the resurrection. And living here, I assert that Jesus lives, that death cannot contain him, that Jesus is Lord. Thus I continue to pray, "Come Lord Jesus."

There is one thing more that we can do. In the narrations of Scripture we can search for clues that will carry us back toward the Easter moment. Using those clues, we can then speculate on how the new consciousness arose. It will be something like reading a detective story, but I think it will illumine Easter in a new way.

Part Four

Clues That Lead Us
Toward Easter

Chapter 14

The First Clue: It Occurred in Galilee, Not in Jerusalem

We have examined the texts. We have looked at the symbols that were employed to explain the experience. Now we begin to probe the event itself. It will require a second look at the texts, but this time from a topical perspective rather than author to author. In this way we can see how ideas developed and discover hints that might otherwise remain hidden.

What occurred on the day that Easter broke upon the human consciousness? Can we find clues that will carry us back to that critical moment? I suppose if one means the kind of clues that will create an absolute certainty, or that will establish a literal facticity, the answer is no. But if one is willing to search the biblical narratives for suppressed or hidden bits of knowledge that illuminate the drama, and even to engage in the act of speculating about various possibilities, the answer is maybe. In this section I will try to piece together the story from data that I believe is available primarily in the biblical tradition itself, illuminated perhaps by history.

I will seek to speak to the basic questions of where, who, how, when, and why. Ultimately, I am convinced, we come to a place where one must stand before the vision of death overcome and say either yes or no to that vision. I have stood there and I have said yes, but that answer has come on many different levels, the last of which occurred only after I probed these texts to prepare to write this book. My research required me to enter in a new way the texts that purport to tell the story of Easter. I had to move again beyond the contradictions and inconsistencies of the texts. I will now seek to carry my readers into that drama by examining five essential clues. I begin with the question of *where,* with an attempt to locate in the geography of the world the place where human beings stood when the experience of Easter broke upon them. This question forces us to look at all issues of location when the story of Jesus is being told.

Was Jesus born in Bethlehem or in Nazareth? Was that which we call the resurrection experienced at an empty tomb in Joseph's lovely garden outside the walls of Jerusalem, or did that experience of resurrection actually occur in Galilee? What issues underlie this debate, which we see raging in the pages of the Gospels themselves? If we can settle this issue we will begin to take a step toward the goal of reconstructing the actual moment that propelled the church of Jesus Christ into being. So our journey toward Easter begins as we seek first to understand the ancient tensions that set Jerusalem and Galilee against each other in the history of the Jewish people.

RIVALRY BETWEEN NORTH AND SOUTH

In the first century, during the earthly life of Jesus, the city of Jerusalem and the region of Galilee were quite separate, distinct, and well defined in the minds of the Jewish people. Each projected an image that had been set throughout a long and sometimes difficult history.

Jerusalem was a city that dominated the province of Judah. It was associated uniquely with the great King David, who gave Israel the only power, status, and military prestige that this tiny nation had ever enjoyed in its history. Yet King David did not reign for his entire kingship from this special city. David was first crowned at Hebron, a town some twenty miles south of Jerusalem, sometime around the year 1000 B.C.E. The land of Canaan, pictured in the Book of Joshua as having been conquered by the victorious Jewish army, was in fact at this time still largely under the control of the Canaanite people. The city of Jerusalem was the city of the Jebusites, not the city of the Israelites, at the time of King David, some two to three hundred years after Moses and Joshua. David, who had been a shepherd boy in Bethlehem some six miles to the south of Jerusalem before a successful military career catapulted him into the leadership of his nation, must often have looked with envy from his pasturelands upon this great city of Jerusalem, built as it was on the top of a hill. From the valley in the south Jerusalem appeared to have been lifted, quite literally, out of the local landscape. Capturing the long rays of the afternoon sun it was aflame with a desert glow as if it were part of heaven itself. It is easy to understand how people began to call Jerusalem both the golden city and the holy city, and how the image of a new Jerusalem descending from the sky became the symbol through which people envisioned the coming of the kingdom of God.

This city was also a fortress. The high ground of the city could be defended for an extended time against a vastly superior military force. An internal water system, combined with stored provisions, enabled the city to withstand an enemy army in positions of siege for months and sometimes even for years. That was quite enough to discourage most foreign generals. The standard military procedure when Judah was invaded was for its army to retreat into fortress Jerusalem and there to out-wait the encroaching enemy. So successful was this tactic over the years that the myth of Jerusalem's indestructibility entered the folklore of the people and began to grow (Mic. 3:11). This was God's city, it was said, and God could not be defeated. Jerusalem, therefore, was very much to be desired as a part of the nation of the Jews, much to the consternation of the Jebusites.

No one understood this better than David, who was both a military and a political genius. As soon as he became king at Hebron he began to map plans to conquer Jerusalem and to make that heretofore foreign, and therefore neutral, city the very center around which all Jewish elements could unite. The story of David's conquest of Jerusalem is told in the Second Book of Samuel (2 Sam. 5:1ff). He went into the city through the internal water supply system, a tactic only an insider could have devised. When Jerusalem surrendered to David, some time around 993 B.C.E., he arranged to have himself crowned king a second time from inside this new capital city. From that moment on, the tradition began to grow in Jewish mythology that this city was the center of the world, the place where heaven and earth touched, the place where God was pleased to dwell.

Solomon, David's son and heir, added to the luster of Jerusalem by building within its walls the temple of God. This structure greatly enhanced the mythology. It featured an outer court, where Gentiles could gather; an inner court, where only the circumcised could tread; and the Holy of Holies, where only the priest who had been ceremoniously purified could enter. It was not long before the temple came to be thought of as the earthly equivalent of heaven itself, and the Holy of Holies nothing less than a replica of God's heavenly throne. We noted this belief earlier when we examined the Epistle to the Hebrews.

Both the city and the temple were powerful symbols of Jewish unity that served to paper over deep divisions, which are quickly revealed by a look behind the literal texts of holy Scripture. The Jewish people were never really a unified nation. Studies now reveal that only a small part of the Hebrew people actually endured slavery in Egypt. This part was related primarily to the Joseph tribes of Ephraim and Manasseh. Joseph, the hero of this narrative, was the favorite son of Jacob by his most beautiful and beloved wife, Rachel, so the tradition stated. Joseph was a Hebrew who, through the combination of his ability and God's providence, was said to have risen to great power in Egypt and to have used that power to save his people from starvation during a time of famine. But the Hebrews, who entered Egypt during Joseph's time, settled in the land of Goshen and in time became the underclass in Egyptian society. After some four hundred years, as the sacred story noted, a pharaoh arose "who did not know Joseph" (Exod. 1:8). That is, he did not appreciate the contributions the Hebrews had made historically to Egyptian life, and he proceeded to reduce the Jewish underclass to the status of slaves. This was the social pressure that set the stage for the Moses-led revolt and the exodus.

After managing to escape Egypt, these Semitic ex-slaves seem to have formed an alliance in the wilderness with another band of kindred Semites. This alliance was sealed at Kadesh, an oasis in the wilderness (Num. 10:11–21:3). The Semites of the wilderness had never known slavery, they had not shared in the exodus from Egypt, and they appear to have been loosely organized both politically and religiously. Perhaps some of the Canaanite holy places where shrines had been erected gave these Jews of the wilderness a sense of identity with the land toward which both they and their newfound slave allies were migrating. The principal holy places to which they referred were in Hebron, Beersheba, and Bethel, and the names associated with each holy place respectively were Abraham, Isaac, and Jacob. As these two groups came together, one out of Egypt and the other out of the wilderness, they merged their sacred stories. In this manner they incorporated the three shrines into a related tradition by making Abraham the father of Isaac, and Isaac the father of Jacob, which enabled these two formerly distinct peoples to see themselves as the descendants of this noble ancestry.

Then, to bring the two groups into a relationship with one another that would recognize both their kinship and their differences, these people developed a mythology that gave Jacob, whose name had been changed to Israel, two wives—Leah, the mother of Judah, who was seen as the patriarch of the dominant tribe in the wilderness tradition, and Rachel, the mother of Joseph, who was seen as the patriarch of the dominant tribe in the Egyptian exodus. These folk legends, developed out of their merged histories, also gave the Jewish federation a theological claim that demonstrated that the land of Canaan, which they were intent upon conquering anyway, was in fact originally theirs by virtue of the claims of their ancestors Abraham, Isaac, and Jacob. This claim must have seemed strange indeed to Canaan's settled Palestinian people, who had inhabited this land for generations.

When this conquest was complete, or at least when the Jewish people had won the right to settle in the land alongside the

Canaanites, these two distinct groups of Jews became divided once again. The tribe of Judah settled in the south; the descendants of Joseph settled in the north. This Jewish nation then went through a period of loose confederation that found expression in the Bible in the Book of Judges. The need for unified action, particularly in matters of military defense, however, led them finally to press their local judges, and especially a man named Samuel, for a king who would be a symbol of their unity. A man named Saul was chosen. It was an interesting choice.

Saul was from the tribe of Benjamin, who, in the folklore of the people, was the younger but nonetheless full brother of Joseph, father of the dominant northern tribe. Israel's beloved wife Rachel died while giving birth to Benjamin, the tradition suggested. But at the same time, the tribe of Benjamin had settled in the south country, as a satellite of the tribe of Judah, so Saul was an acceptable choice to both sides of the primary Jewish division. Saul could not establish his dynastic line, however, and he failed to pass on his kingdom to his son. When the king was killed in the battle of Mount Gilboa, the way was clear for Saul's most successful military general to take over the kingdom. David did just that.

However, as a member of the tribe of Judah, and therefore as one feared by the people of the north as a threat to their sovereignty, David had to take steps designed to allay anxieties before he could accomplish the unification of his kingdom. To conquer a foreign and neutral city, and to make that city the capital of the nation and a symbol around which all Jews could unite, was a wise and politically expedient step for David to take. At least it worked for David and for his son Solomon, and the Jewish nation had political security for a period of almost eighty years.

When Solomon died, however, the weaknesses in the political alliance between north and south once again became apparent. A revolt in the north, led by a successful military man named Jeroboam, took specific northern grievances to Solomon's son and heir Rehoboam, demanding redress (1 Kings 12). Rehoboam rejected these demands, and the tribes of the north seceded from the unified Jewish nation centered in Jerusalem and in the Davidic line. They elected the same Jeroboam to be their first king. A civil war ensued in which Rehoboam tried to reunify the nation by force. He failed, and from that moment on, the northern region, called Israel, and the southern region, called Judah, were separate, competing states—each jealous of the other.

Each region then proceeded to develop quite separately. In the north the city of Samaria was built to be the capital that the northerners hoped would compete with Jerusalem. But it never achieved either the grandeur or the mythology of the holy city. King Jeroboam also never established a dynastic family, so revolution and intrigue constantly marked the political institutions of the north. Religious shrines were set up to wean people away from their yearning for Jerusalem, but these shrines likewise never became popular enough to compete with the temple. So the northern kingdom failed to become centralized, no single city dominated the area, and no religious or political institution became bigger than life.

Some two centuries later, in 721 B.C.E., the province called Israel was defeated by an Assyrian host that was led first by Tiglath-Pileser III and finally by his son Sargon II. Its people were exiled and its land was repopulated. In time, through intermarriage between the original Jewish settlers who were not exiled and the repopulated aliens, a people known as the Samaritans emerged in this region. They were neither ethnically pure nor religiously orthodox, and so they earned from their southern cousins the rejection and prejudice that comes when one group considers itself racially pure and religiously orthodox. The Jews from the south dismissed their former foes to the north as half-breeds and heretics.

Slowly but surely over a number of years, the Samaritan population was squeezed into a narrow central band of the region as Jews reclaimed the north country. Finally two separate, tiny provinces appeared where the northern kingdom of Israel had once existed. They did not receive their official names of Samaria and Galilee, however, nor were they officially divided, until the death of King Herod in 4 C.E.

The name Galilee was derived from the Hebrew colloquial phrase by which the area had been known since the time of

Solomon, *galil hagoyim,* which literally meant "circle of Gentiles." Solomon thought so little of this area in his kingdom that he gave Hiram, king of Tyre, twenty cities of Galilee in payment for the cedars of Lebanon, with which he had built the temple in Jerusalem. The reputation of the region was not enhanced by the fact that Hiram regarded this as a very inadequate payment (1 Kings 9:11ff). In the eighth century before the common era, however, the prophet Isaiah had predicted a new greatness for the region that he called Galilee of the nations (Isa. 9:1ff).

Its name was an apt one, for the region was surrounded by gentile nations. Its borders were never quite secure, and its Jewishness was never quite certain. Indeed in all its history this part of Palestine had a relatively weak Jewish identity. In the time of Joshua this region had been assigned to the tribes of Zebulun, Naphtali, and Asher. Naphtali and Asher were said to be sons of Jacob by two slave girls who served as handmaidens to Jacob's wives, Leah and Rachel, and therefore they were never thought of as full Jews. It was an interesting official way for Jewish historians to suggest that the racial bloodlines in these northern tribes had never been very pure. Zebulun was acknowledged as a full son of Jacob by his first wife, Leah, and therefore as a full brother to Judah. According to the legend incorporated into the biblical narrative, however, Leah had conceived Zebulun when she lured Jacob away from his favorite wife, Rachel, for the night for the price of some mandrakes (Gen. 30:14ff), so his origins were a bit suspect. Again, it was an interesting commentary on the ethnic purity of the people of this region.

Still, over the centuries, Galilee seemed to produce a vibrant, fiercely independent people, who in the first century gave rise to the revolutionary movement known as the Zealots. It was also a region that managed to retain its independence from total Roman domination longer than any other part of the Jewish state. Galilean Jews, however, were thought by the Jews of the south to be without class or tradition, to speak in a country brogue that was scorned, and to be of a region from which nothing good could finally come. Yet there stood Galilee, the remnant of the northern kingdom, still identifiably Jewish at the dawn of the first century, but labeled inferior by the region dominated by Jerusalem.

Compare that regional history with the story of the southern kingdom, known as Judah, as its history developed following the division of the kingdom at the time of the death of Solomon in 920 B.C.E.

This little nation centered in Jerusalem managed to survive the Assyrian host that destroyed its northern neighbor, but it did so at the price of vassalage. By becoming a vassal state, the southern kingdom gained an additional 130 years of identifiable national history. During that history it also managed to retain the Davidic throne and the unifying power of the worship tradition of the temple. In these years Jerusalem successfully resisted several would-be invaders, enhancing its reputation as unconquerable and adding new chapters to its developing legends.

In the latter years of the seventh century, about the year 621 B.C.E., a massive religious reform was carried out in the land of Judah during the reign of King Josiah and, with his support, by a group of religious leaders who came to be known as the Deuteronomists. These reforms had the effect of centralizing Jewish worship even more firmly in the temple in Jerusalem, for it called for the dismantling of all other religious shrines and practices in the land. Jerusalem, from that day on, dominated the region in every way.

Despite all that religious fervor, in 598 B.C.E. and once again for good in 586 the unheard-of, the undreamt-of, and the unbelievable happened. Jerusalem itself was destroyed. The legend died. A Babylonian army under the leadership of a general named Nebuchadnezzar first laid siege to the city and sustained that siege for two full years. Finally supplies were exhausted and starvation became so intense that the desperate citizens resorted to cannibalism. The heroic Jewish defenders at last surrendered, and the Babylonian troops poured into the once-invincible holy city. The king of Judah was captured and his eyes were put out. The Davidic dynasty that had endured for four hundred years was at an end. The temple of Solomon was destroyed, and the people of Judah were marched off into exile in Babylon. None of them would live long enough to return, but their children, grandchildren, and great-grandchildren did.

With this physical and historical disaster the two major props to Jewish identity, the royal family and the temple, disappeared. Interestingly enough, however, from that moment on both entered even more deeply into the realm of mythology, where they continued to live and grow. The reestablishment of a son of David on the throne in Jerusalem began to be expressed in terms of messianic expectations. The ideal king was mythologically portrayed as one who would come at the end of time to restore the fortunes of Judah. The hope to rebuild the earthly temple began to fade into the dreams of a heavenly temple that would descend from the sky on the last day in the midst of the New Jerusalem to inaugurate the timeless kingdom of God. Soon these two images flowed together, and the messiah became the son of man who would come in the clouds of glory as the primary agent for the establishment of the new Israel, the new Jerusalem, and the new age. In time both the city of Jerusalem and the temple were physically rebuilt, but they never achieved the grandeur of either the past or the dreams of the future. These were the nuances and the images that surrounded the rebuilt city and its temple as the first century B.C.E. came to a close.

The drama of the life of Jesus was lived out in these two settings—Galilee and Jerusalem. Both locations were crucial to an understanding of his life, and in the debate that surrounded his life one can hear echoes of the history of both of these places, still exerting their subtle pressures. One can also hear the residue of those strange ancient notes of continuous jealousy, competition, derision, and distrust that did not seem to die with the passing of countless generations.

LOCATING THE ACTION IN GALILEE

In my opinion the crucial events of Jesus' life occurred in Galilee, including both his birth and the experience of his risen presence. Yet the power of Jerusalem was such that in time both events were drawn into the holy city's orbit. Moving both of the interpretive events from Galilee into Jerusalem was not easy, and the original truth of a Galilean setting was neither obliterated nor expunged from the Gospel record. If we will take the time to do so, we can rediscover the Galilean origins of both the Christmas story and the Easter story, and we can also begin to see why ultimately Jerusalem had to take over both of these events and redefine their meaning in its own terms.

Jesus certainly went to Jerusalem to die. The fourth Gospel's author believed that he went there on several other occasions as well. In the synoptic Gospels there are hints that Jesus' first visit to the holy city was not synonymous with his last. Luke suggested that Jesus went to Jerusalem when he was twelve to visit the temple and acknowledges that Jesus had a close friendship with Mary and Martha, who lived in Bethany on the outskirts of Jerusalem. Jesus was also portrayed as able to make arrangements in the city of Jerusalem for the Passover meal, apparently aware of the availability of a large, furnished upper room sufficient to accommodate the disciple band. All of these activities assumed both contact with and relationships in Jerusalem, which surely pointed to his presence in that city on occasions long before the last week of his life.

Jesus also seemed to have had a sense of Jerusalem and its meaning, and that sense was found again and again in words attributed to him. It was not right for a prophet to die outside Jerusalem, he stated (Luke 13:33). To be beheaded in a Galilean prison by Herod, which was the fate of John the Baptist, was not a fitting way to end a life of significant meaning (Matt. 14:10). Jerusalem drew this Jesus like a magnet, so the climax of his life had to be lived out in that city. The Jerusalem climax, in my opinion, was to be limited to the passion and the death of this Jesus. The ultimate moment that made his passion and death meaningful, as well as the place of his birth, however, was located in Galilee, as I shall try now to demonstrate.

Jesus was born in Galilee. The Bethlehem/Jerusalem tradition of his birth was an obvious attempt to interpret and to demonstrate the meaning of his life. The Galilean origins of this Jesus, however, are clear even in the biblical text.[1] Indeed the primary and most indisputable fact of the life of the Jesus of history is that he was identified with the town of Nazareth in the province of Galilee. It is "O Little Town of Nazareth" about which our voices should sing in the Christmas celebration.

Not only was Jesus referred to as the Nazarene and the Galilean, but in John's Gospel, where there are no birth narratives, his origins were clearly in the northern province (John 7:40ff). Even the birth narratives in Matthew and Luke gave tacit agreement to that Nazareth tradition. Matthew had to develop a reason to get the holy family back into Nazareth from its Bethlehem home and its Egyptian rendezvous, because Matthew could not deny Jesus' Nazareth origins (Matt. 2:21ff). Luke, who assumed the truth of a Nazareth home for Jesus even in his infancy, had to develop a narrative to get Jesus' mother out of Nazareth at least for the actual moment of his birth. So in that Gospel we read of a taxation or enrollment that took place when Quirinius was governor of Syria. Today the literalness of that census is almost universally rejected for many reasons, not the least of which is that Quirinius did not become governor of Syria, according to secular records, until 6 to 7 C.E., by which time Jesus would have been some ten years old. Second, there is no record in any secular source that would suggest that a return to the place of origin of one's ancestors was required in any census or for any form of taxation.

There are other elements of that birth narrative that, upon reflection, lead one to dismiss the literalness of Luke's travelogue to Bethlehem. Would a first-century Jewish man in his right mind force a woman in the last stages of her pregnancy to take a hundred-mile journey from Nazareth to Bethlehem? Why indeed would such a woman have been involved in a census for tax purposes, since no woman in that society could own property? Why indeed would such a woman have to be involved in a census for political purposes, since no woman was allowed access to any decision making council?

When we add to these facts a story that included a star that wandered purposefully through the sky, magi who followed that star looking for a newborn king, angelic choruses who broke through the darkness of night to announce a savior's birth, and shepherds who miraculously went from their fields to the exact spot where this child was laid in a manger, wrapped in his swaddling cloths, the dramatic, nonliteral midrashic nature of the birth stories becomes apparent.

When one looks for the reasons behind the development of the Bethlehem and Judaic tradition of Jesus' birth, one must consider the region's ancient connotations. The great King David had been born in Bethlehem. When Jewish people yearned for a new King David, they associated the birthplace of the new royal figure with the birthplace of their historical hero, David. So it was that Micah, writing two hundred years after the death of King David, could suggest that Bethlehem would be the place of origin for the king messiah of the future (Mic. 5:21ff). When the disciples arrived at the conviction that Jesus was in fact this expected king, a Bethlehem birth tradition began to be woven around him in the people's folklore. In time the nativity stories came into being to form the cultural celebration of Christmas so familiar to all people. But the facts of history lead us to dismiss the fanciful claims of a Bethlehem origin and to assert that Nazareth was, in all probability, the place of birth for the one who was indelibly known as Jesus the Nazarene.

When we come to locate the experience that gave rise to the resurrection tradition, it is not quite so simple, and the facts drive us more deeply into the realm of speculation. Once again, however, the weight of evidence has led me to share the conclusion of the vast majority of scholars that Galilee was the primary place where Jesus was perceived by his disciples as having been raised by God from the dead.

Beginning our search with Paul, the earliest Christian writer to be included in the canon of Scripture, we discover that Paul did not give a location for any of his witnesses to whom he asserted the risen Jesus had appeared. By Paul's day the Christian movement was certainly centered in Jerusalem. Indeed the word *Galilee* was not used by Paul in any of the epistles, either in those written by him or in those attributed to him. The only hint we might pull out of Paul is the phrase "he appeared to Cephas" (1 Cor. 15:5). I shall try to show in the next chapter that this may be an allusion to a Galilean tradition, but that possibility cannot be sustained without drawing in many other pieces of data that would not be appropriate at this point in my story.

In the Book of Acts, which features Paul prominently, the word *Galilee* was used on only four occasions, and for our purposes they only offer hints at best, not conclusive proof, of the originality of the Galilean resurrection tradition. The first reference was put into the mouths of the angels in the story of the ascension, when they addressed the disciples as "men of Galilee" (Acts 1:11). That was a strange phrase to use for people who in fact were in Jerusalem. The second reference was a geographical one. Following the conversion of Paul, the editorial comment of the author said: "So the church throughout all Judea and Galilee and Samaria had peace and was built up" (Acts 9:31). It adds nothing to our search.

In chapter 10, however, the primacy of Galilee was asserted in a sermon by Peter. Peter referred to "the word that was proclaimed throughout all Judea, *beginning from Galilee*" (Acts 10:37). That may be nothing more than the author of Acts reminding his readers that Jesus began his public career in Galilee, but it could be a more profound hint that "the good news of peace by Jesus Christ" (Acts 10:36), which surely was not perceived until the Easter moment, in fact began from Galilee.

The final reference to Galilee in the Book of Acts is found in a speech in which the author has Paul assert that "God raised him from the dead; and for many days he appeared to those who came up with him from Galilee to Jerusalem, who are now his witnesses to the people" (Acts 13:30–31). Once more this simply recapped Luke's Gospel tradition that the ministry of Jesus began in Galilee and climaxed in Jerusalem. However, as we shall see when we analyze the Gospels themselves, the journey of Jesus from Galilee to Jerusalem may well be symbolic of another journey of Jesus' disciples from Galilee to Jerusalem for a climax quite different from crucifixion. Their journey was for the purpose of proclaiming that in Galilee the risen Lord had been encountered, and his witnesses had to make that known in the holy city. We hold that possibility in clear relief until we have examined additional data and are in a position to draw a more impressive conclusion.

Turning now to the Gospels with the single question of the location of the resurrection experience in mind, new insights emerge. The author of Mark's Gospel quite obviously believed that in Galilee the disciples would meet their risen Lord. The empty tomb story, located in Jerusalem, was told by Mark, but without any manifestation of the risen Lord in the narrative. Instead, in Mark, the messenger directed the disciples to return to Galilee for a rendezvous with the resurrected one. This author had the bearer of that proclamation even say, "as he told you," which drives us back to an earlier point in Mark's narrative where the Galilean locus of the resurrection had been previously asserted. It was on the Mount of Olives, Mark recorded, after the Last Supper had been concluded, that Jesus said, "You will all fall away; for it is written 'I will strike the shepherd and the sheep will be scattered.' But after I am raised up I will go before you to Galilee" (Mark 14:27–28).

Searching Mark for other hints of Galilee we find primarily references to Jesus' origin there and to his early public activity at or around the Sea of Galilee. One interesting hint that might be explored is signaled by the use of the phrase "sheep without a shepherd" earlier in Mark (6:34). Mark set these words in Galilee in the story of the feeding of the five thousand. That episode concluded with the appearance of the ghostlike Jesus, walking on the water and saying, "Take heart, it is I; have no fear" (6:50). There may well be echoes here of Easter and of the primacy of the original Galilean setting, and to these echoes I will return when I look at the role of Peter as well in my proposed reconstruction of the drama of the resurrection.

In Mark there are three predictions of the resurrection attributed to Jesus and written into the text of his earlier life. All three predictions are related to Galilee. The first came after the transfiguration, before the journey out of Galilee began (9:9). The second occurred as they "passed through Galilee" (9:30); and the third was while they were on the road "going up to Jerusalem" but not yet out of Galilee (10:34). The argument and weight of Mark supports the conclusion that the resurrection first became known in Galilee.

Matthew blurred this location issue a bit, but he still came down on the side of the originality of the Galilean tradition in regard to the resurrection. Matthew based his amplified version of the angelic message on his Marcan source, directing the disciples to Galilee with the promise of a meeting with the risen Christ. He then gave to that meeting substance that was beyond his source material in Mark. This was a style used frequently by the author of this Gospel. In Mark the women worried about how they could remove the stone from the mouth of the tomb. When they arrived, however, they found the stone already removed. No explanation was given to make sense of this wonder. Matthew was not able, it seems, to leave the unexplained mystery alone, so he accounted for the removal of the stone by inserting an earthquake and an angel. Similarly Matthew filled in the blanks of a resurrection experience in Galilee to which Mark had only alluded. This meeting between Jesus and his disciples did take place in Galilee on top of a mountain, Matthew wrote. Jesus came, presumably out of heaven, claiming that "all authority in heaven and on earth has been given to me." He concluded his appearance with the promise of his presence until "the close of the age" (Matt. 28:20).

Between the empty tomb and the details of the promised Galilee appearance, however, Matthew inserted a Jerusalem appearance of the risen Christ to the women near the empty tomb. Matthew changed Mark's account to make the behavior of the women obedient to the command of the angel. In Mark the women said nothing to anyone. In Matthew they "ran to tell his disciples" (28:8). On their journey the women were stopped by the risen Christ. They took hold of Jesus' feet and worshiped him. Then Jesus repeated verbatim the angel's message to inform "my brethren to go to Galilee and there they will see me" (Matt. 28:10). The angel seems to have dissolved into Jesus as if in a scene from a film. This narrative displays an obvious lack of originality and is therefore dismissed by most scholars as an inauthentic part of the tradition, thus leaving the Galilean setting still intact as the original site of the first Easter in the Gospel that bears Matthew's name.

Other references to Galilee in Matthew simply point to Jesus' origins and to the location of his early public ministry. It was done either in the words of the narrator—"Jesus came from Galilee to the Jordan to be baptized" (Matt. 2:13)—or in the words of the crowd, which, when asked, "Who is this?" replied, "This is Jesus the prophet from Nazareth of Galilee" (Matt. 21:11). In the last part of chapter 17, the text says that "as they were gathering in Galilee," Jesus once again predicted his resurrection (Matt. 17:22–23). That is, at the very least, a strange way to describe the life of a group that, up to that moment, had been journeying together all over Galilee. It was as if this was a new coming together. It was soon followed by a very distinct note that said: "When Jesus had finished all of these sayings, he went away from Galilee and entered the region of Judea" (Matt. 19:1). Here the text seems to point to a time of transition, a moment when the past was completed and a new chapter began.

Perhaps here we have echoes of what I believe might have been a new congregating of the disciples in Galilee after the crucifixion and, because of what they experienced there, a second and possibly more triumphant journey back to Jerusalem. There is even the possibility that these two journeys from Galilee to Jerusalem—one before the crucifixion and one after the resurrection—got blended in the tradition so that the content of one became the content of the other. The triumphal mood of what we now call the Palm Sunday procession would make far more sense as the disciples' post-Easter return to Jerusalem than as a journey into the hostile region of Jerusalem where the arrest and death of Jesus were all but certain. Once again, I urge my readers to file this possibility for a future reference. It is a hint to which I shall return. Suffice it now to state that the evidence in Matthew is certainly on the side of the Galilee tradition.

Luke offered a counterpoint to Galilee's original claim for primacy in the resurrection drama. Even Luke, however, bears a strange witness to the authenticity and originality of the Galilee tradition in his very denial of that tradition. Luke centered the resurrection appearances exclusively in the Jerusalem environs, in effect denying the Galilean claim. He went so far as to have Jesus order the disciples "not to depart from Jerusalem but to wait for the promise of the Father" (Acts 1:4). In order to build his claim for the Jerusalem setting, Luke had to skew Mark's words, placed into the mouth of the messenger, directing the disciples to return to

Galilee. These words were given an entirely new meaning in Luke. Luke's angel said, "Remember how he told you, while he was still in Galilee, that the Son of man must be delivered into the hands of sinful men, and be crucified, and on the third day rise" (Luke 24:6–7). Then, Luke said, the women remembered and went and told the disciples, who, we are led to believe, were still nearby in the holy city. When Luke told the story of the Jerusalem appearance of Jesus to the disciples, however, he dropped one more hint that screamed for an original setting in Galilee. In this narrative, Jesus, seeking to give the disciples some sense of his living reality, asked for something to eat and was given a piece of broiled fish. Fish was a food of Galilee, not of Jerusalem, unless a drying process had been used, and then the fish would not have been broiled. Without the conveniences of refrigeration, people ate only what they could get locally. One had to live near the coast or be by the Sea of Galilee to eat fish, for it had to be consumed the day it was caught. By including a piece of broiled fish in his Jerusalem story, Luke suggested, inadvertently I believe, a tradition that pointed to Galilee as the original site of the resurrection.

Searching Luke for other references that could help build a case for the Galilean setting of the first experience of resurrection, we find only one text that might help. It has either an enigmatic or a many-layered meaning. It comes after the temptation story, where the text says: "Jesus returned in the power of the Spirit into Galilee, and a report concerning him went out through all the surrounding country. And he taught in their synagogues, being glorified by all" (Luke 4:14–15). Again, the words in this text fit uneasily into the context of the temptation story. Jesus returning to Galilee, Jesus full of the Spirit, Jesus having "a report concerning him" going "through all the surrounding country," and Jesus "being glorified by all"—these were strange phrases to use when Jesus had just been portrayed as being alone in the desert for forty days and when the Gospel writer had as yet described nothing of Jesus' message or power. If the statement "he taught in their synagogues" was originally "he *was* taught in their synagogues" (Luke 4:15), then a post-Easter context would be far more appropriate for this passage. After the resurrection it was not the message that Jesus proclaimed that was important. The power of the Gospel was that it was Jesus himself that they proclaimed. The person had become the message. Again, this is not a determinative argument and it is admittedly highly speculative. Yet, while specifically denying the setting of Galilee for the Easter experience, Luke nonetheless left a trail of clues that point us to the very tradition he was denying. As we noted earlier, when we include the additional hints in volume two of Luke's corpus, known as the Book of Acts, the case for Galilee is not diminished even by the writings of Luke.

When we turn to the fourth Gospel we once again find a confused and mixed message. John appears at first to agree with Luke by locating the primary Easter events in Jerusalem, both for the women at the tomb (in John's case it was just one woman) and for the disciples (John 20). John's Easter story includes no direction to the disciples to return to Galilee to meet the Lord, as in Mark and Matthew. Nor does John contain a cryptic message about Galilee where the direction to return once existed, as Luke does. Galilee is simply not mentioned in John's description of the first resurrection experiences.

Just when one might think John's witness is clear, along comes chapter 21, an epilogue to the Gospel. I have already discussed the relationship of this chapter to the rest of the Gospel, and I will not repeat that here. Because the story of this epilogue is centered on Peter, however, its analysis will come in the next chapter. For now I will simply note that this chapter is set in Galilee and that it has a very primitive, original quality about it.

Turning to the rest of the fourth Gospel in a search for clues that might also reflect the Galilee tradition, we find that at Cana of Galilee Jesus "manifested his glory and his disciples believed" (John 2:11). To make known his glory was a way in which this author referred to the Easter event (John 12:16). Again, those were strange words to use in the context of a wedding celebration at the very beginning of Jesus' public ministry. Later in this Gospel, John suggested that the first disciple to believe was the beloved disciple, and this belief came only when he had entered the empty tomb

(John 20:8). If Jesus had already manifested his glory, and his disciples had already believed, then the story about the beloved disciple becomes nonsensical. But if this was an echo of the original Galilee tradition of Easter, then it makes abundant sense.

John's Gospel contains other episodes where Jesus went up from Galilee to Jerusalem (John 2:13; 5:1; 7:1, 10), and each of them has language that is not comfortable in its context. I shall examine these passages in more detail as my story unfolds. There does appear in John to be a strong tradition that will support the originality of a Galilean setting for the experience of resurrection.

In my attempt to reconstruct the Easter moment that gave birth to the Christian faith, my first conclusion is that the experience that was later to be called the resurrection was located in Galilee, and from Galilee it must have been carried into Jerusalem and planted there. This immediately means that I can no longer hold the story of the empty tomb, with all of its surrounding details, including the Jerusalem setting, to be anything other than a later legendary addition to the faith story. I will amplify this conclusion in chapter 18, but for now I simply place the Jerusalem narrative in a secondary position. It was not of the essence of the original Easter moment. Galilee where there is no tomb and no burial is my setting for Easter.

Now that the place has been determined, we move to discover who was in that place and try to understand what occurred in their lives so that in the region of Galilee it became the conviction of the first Christians that the living Lord had indeed been seen, that Jesus had been raised by God.

Chapter 15

The Second Clue:
The Primacy of Peter

"He appeared to Cephas, then to the twelve" (1 Cor. 15:5). These words, representing the earliest written record in the Bible of Jesus' resurrection, were penned by Paul in his letter to the Corinthians sometime around the year 56. Paul stated that he was handing on the received tradition, not simply writing his own opinions. His words make it quite clear that when we get as close as we can to the primitive Christian affirmation, we find the figure of Peter standing squarely in the center of that affirmation.

Peter's centrality in the resurrection was also alluded to in the fourth Gospel, whose author certainly had a vested interest in extolling the role not of Peter but of the "beloved disciple," the fourth Gospel's hero. Nevertheless even here there was a tacit acknowledgment of Peter's preeminence in the Christian faith story. In John's resurrection account, the beloved disciple outran Peter to the tomb, after Mary Magdalene reported it empty, but stopped at the entrance and waited for Peter to enter first.

I mention Paul and John first because if anyone had reason not to uphold the centrality of Peter in the dawning moments of Christianity, it would be one or both of these men, who in some sense competed with Peter for the leadership of the Christian movement.

Yet both John and Paul were firm: Peter was central to the meaning of Easter. In this chapter I will seek first to document that reality and then to interpret it. In the process I will search for other clues that might help us get inside Peter's experience to gain a better view of the moment of Easter from his perspective.

SURMOUNTING THE FIRST OBSTACLE: LITERALISM

My first clue comes when I look at the Gospels through the lens of midrash. For centuries we have been taught to read the Gospel stories with minds trained to be linear, without recognizing how badly a linear concept will distort our understanding. The Gospels are not biographies designed to chronicle the beginning, middle, and end of a person's life. Perhaps that needs to be said a million times to counteract the influence of linear thinking.

The Gospels are, rather, timeless re-creations of significant moments in the religious traditions of the Jews. Beyond being alert to this midrashic element, we also need to destabilize, if you will, the time line of the Gospels by removing the linear dimension from the narratives. There was, for example, not one word attributed to Jesus or one verse of the Gospel story that was in fact written prior to the resurrection, regardless of what the text says. No Gospel would ever have been written unless someone, somewhere, had "seen the Lord" in a dramatically different way following the crucifixion. So, the boy Jesus who was lost in Jerusalem for three days before being found in the temple was meant, by Luke, to presage the adult Jesus who was also lost in Jerusalem for three days before being found on Easter day exalted to God's heavenly temple. The words supposedly spoken by the Jesus of history in Galilee in the early phase of his public ministry were in fact the remembered words of the resurrected one, read back into the narrative. We have tended to read the fourth Gospel this way because of its portrait-like interpretive quality. But I am now suggesting that we must learn to read all of the Gospels this way. Linear time, imposed on the texts of the Gospels by those who did not understand how the midrash tradition worked, has not been an asset to this century's understanding of the gospel's ever-deepening truth.

We also need to keep in mind that it was the community of Christians who produced the Gospels some thirty-five to seventy years after the end of their Lord's earthly life. It was the resurrected Lord about whose baptism they wrote. It was the resurrected Lord whose words, teachings, and parables they recounted. It was the resurrected Lord who was betrayed, denied, and forsaken. For them the meaning of Jesus did not unfold dramatically at the end of their narrative. The meaning of Jesus is what drove them to write the narratives in the first place. So there was always a timelessness about the words of the Gospels, which Western eyes frequently have been unable to see. Hence the Gospel writers may well have placed resurrection stories into the body of the story of Jesus' life rather than saving them for recounting after the crucifixion. By being made aware of that possibility, we can recognize it when we encounter it.

So it is that in order to understand the place of Simon called Peter in the drama of Easter, one may well have to examine every Gospel reference to him. When chronology is finally excised from the text, incredible new possibilities for meaning appear. Once this perspective has been grasped, then questions of real significance can be asked. Did it make any sense, for example, for Simon to be given the nickname "Cephas" or "Peter," which meant "rock," prior to the moment of Easter? Why would anyone say to Simon that he was the rock upon which the church would be built before the events of the passion and resurrection, when presumably no one even knew or suspected that there would be a movement toward an institution that might be called a church? What was the basis for the story of Peter walking on the water toward a ghostlike figure that he recognized as his Lord? What did it mean for Peter to offer to build three booths, or tabernacles, to house Elijah, Moses, and Jesus, two of whom were already believed to have been exalted into heaven, if the third figure was not also already believed to have been exalted into heaven? Do any of these episodes make any sense as literal stories from a time before Easter? Finally, what does it mean when two Gospels recount the same story, but in one it is a resurrection story, and in the other it is from the early days of Jesus' earthly ministry?

With these daunting questions troubling our complacency, let me lift Simon called Peter out of the Scriptures so that we might see him as both man and symbol, as the rock of faith upon whom the Christian enterprise seems to stand.

SEEKING PETER'S IDENTITY

His name was Simon Bar Jonah, or Simon the son of John. He was married, and he seems to have lived with his mother-in-law. He had a brother named Andrew. He worked as a fisherman on the Sea of Galilee. He was a Galilean who hailed, according to the fourth Gospel, from the town of Bethsaida, a fishing village on the north shore of the lake. Other Gospels suggested that Peter lived in Capernaum in his adult life, which was only three miles removed from his village of origin and slightly more than twenty miles from the inland town of Nazareth.

The name Simon was a common one. It appeared twice even in the list of the twelve. There was Simon called Peter and Simon called both the Cananaean (Matt. 10:4) and the Zealot (Luke 6:15). This name also made a frequent appearance in various parts of the New Testament. There was Simon, the brother of Jesus (Mark 6:3), Simon the Pharisee (Luke 7:40), Simon the tanner (Acts 9:43), Simon the leper (Matt. 26:6), Simon Magus (Acts 8:9ff), Simon Iscariot (John 6:71), and Simon of Cyrene (Mark 15:21). Dale Miller has argued that all of the Simons in the New Testament were various aspects of the life and personality of Simon Peter.[1] It is an intriguing argument, but not yet persuasive for me.

When we search the Scriptures looking for hints of what the name Simon might have meant in Hebrew history, we discover that it appears in the Old Testament under several different spellings: Simeon, Shimei, and Shammah. It is a name without great distinction. A Simeon is one of the sons of Jacob, and therefore one of the tribes of Israel. But that Simeon is not portrayed as exercising a major role in the Jewish story either as an individual or as a tribe. In the form of Shimei the name Simon is attached to a strange figure described in the Second Book of Samuel (16:5–14) who was best known as the one who cursed David, the Lord's anointed, as David fled the capital under pressure from his son Absalom. Shimei's cursing of the Lord's anointed may have colored the portrait of Simon Peter, who, in his act of denial of the Lord's annointed, was also portrayed as cursing vehemently (Mark 14:71).

Certainly very few, if any, conclusions can be drawn from this analysis save the general one that the name Simon did not appear to be one that carried positive connotations in biblical history. I would suggest that neither did Simon the apostle until he did whatever it was that he did to force the change in his name from Simon to Cephas; from the one who cursed the Lord's anointed to the one who became the rock of faith upon which could be built the truth of the good news that Jesus came to bring. We look now at the way Simon becomes Peter in the Gospels.

In every listing of the disciples of Jesus, Simon called Peter was placed first. In Mark and Matthew, Simon was the first disciple to be called from his job catching fish to his role as a follower of Jesus. Although Simon was first, we need to note that Andrew, James, and John joined him quickly in the original call. Luke, however, changed that call dramatically. He portrayed Simon first as a friend with whom Jesus was staying in Capernaum, whose mother-in-law Jesus healed during that stay. It was during that same visit, according to Luke, that the crowd pressed upon Jesus to "hear the word of God." Jesus then stepped into Simon's boat in order to teach the people from that pulpit. When he ceased speaking, said Luke, Jesus said to Simon, "Put out into the deep and let down your nets for a catch" (Luke 5:4).

Here a story remarkably similar to the postresurrection narrative in John 21 was related. Simon objected to Jesus' direction, but he obeyed. A miraculous catch, breaking their fishing nets, was the result. When Simon beheld this miraculous sight, he fell at Jesus' feet in a posture of worship that seems inappropriate at this point in Jesus' historic life, and Simon said words that, in this context, sound strange indeed: "Depart from me, for I am a sinful man, O Lord." What had elicited so abject a confession? If placed after his act of denial during the crisis of the crucifixion, the words would have been quite appropriate. In any event, let it be noted that contrary to Mark and Matthew, in Luke's Gospel the suggestion that from now on "you will be catching people" was said to Simon alone. This was Luke's version of the enigmatic call of Peter, who, according to the text at that point, "left everything and followed him" (Luke 5:11). Was this a confused memory where Simon's first association with Jesus had been blended into Simon's postresurrection change?

When we reach the fourth Gospel, we find that it deviates ever so slightly from the primacy-of-Peter theme in that Andrew, Peter's brother, who was identified as one of two disciples of John the Baptist, became the first disciple to be selected by Jesus. My presumption is that the other, unidentified discile in this narrative was John, the son of Zebedee, extolled constantly in the fourth Gospel as the beloved disciple but frequently portrayed as the nameless one. If that is accurate, Andrew and John Zebedee were the first of the twelve chosen by Jesus to be his disciples. Andrew then went and got his brother Simon and took him to Jesus. Jesus, who presumably had never before seen Simon, said to him, "So you are Simon the son of John? You will be called Cephas" (Petras in Greek, which means "rock"; John 1:42). This may be nothing more than a subtle attempt by the disciples of John Zebedee to lift up their hero by placing him into the apostolic band prior to Peter. But it may also point to a role, now lost forever, played by Andrew in bringing Peter into the resurrection faith. Certainly the changing of Simon's name to Peter in this first conversation with Jesus does not ring with authenticity.

PETER'S CENTRALITY

As the story of Jesus unfolded in each of the Gospels, Peter, James, and John, with Andrew always in the background, emerged as the inner core of the apostolic band, but in each instance Peter was listed first. This threesome shared with Jesus in the account of the raising of Jairus' daughter from the dead, as narrated in all three of the synoptic Gospels. Peter, we are told, understood this resurrection episode as a resuscitation. There are slight differences in the three narratives. Mark and Luke named the ruler Jairus and had him bring the request to Jesus while his daughter was ill, even though she died before Jesus arrived. Matthew left the ruler nameless and had him come to Jesus only after his daughter was dead. Luke interpreted her rising to mean that "her spirit returned," and also had Jesus instruct them to give her something to eat, which resembles Luke's portrait of the resurrected Jesus, who asked his astonished disciples for food (Luke 24:41).

Peter, James, and John also shared in the stories of the transfiguration and the garden of Gethsemane. In each episode Peter is clearly the central figure and is usually the only one to speak. At Caesarea Philippi, Peter made the Christ-confession, to which we have already referred. At this point let me simply raise the question as to whether Jesus' words to Peter in Matthew make any sense except as a postresurrection affirmation into which Peter had brought the Christian community. (See Matt. 16:13–20.)

Was the title Christ applied to Jesus except after his exaltation? What did it mean for Jesus to say, as Matthew has it, "Blessed are you, Simon Bar-Jonah! For flesh and blood has not revealed this to you, but my Father who is in heaven. And I tell you, you are Peter, and on this rock I will build my church, and the powers of death [the gates of hell] shall not prevail against it" (Matt. 16:17–18).

In Mark's narrative of this confession, what did it mean for Jesus to begin to urge Peter to take up the cross? Jesus had not yet mounted a cross. Was crucifixion inevitable? Hardly. John the Baptist lost his life to beheading (Mark 6:14–29). Stephen lost his life to stoning (Acts 7:54–60). The words "Take up your cross" were those of the Christian community, not of Jesus.

Furthermore, as we noted when tracing the history of the title Christ, the admonition not to be ashamed of Jesus came primarily out of the means of his death. It was certainly a reference to the taunts hurled at Christians by their Jewish critics, quoting Deuteronomy in regard to the curse pronounced on anyone who had been hung upon a tree. "We are not ashamed of a crucified Lord" could be stated only in the power of the Easter experience, and it was placed by the Gospel writer into the middle of a confession of the messianic nature of Jesus by none other than Peter. Perhaps this same reference to the curse on one who had been hung upon a tree can be found as a hidden note in that strange Marcan story about Jesus cursing the fig tree (Mark 11:12–26). I shall return to the origin of this story later. My concern now is only to note how it was used in the Gospels. Mark is stating somewhat defensively that it was not the body hung upon the tree but the tree itself that was cursed. It is also worth noting that in this episode it is Peter who was portrayed as "remembering" Jesus' words. When Peter called the dead fig tree to Jesus' attention, he was made to listen to Jesus say, "Have faith in God" (11:22).

In Mark's Gospel, Peter was listed first among the disciples who asked Jesus to tell them when the end of the age would come (13:3). Jesus responded with the words that we now call the little apocalypse (13:3–37). He talked about the cataclysmic events that would precede the end of time. He pictured the persecution the disciples would endure. He asserted that the Gospel must be preached first to all nations. He instructed the disciples on how to behave when put on trial. Finally, when the sun and moon were darkened and the stars began to fall, then the Son of man would come in clouds with great power and glory. All this would happen before this generation had passed away. Once again we find words that were hardly spoken by the Jesus of history. Rather, they reflect the events of the Galilean war in 66 C.E. that finally led to the destruction of Jerusalem in 70.

Each Gospel contains a dramatic portrayal of Peter's denial of Jesus. In Mark, Peter protested his loyalty and was told he would deny Jesus three times. When that came to pass, Peter exited the Gospel of Mark to the accompaniment of Mark's words "He broke down and wept" (14:72). Matthew's version is much the same, save that Peter's protestations of loyalty are a bit more verbose, "Even though I must die with you I will not deny you" (26:35), and his tears of remorse, a bit more intense, "He went out and wept bitterly" (26:75). Matthew had great difficulty not heightening his story. In Luke the conversation about Peter's loyalty took place around the table at the Last Supper, and not after they had gone out to the Mount of Olives, as was the case in Mark and Matthew. Before Peter swore fidelity, Luke had Jesus say words quite unique to this Gospel but very revealing: "Simon, Simon, behold, Satan demanded to have you, that he might sift you like wheat, but I have prayed for you that your faith may not fail; and when you have turned again, strengthen your brethren" (Luke 22:31–32). This statement seems to imply that Peter would be the one to call the disciples back into faithfulness.

John's story of Peter's denial was also unique and revealing. In some sense it permeated the entire Gospel. In chapter 6, following the feeding of the five thousand and Jesus' teaching about the necessity of eating his flesh and drinking his blood, a passage that was surely related to the Last Supper as I shall seek to demonstrate later, came the statement "After this many of his disciples drew back and no longer went about with him" (John 6:66). Jesus turned to his disciples and said, "Do you also wish to go away?" It was Peter who held them together by saying: "Lord, to whom shall we go? You have the words of eternal life; and we have believed, and have come to know that you are the Holy One of God" (John 6:67–69). These are remarkable words if one insists on locating them in a chronologically earlier phase of Jesus' ministry. They were spoken by one who we are told had yet to deny that he even knew Jesus. Are they not clearly words of a Peter who, after the experience of Easter, called the disciples back into existence? Linear time is challenged once again.

Peter's internal wrestling was given another slant in John 13. The setting is the meal in preparation for the Passover. There is no Last Supper in the fourth Gospel. Instead John related the story of Jesus washing the disciples' feet. Peter drew back from Jesus in this episode as if to prevent this procedure. Jesus said, "If I do not wash you Peter, you have no part in me." Peter then rushed forward and asked to be washed all over. It was a strange ambivalence, not unlike the ambivalence of pledging loyalty and then falling away and then rushing back.

It is in this same chapter that Peter's denial is foretold. This came after Jesus had spoken of being glorified and had said that the disciples would seek him but that they could not come to where he was going. Peter then joined the conversation by asking: "Lord, where are you going?" (John 13:36). Jesus replied: "Where I am going you cannot follow me now; but you shall follow afterward." "Lord, why cannot I follow you now?" Peter inquired; and Jesus answered that it was because he denied him three times (13:36–38).

A third revealing touch was included in John 16:31–33, a passage that separated the prediction from the actuality of Peter's denial, in the midst of what is called the farewell discourses. Postcrucifixion nuances are clearly present in chapter 16 when Jesus says that the Spirit "will glorify me" (v. 14); and, "A little while and you will see me no more; again a little while, and you will see me" (v. 16); and, "Because I go to the Father" (v. 17). The disciples were portrayed as not understanding, and so they asked for an explanation. Without explaining, Jesus went on to say that they "will weep and lament, but the world will rejoice"; that they "will be sorrowful, but your sorrow will be turned into joy" (16:20). Jesus continued: "You have sorrow now but I will see you again and your hearts will rejoice, and no one will take your joy from you" (16:22). He then said that when joy had replaced sorrow, the disciples would ask the Father in Jesus' name and the Father would give them whatever they asked (16:24). "I am leaving the world and going to the Father," Jesus concluded (16:28). Surely that was how the author of the fourth Gospel understood the resurrection.

To these words in that strange context the disciples indicated that now they understood, that now Jesus was talking plainly. Jesus responded with words that ring with accurate, descriptive history: "Do you now believe? The hour is coming, indeed it has come, when you will be scattered, *every man to his home,* and will leave me alone" (John 16:31–32). If Peter had scattered to his own home at the time of trial, it would have been to the region about the Sea of Galilee. That becomes important when we get to the end of John's Gospel.

The story of Peter's actual denial was then recorded in chapter 18. When he had denied Jesus three times, Peter disappeared from the scene until he made a cameo appearance at the tomb on the first day of the week, in chapter 20. He was not mentioned by name at the two postresurrection gatherings of the disciples, either on Easter evening or on the occasion eight days later in which Thomas was the focus of attention (John 20).

The fourth Gospel did climax the Peter narrative, however, in what is called the Johannine epilogue in chapter 21. We have already noted the debate as to how this chapter fits into the original corpus of that Gospel, and even whether it is the product of the same author. Yet chapter 21 was written in such a way as to connect it to what had gone before. We know from textual studies that the fourth Gospel never circulated without chapter 21, so if this chapter was an epilogue, it was appended very early in the life of the Gospel. An internal study of the chapter, looking particularly at vocabulary and style, is not persuasive in suggesting authorship by another or different hand from the first twenty chapters. This chapter appears to be quite Johannine. Yet some clear problems are present when chapters 20 and 21 are related to each other in time, as a chronological description of events.

Chapter 21 is set in Galilee, while chapter 20 is set in Jerusalem. Since I have already sought to demonstrate the primacy of the Galilean tradition as the place where the first experience of resurrection occurred, it may be that what we have in John 21 is the memory, now clearly embellished, of this authentic early tradition. Moreover, the behavior of the disciples in chapter 21 makes little or no sense if we see it as a sequel to events in chapter 20. It reads as if those events had not occurred or, at the very least, as if those events had no impact. Despite two appearances to the disciples in chapter 20, one without Thomas and one with him, where the risen Christ breathed on them to impart the Holy Spirit, and where Jesus confronted Thomas with the invitation to touch his wounds, designed to verify both his identity and his continuing presence, the disciples as portrayed in John 21 were strangely unmoved. Even Thomas's cry of faith, "My Lord and my God!" had not served to put any particular new energy into Thomas's life. What we have here is a strange placement of a text that contains key insights and probably primitive traditions.

Given all that, John 21 opens with Peter at home near the Sea of Galilee, in the company of six of the disciples, including Thomas, announcing, "I am going fishing," to which the others responded, "We will go with you." We need to recall these were not sport fishermen, wanting a day of recreation. They were commercial fishermen earning a livelihood from their trade. Peter was saying that the time had come for him to pick up the pieces of his life. It was as if he had finally recognized that the Jesus adventure was over. In my opinion, that captured precisely the mood of Peter and some of the disciples who fled Jerusalem for Galilee when Jesus was arrested. The grief rising out of the trauma of Jesus' crucifixion had finally begun to lift, and the time had come for Peter to return to the routines by which his life had been governed before he met Jesus of Nazareth. This setting and this behavior is nonsensical if it is placed after the Jerusalem appearance of the risen Christ. This epilogue, therefore, points me once again to a narrative that may have its origins in a quite primitive tradition, not secondary at all, as it came to be regarded by either its author or the one who attached it to the Gospel of John.

After fishing through the night and catching nothing, the disciples received instructions from a figure on the shore to try the right side of the boat. With some mild protest they complied and hauled in a great catch of fish. As I noted earlier, this narrative is almost identical with a story that also resulted in a great catch of fish, but Luke placed that story into the early Galilean phase of Jesus' earthly ministry, even though it elicited from Peter an ecstatic cry that sounds very much like a postresurrection confession. This suggests to me that the episodes that got written into the Gospels much later floated freely in the oral period and were not time-bound. It also indicates to me how these narratives might have been changed in the oral tradition, at least raising the possibility that stories in the New Testament, with quite different content in their present form, might point back to a common origin.

With that possibility in mind, I went back to the Gospels with these two similar stories, one from John, set in a postresurrection context, and one from Luke, set in Galilee early in Jesus' earthly ministry, and began to search out other episodes that had similar features to these two and that might particularly involve Peter.

A POSSIBLE MEANING FOR THE LAKE STORIES

I found that for which I was looking. The narratives set on or by a lake, which locates them in Galilee, must be looked at together. The first event was Mark's account of Jesus calming the great storm that had whipped up both wind and wave and threatened the boat in which Jesus and the disciples were present (Mark 4:35–41). That story was retold in Matthew (8:23–28), but there it was placed immediately after Jesus had entered Peter's house and healed his mother-in-law. It was again told in Luke (8:22–25). Next there was Mark's story of Jesus walking on the water (6:45–52), where once again a storm made difficult their passage to Bethsaida (Peter's hometown). The disciples believed Jesus to be a ghost, so Jesus identified himself by responding, "Take heart, it is I, have no fear." The story concluded with the statement that the disciples were astounded, for "they did not understand about the *loaves.*" This narrative was set immediately following the story of the feeding of the five thousand.

Matthew accepted Mark's context of just after the feeding of the multitude. He told Mark's story of Jesus walking ghostlike on the water, calming the terrified disciples with the same words, "Take heart, it is I; have no fear." But then Matthew added a whole new dimension. Peter, who was not convinced by Jesus' assurances, said, "Lord, if it is you, bid me come to you on the water." Jesus invited him to come, and Peter walked on the water. But when Peter saw the wind, he became fearful and cried out, "Lord, save me." Jesus reached out his hand and said, "O man of little faith, why did you doubt?" They then got into the boat and the wind ceased. Those in the boat, now presumably including Peter, worshiped Jesus and said, "Truly you are the Son of God" (Matt. 14:22–33).

John also included this story, injecting it, as do the other writers, into the feeding-of-the-multitude narrative. Similarities include the disciples' fear when they saw Jesus walk on the water, Jesus identifying himself, and the disciples taking him into the boat. Then immediately they were at their destination, for obviously the wind that had prevented their passage had ceased. Then there was a protracted conversation with those who had seen only one boat on the lake and who had seen that Jesus had not entered that boat. So they sought Jesus, wondering how he had gotten to the other side of the sea, a question that surely has to be read in terms of the resurrection. The conversation climaxed with Jesus asserting, "I am the bread of life" (John 6:16–40).

In his version of the feeding of the multitude, Luke had no story of a seaside adventure, of calming the storm or walking on water; but, interestingly, Luke inserted into that position in his narrative the confession of Peter that Jesus was "The Christ of God" (Luke 9:18–22) and then moved directly into the account of the transfiguration.

There are similar themes in all of these stories, even beyond their lakeside setting. All of them reflected a traditional messianic symbol of mastery over water, including the ability both to calm the waves and to walk on the sea or through it. These stories also seem to have some connection with food, and Peter plays either a cryptic or an overt role in each of these accounts.

I will return to the food reference in the next chapter, but let me now lift out of the Hebrew past that peculiarly Jewish tradition that suggested that the messiah would have mastery over the water.

The Book of Job, which most scholars believe appeared in its final form in the sixth century B.C.E., referred to the God who "stretched out the heavens and trampled the waves of the sea" (9:8). Those parts of the Book of Isaiah that we call 2 Isaiah, which also appear to be a sixth-century B.C.E. creation, picked up this same theme. The "servant figure" was introduced in Isaiah 42 and, as already noted, provided an important interpretive clue by which Jesus came to be understood. Then, in chapter 43, God said to Israel, "When you pass through the waters I will be with you; and through the rivers, they shall not overwhelm you" (v. 2). Later in that same chapter the prophet introduced a word from God by describing the Lord as one "who makes a way in the sea, a path in the mighty waters" (v. 16).

In chapter 51, just prior to the two chapters that contain passages used by early Christians to describe Jesus' crucifixion and burial, the prophet wrote:

> *Was it not thou . . . that didst make the depths of the sea a way*
> *for the redeemed to pass over?*
> *And the ransomed of the Lord shall return,*
> *and come to Zion with singing;*
> *everlasting joy shall be upon their heads;*
> *they shall obtain joy and gladness,*
> *and sorrow and sighing shall flee away.*
> *"I, I am he that comforts you;*
> *who are you that you are afraid of man who dies,*
> *of the son of man who is made like grass,*
> *and have forgotten the Lord, your Maker,*
> *who stretched out the heavens*
> *and laid the foundations of the earth. . . .*
> *He who is bowed down shall speedily be released;*
> *he shall not die and go down to the Pit,*
> *neither shall his bread fail.*
> *For I am the Lord your God,*
> *who stirs up the sea so that its waves roar—*
> *the Lord of hosts is his name." (Vv. 10–15)*

Given the midrash tradition of searching the Scriptures to interpret God's action in the present, this passage is quite likely to have been used by early Christians to shed light on Jesus of Nazareth. Mastery over the sea, bread that does not fail, the Son of man who is made like grass, that is, one who can actually die yet one who does not go down into the Pit—all are symbolic phrases far too familiar in the telling of the Christ story to be coincidental.

The Book of Psalms, most of which came from the period after the Babylonian exile, continued this theme. It must be noted here that a storm on the sea was a metaphor for evil forces at work. Salvation was seen in God's power over those evil forces and God's ability to make those evil forces obey the divine command. So we read "[God] reached from on high, [God] took me, [God] drew me out of many waters" (Ps. 18:16). "Save me, O God! For the waters have come up about my neck. I sink in deep mire where there is no foothold; I have come into deep waters and floods sweep over me. I am weary with my crying; my throat is parched. My eyes grow dim with waiting for my God" (Ps. 69:1–3).

It is not inconceivable to me that these two passages gave rise to the story of Peter trying to walk on the water to reach Jesus—a Peter who believed that the crucifixion was final and that there was no help in Jesus. This would be an accurate picture of the Peter who fled Jerusalem for Galilee and who lived for a time in the unrelenting depression of believing that Jesus had, in fact, gone down to the eternal Pit while his eyes grew dim waiting for his God. It is certain that this psalm was part of the Scripture that fed the early church's interpretation of Jesus, for in verse 21 it says: "For my thirst they gave me vinegar to drink," which the fourth Gospel incorporated into the story of the crucifixion (John 19:28–30).

Other passages in the Psalter confirm the expectation that the messiah, God's representative, might have power over the sea. "When the waters saw thee, O God, when the waters saw thee, they were afraid, yea, the deep trembled. . . . Thy way was through the sea, thy path through the great waters; yet thy footprints were unseen" (Ps. 77:16, 19). "Thou dost rule the raging of the sea; when its waves rise thou stillest them" (Ps. 89:9). "Mightier than the waves of the sea is the Lord" (Ps. 93:4).

Behind these different and yet similar Gospel episodes I find a common theme that comes together for me in the final chapter of John in still another form. That chapter was also set by the lake. The disciples were struggling not against the raging elements but against an empty catch. Jesus appeared by the lake and directed them to cast their nets yet one more time. They did as he directed and the nets were filled. Peter, upon being told that "It is the Lord," leapt into the water to go ashore. He did not walk; he swam. The other disciples, bringing the heavily laden boat, also came ashore at Jesus' invitation: "Come and have breakfast," Jesus said. None of them dared to ask who he was, because "they knew it was the Lord." Jesus then took bread and gave it to them. And then the memorable conversation with Peter was recorded in triplicate:

"Peter, do you love me?"
"Yes, Lord, you know I love you."
"Feed my sheep."

Somewhere in the dark recesses of time after the earthly life of Jesus had ended, and some forty to seventy years before the writing of the Gospels was undertaken, the event occurred that created the Christian movement.

The details were, and still are, sketchy—"The crucified one lives" was the heart of their message. Scrape the veneer off their stories and we come to the probability that the moment that convinced them of this truth occurred in Galilee and that Simon was the primary person in whom this truth first dawned. Because of that, Simon became known as the rock upon which the Christian faith rested, and so the nicknames Cephas, Peter, Rock were attached to him. When he turned, he strengthened his brethren. When he stopped denying, he was reborn. When he ceased to doubt, he no longer sank into the waters of despair. Jesus appeared first to Cephas. The second detail in the attempt to reconstruct the moment of Easter is now in place. Peter stands, probably alone, in that moment.

Chapter 16

The Third Clue:
The Common Meal

"When he was at table with them, he took the bread and blessed, and broke it, and gave it to them. And their eyes were opened and they recognized him; and he vanished out of their sight. . . . And they rose that same hour and returned to Jerusalem. . . . Then they told what had happened on the road, and how he was known to them in the breaking of the bread" (Luke 24:30–31, 33, 35).

Of the many points connecting the experience of Jesus' resurrection with the reenactment of the common meal, this episode is the clearest and the most overt. It is also a narrative strangely cast and deeply disturbing to those who want to literalize the empty tomb and the flesh-and-blood body of the risen Lord.

Look for a moment at the questions that this passage raises: The two disciples, Cleopas and his unnamed companion, were journeying from Jerusalem to Emmaus, a distance of some seven miles. Suddenly Jesus drew near and went with them. I suppose Jesus could have simply been walking along that road and overtaken them, though the implication of the text is that he simply appeared out of nowhere to walk with the two pilgrims. It must be noted that if he did simply overtake them, his body would require the necessary functioning skeletal system to enable him to walk. They talked together on this walk, which would also require a functioning set of vocal cords and a larynx. Presumably Cleopas and his friend saw this stranger and saw the road along which they were walking. There is no sense whatsoever in this narrative that these two disciples were either physically blind or that they went through this adventure with their eyes closed.

Arriving at a house that appears to have been their destination, they invited their walking partner inside. Acting as if this was their home, they urged the stranger to "stay with us for it is towards evening and the day is now far spent" (v. 29). The invitation was accepted, said the narrative. Then suddenly the invited guest began to act like he himself was the host. He took the bread and offered the ceremonial blessing, a task usually performed by the head of the family. Indeed, in this narrative, words were used that are generally recognized as the highly developed technical words of the early Christian liturgies. The stranger took bread, blessed it, broke it, and gave it. Something happened in that moment, the text stated, that caused the eyes of Cleopas and his companion "to open." What kind of opening was that? It clearly was not physical. It was more like insight than sight, more like second sight than first sight.

Inspired by the meanings uncovered when the Gospels are looked at as examples of early Jewish Christian midrash, we now search the Scriptures to see if there are other episodes in the sacred text in which people who are not blind have their eyes "opened" to new dimensions of reality. That search is quickly rewarded.

OTHER MOMENTS OF INSIGHT WHEN EYES ARE OPENED

In the story of Adam and Eve in the garden of Eden (Genesis 2, 3), there are two forbidden trees, not just one, as most of us think. The first was the familiar tree of the knowledge of good and evil; the other was the enigmatic tree of life. The second tree does not appear in the story until the last moment, in Gen. 3:22. Eating of the fruit of the tree of the knowledge of good and evil brought with it the punishment of death. So presumably in this myth Adam and Eve possessed the gift of eternal life before they ate of that tree. Once they had eaten, however, they were banished from the garden. An angelic figure, called in the text a cherubim and armed with a flaming sword, was set to guard the way back into the garden and, therefore, the way back to the second tree, the tree of life. In this way the tree of life was divinely protected lest the disobedient primeval parents would come to possess not only the knowledge of good and evil but also the gift of life.

But in this story, when Adam and Eve ate the forbidden fruit, the text said "their eyes were opened." Is it possible that in Luke's resurrection story the bread taken, blessed, broken, and given was thought of as the fruit of the tree of life that opened the eyes of those who lived east of Eden, to enable them to see their way back into the kingdom of God as understood under the symbol of the garden of Eden?

In any event, in this vignette the breaking of the bread provided the occasion for a new kind of sight; for a vision beyond the limits of the physical into the deeper meanings of God. Cleopas and his partner "see" what they had not seen before, and when they "see," they recognized their invited guest as Jesus, risen from the dead. At that moment "he vanished out of their sight." Where did he go? To the place, presumably, from whence he had come. Where was that? The text is noncommittal, but it implies that heaven and the abode of God are all about us but our eyes cannot or do not see. What kind of body did the risen Christ possess? One that could appear and disappear, the text implied, and one that could be recognized in the breaking of bread. When Cleopas and his partner returned to Jerusalem, they made this insight quite certain. Jesus, risen from the dead, was "known to them in the breaking of the bread" (v. 35).

This is not the only episode in the New Testament where the resurrected Jesus and the sharing of food were placed in juxtaposition. It occurred in the secondary ending in Mark, where the text said that Jesus appeared to the disciples "as they sat at table"

(16:14). It appeared in Luke's account of Jesus' appearance to the eleven in Jerusalem when he requested food and they gave him a piece of broiled fish "and he took it and ate before them" (Luke 24:42, 43). It may be covertly present in John 20, where two appearance stories are told. The time for both of these stories is set when the evening meal would normally be served. The first event occurred, said the text, "on the evening of the first day of the week, the doors being shut"(John 20:19). The second event came eight days later, when his disciples were again in the house with the doors shut (20:26). In the Jewish world, eight days later would be the first day of the second week, at the same hour, the hour of the evening meal. There is here just a hint, nothing more.

In the epilogue to the fourth Gospel, however, the connection of food with the resurrection is clear and more overt. When the disciples accepted Jesus' invitation to dine with him by the lake, and when in the course of that meal Jesus took and gave the bread to them, the text said: "Now none of the disciples dared ask him, 'Who are you?' They knew it was the Lord" (21:12). There was one additional unique twist in John's epilogue. The liturgical formula so omnipresent in the New Testament where Jesus takes, blesses, breaks, and gives the bread was violated. In this text Jesus only "took and gave."

To understand this we need to recall that the fourth Gospel is the only Gospel that contains no account of the Last Supper. Never in the Gospel of John does Jesus gather his disciples around a table prior to Good Friday and identify broken bread with his body and poured-out wine with his blood. In that position John inserted instead the account of Jesus washing the feet of the disciples. For John there was only one moment when the bread of life was taken, blessed, broken, and given, and that moment was on the cross of Calvary. In John's epilogue, the blessed and broken bread of life was present at this meal; indeed he was the host presiding at this table. He needed only to take and give. We will encounter this idea in John once more when we examine other feeding stories in his text.

Moving on to the Book of Acts, there are two references that seem to bring together in a unique way food and the risen presence of Jesus. Both references point, I believe, to an original and primitive connection. The first reference is weak, but the second is so strong that it cannot be avoided.

In chapter 1 the text said: "And while staying with them he charged them not to depart from Jerusalem"(v. 4). The Greek word translated here as "staying" is *synalizomenos*. The more common translation of this word is "eating," which a footnote in the Revised Standard Version of the Bible makes clear. This verse is the preamble to Luke's story of the ascension. The risen Christ was known by them through the medium of a shared meal.

When we move on to chapter 10 of Acts, to a sermon attributed to Peter, we discover that these enigmatic words have been employed: "They put him to death by hanging him on a tree; but God raised him on the third day and made him manifest; *not to all the people but to us who were chosen by God as witnesses, who ate and drank with him after* he rose from the dead" (Acts 10:39–41). This is a remarkable statement. It first affirmed the divine initiative—God raised him, Jesus did not himself do the rising. It suggested also that subjectivity was involved in the concept of "seeing" the risen Christ. The God who raised him also "made him manifest," but only to those "*chosen as witnesses*." The risen Christ was not made manifest to "*all the people*." He was not, this text appears to say, objective, physical, or photographable. It took the action of God to make him "seen" or "manifest." Something had to happen to these "witnesses" to open the eyes of nonblind people to see what normal eyes could not see. The risen Christ could be envisioned only by eyes that in some unique way had been divinely opened. Finally, the text suggested that the witnesses to the resurrection were those who "*ate and drank with him after he rose from the dead*." Once again, the connection is clear. Somehow, seeing the risen Christ was associated with sharing the common meal, with participating in the meaning of the broken bread.

The final connector of food with the specifically risen Jesus was recorded in the book called the Revelation to John. In this text the victorious Christ, who "has conquered" and has sat down with his Father on his throne, says to the church at Laodicea: "Behold, I stand at the door and knock; if any one hears my voice and opens the door, I will come in to him and *eat* with him, and he with me" (3:20)

THE FOURFOLD FORMULA: TAKE, BLESS, BREAK, AND GIVE

From the earliest moment there appears to have been an indelible connection between the experience of Jesus alive after Good Friday and the experience of gathering in the Lord's name to break bread and eat together. Accepting the inappropriateness of reading the Gospels with a sense of linear time, we now look in the body of the Gospels for other food-resurrection connections. We need to remind ourselves to break the pattern that history has encouraged; that is, to stop seeing the Gospels as chronologies of Jesus' life, describing events in sequence from his birth to his death and his resurrection. In reality, every Gospel was written in the light of Easter, and the meaning of Easter can be found over and over again in the corpus of the text itself if we only have the eyes to see.

The first and most obvious event to which we must turn is the meal that has come to be called the Last Supper. An account of that meal was given by Paul and the writers of three synoptic Gospels.

In the First Letter to the Corinthians (11:23–26), which is the earliest written account of this meal (56 C.E.), Paul introduced the episode, as we noted earlier when we analyzed his thought about the resurrection, by saying: "For I received from the Lord what I also delivered to you, that the Lord Jesus on the night he was betrayed took bread." Paul was saying that this was the authentic, sacred tradition of the primitive Christian community, and it was to be treated with a special kind of respect. It was "received," and it was to be "delivered" as it had been "received." In a day before the printing press, when written messages were scarce indeed, sacred tradition was handed on by word of mouth with a reverence for its accuracy that was not to be ignored. Four chapters later in the same epistle, Paul introduced the story of Jesus' resurrection in the same way: "For I *delivered* to you as of first importance what I also *received,* that Christ died for our sins in accordance with the scriptures, that he was buried, that he was raised on the third day" (1 Cor. 15:3ff). So it is fair to say that in Paul the reenactment of the Lord's Supper and the accounts of witnesses who attested to the resurrection were together accorded the status of the "received" tradition that must be "delivered" in an exact way.

It is also worth noting that by the time Paul wrote this letter, the four liturgical verbs were already clearly in place. Jesus, in this final meal, took, blessed (gave thanks), broke, and gave.

Moreover the broken bread was identified with the body of Jesus, which had been given or broken "for you." The cup was called "the new covenant in my blood." "Do this in remembrance of me" was the command.

We should also note that this reenacted liturgy was not to be done to celebrate the resurrection but rather to "proclaim the Lord's death until he comes." It was the means by which the Christian community came to understand his death. In that understanding lay the hope that this Jesus was with God, and that from God he would come at the end of the age. The Jesus who would be portrayed two decades later as walking out of the tomb was simply not contemplated in this early Pauline text. But the understanding of that death, and therefore an understanding of Jesus' triumph over that death, which identified him with the yet-to-come Lord of Judgment called the Son of man, was present in Paul's text describing the sacramental meal.

Going back now to traditions about Jesus' life that the Gospel writers located before his resurrection, we take with us the four liturgical verbs—take, bless, break, and give—to provide us with clues to deeper meanings. These key words indicate that we are dealing not with a normal meal but with a unique meal that is somehow a signal to understanding the original meaning of the resurrection.

We look first at the synoptic tradition of the institution of the Lord's Supper. Mark, the earliest Gospel, employed in the telling of that story the four crucial verbs; Jesus took, blessed, broke, gave (Mark 14:22). The meal ended by Jesus saying, "I shall not drink again of the fruit of the vine until that day when I drink it new in the kingdom of God" (14:25). One might well ask to what "that day" referred. My suspicion is that "that day" meant either the day of the resurrection or the day of the second coming. Those two days quickly became confused in Christian history, as I hope to demonstrate.

Matthew's version of the Last Supper made only one significant change in Mark's text. Matthew amended the closing statement of Jesus to say that the next time he would drink the fruit of the vine it would be "with you" in his "Father's kingdom" (Matt. 26:29).

Luke's only change in the Last Supper narrative was to have Jesus use two cups instead of one. My supposition is that Luke was a Gentile with strong Jewish connections, but not strong enough to get all the rituals, like the Passover, correct. In chapter 2 of his Gospel he also confused the rites of purification and presentation. Beyond that minor point, Luke also contains a unique twist in the final words of the earthly Jesus. "You are those who have continued with me in my trials; and I assign to you, as my Father assigned to me, a kingdom, that you may *eat and drink at my table in my kingdom* and sit on twelve thrones judging the twelve tribes of Israel" (22:28). Luke was saying, it seems to me, that eating and drinking at the Lord's table was part of what it meant to be in the kingdom of God. That in turn seems to suggest that in the act of eating and drinking in the name of the Lord, here and now, we are sharing a foretaste of that kingdom. Perhaps in such a setting our eyes might well "be opened" to behold the one who, though crucified, was seen in fact to be reigning as the Lord of heaven.

There are other feeding/eating episodes in the Gospels that now cry out for explanation. In Mark, Jesus fed two multitudes. One story had five thousand "men," who were fed with five loaves and two fish, and after which twelve baskets of fragments were gathered (Mark 6:30–44). The other episode had four thousand "people," who were fed with seven loaves and a few small fish, and afterward seven baskets of fragments were gathered (Mark 8:1–10). In both of these narratives Mark had Jesus use the liturgical formula. He took, blessed, broke, and gave the bread.

There are two other notes in Mark that suggest that we are dealing with a postresurrection understanding, now being read back into an earlier episode. In the feeding of the five thousand, Jesus was said to have had compassion on the crowd because they were "like sheep without a shepherd" (Mark 6:34). That note was also struck in Mark's account of the Last Supper, when Jesus said to the disciples, "You will all fall away; for it is written, 'I will strike the shepherd, and the sheep will be scattered'" (Mark 14:27). Surely that duplication of almost identical words as part of two distinct episodes, in each of which Jesus took, blessed, broke, and gave, is not coincidental.

In the episode describing the feeding of the four thousand, Jesus said, "I have compassion on the crowd, because they have been with me now *three days*, and have nothing to eat" (Mark 8:2). When Mark's Gospel was written, the phrase "three days" was the language of the resurrection. It was not an accidental phrase and must be understood here in that context.

When one adds up the strange symbols—five loaves here, seven loaves there, five thousand men here, four thousand people there, twelve baskets of fragments here, seven baskets of fragments there, sheep without a shepherd here, three days there—it becomes clear that these feeding stories were not to be understood either literally or as stories about a supernatural miracle. They had some connection with both the Last Supper and the resurrection.

Matthew followed Mark's format and included in his Gospel both the feeding of the five thousand and the feeding of the four thousand. In both instances he used the fourfold liturgical code: Jesus took, blessed, broke, gave (Matt. 14:10; 15:36).

Luke omitted the second feeding-of-the-multitude story and recorded only the story of the five thousand, but once again, in an ever-consistent way, the formula was employed: Jesus took, blessed, broke, gave (Luke 9:16).

John also recorded but one feeding story. But in his description of that single episode, he confirmed every suspicion that the feeding of the multitude by Jesus with bread in the wilderness was a sign of the resurrection, a symbol of the heavenly banquet. Even though John omitted the Last Supper from his narrative, we do have, at the place where the Last Supper would normally be included, a midrashic connection with food that helps us to know that the common meal was in fact not only in John's mind but was actually the setting for his words. John had Jesus say at the events that night, "I am not speaking of you all; I know whom I have chosen; it is that the scripture may be fulfilled, 'He who ate my bread has lifted his heel against me'" (John 13:18). Shortly thereafter he dipped a morsel and gave it to Judas as a way to indicate who the betrayer would be. The verse that created that midrash is Ps. 41:9, where the psalmist wrote: "Even my bosom friend in whom I trusted, who ate of my bread, has lifted his heel against me." But this psalm went on to include words that most assuredly would be seen as a resurrection reference: "But do thou, O Lord, be gracious to me *and raise me up,* that I may requite them" (Ps. 41:10). Even John, the one Gospel making an eyewitness claim (John 21:24), used the midrash method.

Without a Last Supper in the narrative, the fourth Gospel attached to the feeding-of-the-multitude story all of the teaching that Paul and the synoptic writers had placed around the Last Supper. For this author the feeding of the multitude was a clear sign that resurrection and the common meal were intimately interrelated. John even stated that the feeding of the five thousand took place at the time of the Passover, which was the synoptic Gospels' setting for the Last Supper. John disputed that synoptic claim by placing the crucifixion itself on the day before the Passover, when the Paschal Lamb was slain, but he located the story of the five thousand during the Passover.

In John's story of the feeding of the five thousand, Jesus takes, blesses, and gives. He does not "break"! John told this episode as an event in the early part of Jesus' life and not as a postresurrection story. So Jesus could take the bread, bless the bread, and give the bread. But for John, the bread of life could only be broken once, and that occurred when the crucifixion was accomplished. For John the crucifixion was the breaking once and for all of the person whom John believed to be the bread of life. Hence there was no breaking of bread in John's story of the feeding of the five thousand.

When we look at the details around that episode in the fourth Gospel, John's purpose in writing becomes very clear. When the people saw the miracle of the loaves, they immediately said, "This is indeed the prophet that should come into the world" (John 6:14). John had correlated the feeding of the multitude in the wilderness with the Exodus story of Moses giving manna in the wilderness to the people of Israel (Exod. 16:13ff), which was surely the midrashic tradition behind each Gospel's feeding of the multitude stories.

In time the Jewish tradition came to view as heavenly food the bread given in the wilderness that they called manna. It was "the bread of angels," and the ability to provide such bread was incorporated into the expectation of the messiah, a prophet like Moses, whom God would someday raise up. These themes were caught by the psalmist, who wrote, "Can God spread a table in the wilderness? . . . Can He also give bread?" (Ps. 78:18ff). There were other elements in the wilderness story from Exodus that seem to be echoed in John's account of the feeding of the multitude. When Moses spoke of that heavenly food, he said, "in the morning you shall see the glory of God" (Exod. 16:7), a verse that would undoubtedly have been seen by the early Christians as anticipating their experience of resurrection.

In that ancient wilderness tale God provided not just bread but meat (Exod. 16:13), and in time this meat came to be referred to by the psalmist as flesh, which God's people ate (Ps. 78:27, 29). The fourth Gospel played on all of these themes. Jesus as Messiah could give bread, but he also could give his flesh for the life of the world. John now moved beyond the feeding of the multitude and began to belabor these points, as if to say, Please do not misunderstand what I am saying: It is the Son of man who gives the bread that endures to eternal life. On this Son of man God has set his seal (John 6:27). That is, God has vindicated him. My Father thus gives the true bread; the bread of God is that which comes down from heaven and gives life to the world (John 6:30–34).

Then, in John's story, the crowd asked for this heavenly bread, and Jesus responded: "I am the bread of life; he who comes to me shall not hunger. . . . The bread which I shall give for the life of the world is my flesh" (John 6:35, 51b). Again and again John portrayed Jesus as driving this point home. "Unless you eat the flesh of the Son of man and drink his blood, you have no life in you; he who eats my flesh and drinks my blood has eternal life, and I will raise him up at the last day" (6:53, 54); that one "abides in me, and I in him" (John 6:56). When the disciples complained that this was a hard saying, Jesus responded: "Then what if you were to see the Son of man ascending to where he was before? It is the spirit that gives life, the flesh is of no avail" (John 6:62–63).

There they are—all of the symbols together: my flesh is food indeed, God's bread is spirit, the body that died is not important. I have ascended so that I might come to you as spirit to feed you, to give you life, to be your heavenly food. Then, said the fourth Gospel, Peter understood, and when asked if he would go away from this Jesus, he responded: "Lord, to whom shall we go? You have the words of eternal life; and we have believed, and have come to know, that you are the Holy One of God" (John 6:68–69). That could not be a word spoken before Easter no matter where it has been placed in the Johannine text.

Resurrection, bread, ascension, spirit, and the confession of Peter are the elements that came together at the dawn of the Christian story, John suggested. It was in Galilee. It involved Peter. It had something to do with broken bread and with seeing Jesus as heavenly food. When we journey into the heart of the Scriptures, we discover that somehow bread, in the form of a loaf broken sacramentally, became the means through which eyes were opened to see Jesus as the bread of life, as the one upon the cross who was taken, blessed, broken, and given. We will know him thus as alive and therefore eternally available to us, for his life has now been lifted into the very life of God. From that heavenly place "he made himself known to them in the breaking of bread." The third clue has fallen into place.

Chapter 17

The Fourth Clue: The Third Day—
An Eschatological Symbol

"And he began to teach them that the Son of man must suffer many things, and be rejected by the elders and the chief priests and the scribes, and be killed, and after three days rise again" (Mark 8:31).

". . . after three days rise again" is a fascinating phrase in Mark's story. If we take those words literally, the story of Jesus' resurrection would have to be located on the second day of the week, a fact that few people seem to realize.

In Matthew's Gospel, Jesus is quoted as saying to some of the scribes and Pharisees: "For as Jonah was three days and three nights in the belly of the whale, so will the Son of man be three days and three nights in the heart of the earth" (12:40). If these words are to be taken literally, then the resurrection of Jesus would have to be located at sundown on Monday. Even then, the stated order would have to be reversed so that it would read three nights and three days. There is not much chance that the text with which I opened this chapter can be explained as an offhand comment that proved not to be literally accurate, because Mark had Jesus repeat it in chapter 9, verse 31: "The Son of man will be delivered into the hands of men, and they will kill him; and when he is killed, *after three days* he will rise."

If one is still not certain that this is what the early tradition thought, one has only to skip over to Mark 10:33, 34, where again, Jesus is speaking: "Behold, we are going up to Jerusalem; and the Son of man will be delivered to the chief priests and scribes, and they will condemn him to death, and deliver him to the Gentiles; and they will mock him, and spit upon him, and scourge him, and kill him; and *after three days* he will rise." If one can count to three, this locates the day of the resurrection on Monday, the second day of the week, not on Sunday, the first day of the week.

Maurice Goguel, a ranking biblical scholar in the first half of this century, argues that in Mark "after three days" did not refer to a period of seventy-two hours but simply meant "after a brief delay."[1] That may well be, but it is clear that this time designation got literalized very early and that efforts were made to bring the tradition of the first day of the week together with the symbol of three days. That blend was accomplished by shifting "after three days" to being understood as *"on the third day,"* and that new understanding was passed on in the written tradition. "After three days" and "on the third day" do not mean the same thing, but they sound similar, and most people will not question the difference. So the harmonization took place rather early in the Christian movement. Even so, the first day of the week could become the third day only by counting Friday as the first day, which severely presses the definition since the sun went down ending that day near the moment of Jesus' death.

Paul referred to the third day as early as 56 C.E. in his letter to the Corinthians (1 Cor. 15:4). Therefore we can conclude that at least in the hellenized and gentile communities the harmonizing of the first day and three days had already occurred. Mark's Gospel, though written later than any of Paul's Epistles, nonetheless reflected the more primitive Palestinian tradition. We can observe the shift taking place when we note that both Luke and Matthew changed Mark's "after three days" into "on the third day" (see Matt. 16:21; 17:23; 20:19; and Luke 9:22; 18:33; 24:7, 46). The change was deliberate, consistent, and quite specific, since both Matthew and Luke had the text of Mark in front of them as they wrote. Yet, by including the Jonah text, Matthew gave evidence that the version reflected in Mark was in fact more primitive.

Matthew also slipped back into this earlier tradition when he told the story of the Pharisees seeking guards for the tomb. They asserted that Jesus once said: *"After three days* I will rise again" (Matt. 27:63). Mark, Matthew, and John also include Jesus' reference to rebuilding the temple in three (presumably full) days (Mark 14:58; Matt. 26:61; John 2:20). Even Luke, I believe, revealed knowledge of the originality of the tradition of three full days when he employed it in the story of the boy Jesus in the temple (Luke 2:41–51). "After three days" the boy Jesus, who was lost, was found in God's temple. This child Jesus was then quoted as saying to his mother: "Did you not know that I must be in my Father's house?"

When we put together the narratives of the Gospels, the time between crucifixion on Friday and the empty tomb at dawn on Sunday was barely thirty-six hours, one and a half days at most. The first thing that must be registered, therefore, is that among early Christians the key phrases "the first day of the week," "after three days," and "on the third day" represent competing time references that were not reconciled until after some time had passed.

It becomes clear as we read the Easter narratives that the phrase "on the first day of the week" entered the Easter tradition along with the story of the empty tomb. The empty tomb was a Jerusalem story and was part of the Jerusalem tradition that, as I have already suggested, was quite secondary in time to the more primitive Galilean tradition. Since the empty tomb story was not an original part of the resurrection tradition, "on the third day" had to have been a later attempt to reconcile the primitive phrase "after three days" with the more recent addition "the first day of the week" or, to put it more concretely, to reconcile an ancient tradition with a secondary tradition.

Reginald Fuller has argued that the celebration of the Lord's day on the first day of the week was a Hellenistic Christian institution that was unknown to the Palestinian Christians but was, in fact, quite familiar to Paul, who moved in gentile circles.[2] Indeed

Paul referred to the first day of the week as the day on which Christians put their offerings aside to be accumulated for final collection on his visit. That reference may imply that this was the day on which the Christians gathered for worship. This reference is contained in the same epistle in which Paul said that he had received that tradition that Jesus was raised "on the third day" (1 Cor 16:2; 15:4). If "after three days" represented a Palestinian tradition, it would be fair to say that it antedates the Christian observance of the "first day of the week" and that it was grafted uneasily onto that tradition by the subtle shift to "on the third day." For the original meaning of three days, however, we must look beyond liturgical practices. We must search deep into the heart of Jewish thinking.

THE JEWISH MEANING OF THREE DAYS

In Hebrew thought, could the phrase "three days" constitute a reference to calendar time? I argue that it does not, and to support that conclusion I point my readers to the ancient Talmudic texts of the Jewish people that talked about the general resurrection at the end of the world. It would take place, said these texts, at dawn following the third day after the end of the world, or three days beyond the cessation of time. I understand that to use a time-defined word like *day* to refer to a dimension beyond time is nonsensical. That, of course, is always the problem when earthbound words are used to describe transcendent moments. That was exactly why the language of the Jewish apocalyptic tradition that dealt with the end of the world, and therefore with the end of time, was so bizarre and why the words used to describe the resurrection, when literalized, also become bizarre. The symbol of "three days" was an eschatological symbol for the Jews. The morning after the third day was the decisive, critical moment in the events that marked the final things in Jewish mythology. The symbol "three days" for Jewish Christians would not have been a matter of chronology; it would have been, rather, a dogmatic assertion that Jesus was the one who brought the dawn of the kingdom of God. Despite the

213

implications of the "three days" symbol, the fact remained that the new Jerusalem did not descend out of the sky at the moment called Easter, and the kingdom of God did not get ushered in at the time of Jesus' death and resurrection.

So what were the early Christians asserting when they used the "three days" formula? They were saying that Jesus had entered the realm of heaven from which he had manifested himself to his disciples after his death. It meant that his disciples saw Jesus as a symbol and a pledge that the God who ruled the heavens had taken Jesus into the meaning of God. It meant that the righteous one who was crucified had been vindicated. It meant that his teaching had been affirmed. It meant that the God who had been defined by Jesus, not the God who was defined by the religious establishment of the Jews, had been revealed as the true God. Finally, and most specifically, it meant that what the Jews thought would happen to everyone at the general resurrection three days after the end of the world had in fact happened now in this one special instance to this one son of Israel. It meant that Jesus was the "firstfruits of those who have fallen asleep" (1 Cor. 15:20).

To locate the phrase "after three days" in the vocabulary of Jewish thought about the end of the world is to raise a question about its even earlier origin: How did the "three days" reference get incorporated into Jewish eschatology? That question drives us once more into the midrash tradition of the Jewish Scriptures.

There was a sense in Jewish life and folklore that after three days the crucial moment arrives, particularly when one is dealing either with God or with a turning point in national history. Whenever the people of Israel thought of God or tried to make sense out of the way they perceived God to be relating to them or their history, they appear to use the symbol of three days, and this unit of time is found throughout the Hebrew Scriptures.

A three-day journey was considered a safe distance for Jewish heroes to travel out of danger, like Jacob and Moses from their enemies, Laban (Gen. 30:36), and Pharaoh (Exod. 3:18). Joseph imprisoned his brothers for three days as a test when they came to Egypt to buy grain during the famine (Gen. 42:17, 18). In that story, it was on the third full day that Joseph announced to his jailed brothers his verdict that would be carried out after the passage of that third day: "Do this and you will live, for I fear God." The third of the three days began to connote judgment, the critical day on which the new reality would begin to dawn, a reality that would be fully revealed only when the third day was past.

The "plague of darkness" that Moses was said to have visited upon Egypt was a "darkness to be felt for three days." "Nor," says the text, "did any rise from his place for three days" (Exod. 10:22ff). The Gospel writers surely harked back to this when they told of darkness covering "the whole land" at the time of the crucifixion (Mark 15:33; Matt. 27:45; and Luke 23:44). "No one" did rise "from his place for three days," according to the tradition.

It was also on the third day that David was informed of the death of Saul on Mount Gilboa, which meant that after three days David could proclaim himself king. In that episode the messenger, an Amalekite, was accused of slaying Saul, who was referred to in this sacred story as "the Lord's anointed" (2 Sam. 1:1–16). The "anointed one" was the literal translation of the Hebrew word *mashiach*, which in Greek is rendered "Christ."

When the land of the Jews was split into the two hostile nations of Israel and Judah, the division took place after three days. "Depart for three days," Rehoboam said, and "then come again to me" (1 Kings 12:5). Ezra, on his journey to the promised land from the Babylonian exile, paused for three days by the river Ahava to make sure he had proper ministers for the temple of God before pressing on to his destination (Ezra 8:15). When Ezra arrived, all the returning exiles had to assemble within three days or else be banned from the house of Israel, which would be established after three days (Ezra 10:8, 9). Jonah was imprisoned in the belly of the great fish for three days and three nights before he was delivered by the Lord (Jon. 1:17). Finally after three days and nights of fasting, Queen Esther acted to save her people from the wicked Haman (Esther 4:16).

Blurring this image to some degree, we must admit that there were also some biblical references in which it was the third day itself, not the dawn after the third day, that became the decisive-action moment. Early Christians clearly could have used these texts as a midrashic justification when in order to harmonize the primitive resurrection theme of "after three days" with "the first day of the week" they began to speak of the resurrection as occurring on "the third day." In the Joseph story both the pharaoh's butler and his baker had their destiny of either life or death carried out on the third day (Gen 40:12, 13, 18, 19). Yahweh's appearance on Mount Sinai to give the law occurred on the morning of the third day. This appearance was preceded by thunder, lightning, thick clouds, and loud trumpets. Only then did Moses bring the people out to meet God (Exod. 19:16). In preparation for this theophony, the people were told to go through rites of ceremonial cleansing to be ready for the third day: "for on the third day the Lord will come down upon Mount Sinai in the sight of all the people" (Exod. 19:11).

When King Hezekiah of Judah became ill, Isaiah the prophet went to him to tell him to set his house in order, for he would die. Hezekiah wept and prayed, reminding God of how faithful a king he had been. The Lord then told Isaiah to return with a new message: "I have heard your prayer, I have seen your tears; behold, I will heal you; on the third day you shall go up to the house of the Lord" (2 Kings 20:1–5). Hezekiah, wanting to make sure he did not misunderstand the message, inquired, "What shall be the sign that the Lord will heal me, and that I shall go up to the house of the Lord on the third day?" (2 Kings 20:8). Isaiah provided a sign that had to do with shadows moving backward—an indication that time had been suspended or reversed.

The prophet Hosea, declaring that Yahweh promised to give new life to his people, said, "After two days he will revive us; on the third day he will raise us up, that we may live before him" (Hos. 6:2).

It is clear that the phrase "three days" was constantly used in the tradition of the Jews. The third day was in many instances either the critical day of judgment or the day when the new reality dawned. The third day was thus lifted into the mythology of the Jews in regard to the end of the world. The third day came to be identified as the prelude to the day of the Lord. The day of the Lord would be the day on which God acted decisively to save the world. For evildoers the day of the Lord was to be dreaded. For the oppressed righteous, however, the day of the Lord was to be anticipated with hope. "On that day the Lord their God will save them, for they are the flock of his people" wrote Zechariah shortly after his verses about the king coming lowly and riding on an ass—a passage that certainly got incorporated early into the Christian story (Zech. 9:16). Zechariah the prophet also wrote: "And I will pour out on the house of David and the inhabitants of Jerusalem a spirit of compassion and supplication, so that, when they look on him whom they have pierced, they shall mourn for him, as one mourns for an only child, and weep bitterly over him, as one weeps over a firstborn. On that day the mourning in Jerusalem will be as great as the mourning for Hadadrimmon in the plain of Megiddo" (Zech. 12:10ff). Zechariah went on a bit later to say that they would "strike the shepherd, that the sheep may be scattered" (13:7), a verse that we have met already in the Gospel text. "That day" was a clear reference to "the day of the Lord." It was identified with the reign of God, which would begin three days after the end of the world. Malachi could write about that day, "But who can endure the day of his coming, and who can stand when he appears?" (Mal. 3:2).

So in Jewish history the dawn after the third day, or in some instances even the third day itself, gradually came to be identified with "the day of the Lord," and in time that convenient merger enabled the Christians to tell their story in terms of that apocalyptic symbol. In Jesus they saw God at work. To make sense of his crucifixion they employed the apocalyptic symbol and spoke of darkness covering the whole earth. But after three days, they asserted, God raised him and made him sit at God's right hand. From that position of heavenly exaltation this Jesus would come a second time, but the second coming would be the final day of the Lord, and he would gather all the nations before him and separate the sheep from the goats in the ultimate judgment (Matt. 25:31ff). So it was that the symbols of the Jewish past—three days, the day of the Lord, exaltation, Son of man, and second coming—all gathered around the life of Jesus as they tried to interpret what Jesus' life meant and, even more, what they understood his death to mean.

To literalize these symbols would be to miss their meaning. To open these symbols to the past is to enter through them into another worldview where new sights and new sounds, not experienced before, could be seen and heard.

A SYMBOL THAT CONFIRMED THE REALITY OF THE NEW AGE

Had there been no reality to Jesus, or to his death, or to whatever the Easter experience was, then none of these symbols would have gathered around this life. To analyze the symbols is in no way to discredit that reality; it is rather to tease apart myth and reality. It is to suggest that reality cannot be found in the literalizing of the mythical symbols but only in opening the symbols to their original meanings. In the Jewish apocalyptic tradition, neither "after three days" nor "on the third day" was a measure of time, regardless of whether they referred to thirty-six hours or seventy-two hours. Both phrases represented an affirmation of faith about who this Jesus of Nazareth was believed to be by those who used these symbols. It was the assertion that the day of salvation, the day of the Lord, had already begun to unfold within human history. It was to suggest that, from the time of Jesus' death forward, life had a radical newness. That was the belief born in the experience of Easter. I have yet to speculate on exactly what that Easter experience was, but I have asserted and do assert that something happened— something that was not only real but that also invited those who shared in it into a new reality that they could describe only with mythological words.

Before leaving the "three days" symbol, one other aspect of Jewish thought needs to be mentioned. Jewish people believed that one who had died was not to be considered really dead until after the third day. The deceased person's *nephesh*, or life force, was thought to hover over the grave for three days before finally departing for the regions of Sheol. After three days, decomposition was thought to be so advanced that no resuscitation was possible, except by divine intervention. Advanced decomposition in this primitive society was thought to be the sign that the dead person's nephesh had in fact departed. We can see evidence of this folk wisdom in the Lazarus story in the fourth Gospel (John 11).

In language obviously not accidental, Jesus received the message that his friend Lazarus was ill. Receiving that message, Jesus waited "two days longer in the place where he was" (John 11:6). Then he started for Judea on the third day, knowing, said that text, that Lazarus was dead. When Jesus arrived, having traveled only at night for fear of arrest, he found that Lazarus had "been in his tomb for four days" (John 11:17). That would mean one day beyond any hope of resuscitation. Jesus went to the tomb, which had a stone laid upon it, like a more famous tomb mentioned later in John's narrative. "Take away the stone," Jesus ordered (John 11:39). Martha, Lazarus's sister, protested: "Lord, by this time there will be an odor, for he has been dead four days" (11:39). Jesus then called Lazarus back to life with his burial bandages still wrapped around him, including a separate cloth for his face. It is clear that the fourth Gospel intended to contrast this resuscitation of a dead man into life four days after his death with the exaltation of Jesus on the third day into the presence of God, whence he could make himself known to his disciples as both whole and alive. Indeed, in both stories, bandages are mentioned, including the face covering, a stone had to be rolled away, and a woman named Mary stood outside the tomb weeping.

The tradition that death was real only after a passage of time is also present in the Psalms. "My body also dwells secure. For thou didst not give me up to Sheol, or let thy godly one see the Pit. Thou dost show me the path of life; in thy right hand there is pleasure forever more" (Ps. 16:9–11). There is no question that this psalm was taken into the "three day" symbol and interpreted as referring to Jesus of Nazareth, for it is quoted twice in the Book of Acts (2:25; 13:35), and on both occasions as a reference from David about Jesus. The one God raised up, says the Book of Acts (13:37), saw no corruption. That is, this body did not begin the process of decomposition, because the divine action came before three days had past.

Another psalm that seemed also to speak to the wholeness of the body of the one who was raised, said, "Many are the afflictions of the righteous; but the Lord delivered him out of them all. He keeps all his bones; not one of them is broken. The Lord redeems the life of his servants; none of those who take refuge in him will be condemned" (Ps. 34:19–22). Clearly this psalm was also incorporated into the Jesus story, as a casual reading of John 19:33–37 will reveal. This passage states that the bones of Jesus' legs were not broken, since he was judged to be already dead. The third day was crucial to the theme of physical wholeness.

The "raising" that Jesus said would occur "after three days" was not a resuscitation but an eschatological exaltation into the presence of God. It was a heavenly Jesus that they were convinced they had seen. As time went on, however, both the time reference and the exaltation itself were literalized, and adjustments were made to enable the literalized details of the story to fit the literalized symbols by which the details were being interpreted. In that adjustment "after three days" became "on the third day," and then "the day of the Lord" became "the first day of the week." It was an interesting progression.

Our clues begin to mount up. Whatever Easter was, it occurred in Galilee; the central figure in the drama was Peter; the event had some connection with the eating of a common meal; and it was not related to the crucifixion by a fixed number of days, for the symbols "three days" and "the day of the Lord" were both lifted out of Jewish mythology. These are the conclusions to which our study has drawn us. We need now only to examine the tradition of Jesus' burial before we attempt to put the clues together in a meaningful pattern.

Chapter 18

The Fifth Clue: The Burial Tradition As Mythology

"He was buried." With that simple, unembroidered statement, Paul proclaimed the obvious (1 Cor. 15:4). In Jewish society, after one died, one was buried, and on that very same day. The Jews did not place their dead outside the camp at night to be devoured by predators, as was done in some parts of Africa, or dispose of them in the sea, as practiced by certain island people. Nor did the Jews use funeral pyres. The dead were simply to be buried in the earth. Paul captured this Jewish attitude in his unadorned, direct statement, written about the year 56 C.E., that the Christ who had died "was buried." There is no indication in Paul that the tomb was unique, unusual, or noteworthy. Indeed there is no mention of a tomb at all.

By the time Mark wrote his Gospel, however (ca. 70 C.E.), a tradition about how this Jesus was buried began to evolve. No part of Jesus' life was exempt from legendary accretions. In its earliest Gospel version, this burial tradition starred a man named Joseph of Arimathea. He was described in Mark's text as "a respected member of the council, who was also himself looking for the kingdom of God" (15:43). Prior to this mention in Mark's story, Joseph of Arimathea had not, to our knowledge, ever achieved notice in Christian writing. Yet once he made this brief cameo appearance as a bit player in the critical week of Jesus' life, he immediately entered the developing Christian mythology. The mythology of this Joseph reached its apex in the fanciful tale of his having planted Christianity in what is now the British Isles before the first century was complete. In some traditions it is said that Joseph planted his walking staff in the soil of Glastonbury, England, and that the staff sprouted, growing into the blackthorn tree. The thorns of this tree were thought to point directly to the crown of thorns described in the passion drama. Much of Glastonbury's tourist appeal even today is built on this legend.

Mark tells us that Joseph "took courage and went to Pilate, and asked for the body of Jesus" (15:43). Pilate, surprised that Jesus was already dead, inquired of the centurion to be assured of the death, and then granted Joseph his request. Joseph then performed the Jewish burial rites. Jesus was wrapped in a shroud, which, the tradition stated, was to be generously suffused with spices and sweet-smelling fragrances.

Jewish embalming was quite unlike Egyptian embalming. There was no attempt to preserve the body from decay. Human life was molded out of the dust of the earth, said the Jewish myth of creation, and therefore it was to be returned to the dust of the earth.

The only Egyptian-embalmed mummies that the Hebrew Scriptures knew were the bodies of their patriarchs Jacob and Joseph, whose lives had been involved with Egypt. Jacob was carried back to Israel from Egypt for burial, after forty days of embalming and an additional thirty days for weeping, to the cave of Machpelah near Hebron, in the land of Canaan (Gen. 50:1–14). The body of Joseph was embalmed and put into a coffin in Egypt (Gen. 50:26). When the exodus took place, as much as four hundred years later according to some estimates, the "bones of Joseph" went with Moses and the Israelites (Exod. 13:19). Egyptian embalming mutilated the body with the removal of the brains and intestines, while the Jewish burial tradition treated the body as if the whole of it was sacred, so no parts were removed. For the Jews any effort was primarily to mute the odors of decay, not to slow or halt the process of decomposition.

When Joseph of Arimathea had finished his work of preparing the body, Mark said, he laid Jesus "in a tomb which had been hewn out of the rock; and he rolled a stone against the door of the tomb" (Mark 15:46). Once this was done Joseph disappeared from Mark's narrative as quickly as he had appeared.

Matthew added a bit to Joseph's identity by describing him as "also a disciple of Jesus" (Matt. 27:57), and he made the tomb "his own new tomb, which Joseph had hewn in the rock" (27:60). The stone that was used to cover the tomb became in Matthew the "great stone" (27:60). Then Joseph departed from that text.

Luke also added to the tradition. Arimathea became a "Jewish town" (Luke 23:50). Joseph was described "as a good and righteous man, who had not consented to their purpose and deed, and he was looking for the kingdom of God" (23:51). It is clear that both the stature and the legend of Joseph were growing. The tomb became, in Luke, one "where no one had ever yet been laid" (23:51).

By the time the fourth Gospel was written, a brand-new element had entered the burial legend. There the Joseph of Arimathea story is joined by the tradition involving Nicodemus. John introduced this story by reminding his readers of Nicodemus's earlier visit to Jesus "by night" (John 3:1–15). Then John said that Nicodemus "came bringing a mixture of myrrh and aloes, about a hundred pounds' weight" (19:39). This burial was going to be excessively proper! There are echoes in this burial story that make us aware that John used the method of midrash and built this narrative on Hebrew sources. A tomb that had been "hewn," and a bier on which "various spices prepared by the perfumers" was present, were both mentioned in the burial of King Asa of Judah (2 Chron. 16:14) and may have influenced the Nicodemus story. Also, the psalmist speaks of the king whom God has anointed (i.e., made *mashiach* or Christ) "with the oil of gladness above your fellows; your robes are all fragrant with myrrh and aloes" (Ps. 45:7, 8).

There were also some early Christian references that could be related to the burial tradition. In the Epistle to the Ephesians, Christ was referred to as "a fragrant offering and sacrifice to God" (Eph.5:2). In the even earlier Second Epistle to the Corinthians, Paul referred to the "aroma of Christ," a "fragrance" to those "perishing" as well as to those being "saved" (2 Cor. 2:14–16). These may have helped shape John's burial story.

The New Testament has yet a third burial tradition. It is found in the Book of Acts, in one of Paul's sermons. It is a bizarre tradition because it contradicts the story told in the Gospel of Luke, which, presumably, was written by the same author. Yet here it stands in Acts, a totally different account of Jesus' burial, reflecting the probability that the sermons of Peter and Paul in the Book of Acts had a history somewhat different from the balance of that book. In this sermon, Paul said, "Though they could charge him with nothing deserving death, yet they [i.e., those who lived in Jerusalem and their rulers] asked Pilate to have him killed. And when they had fulfilled all that was written of him, they took him down from the tree, and laid him in a tomb. But God raised him from the dead" (Acts 13:29–30). According to this interpretation, Reginald Fuller argues, "the burial of Jesus was the last act of the crime, the final insult done to him by his enemies."[1] Fuller goes on to make a case for the tradition recorded in this sermon from Acts being more primitive than the tradition recorded in Mark, despite the fact that the Book of Acts itself was written at a later date. It is far easier, Fuller observes, to change a hostile tradition that is too painful for comfort into a less painful, and thus more positive, tradition than it is to move the tradition in the opposite direction.

I am completely persuaded by Fuller's argument, not only for the reason that he states but for many other reasons as well. Surely it was a scandal in the life of the early church that the disciples had forsaken Jesus and fled when he was arrested. Mark, the earliest Gospel, was the most specific in identifying that scandal: "They all forsook him and fled" (Mark 14:50). Mark did tell the story of Peter following "at a distance" (14:54), but that was only to give the details of Peter's threefold denial, ending with Peter breaking down, weeping, and disappearing from that Gospel.

The original note of the disciples' complete abandonment of Jesus was repeated in Matthew (25:56). Luke, however, softened this behavior by suggesting that the disciples tried to resist with swords, even to the extent of cutting off the ear of the high priest's slave (Luke 22:49, 50). But Jesus put a stop to their resistance, healed the slave, and submitted to arrest. No reference to apostolic flight was recorded in Luke.

John did Luke one better. In the arrest story of the fourth Gospel Jesus asked, "Whom do you seek?" When they replied, "Jesus of Nazareth," Jesus responded, "If you seek me, let these men go" (John 18:6–8). The story of the use of swords was also told by John. In this story Simon Peter was given the heroic role of resistance. And the slave who lost his ear received the name Malchus (John 18:10). Jesus rebuked Peter and ordered him to put up his sword with the submissive-sounding words "Shall I not drink the cup which the Father has given me?" (John 18:11). It is clear that the reputation of the disciples improved with the passage of time. The probability is high that the earlier and less flattering narrative is in fact the more accurate one.

So it is with the burial tradition. There is a strong probability that the story of Joseph of Arimathea was developed to cover the apostles' pain at the memory of Jesus' having had no one to claim his body and of his death as a common criminal. His body was probably dumped unceremoniously into a common grave, the location of which has never been known—then or now. This fragment in Paul's sermon in Acts thus rings with startling accuracy.

I have already pointed out the fact that the empty tomb tradition does not appear to be part of the primitive kerygma. It was attached to the Jerusalem tradition, which I have suggested was quite secondary to the Galilean tradition.

The difficulty the Gospel writers had in trying to decide why the women went to the tomb at dawn on the first day of the week is just another problem for those who seek to find history here. Mark said they went "to anoint him" (Mark 16:1), though Mark also implied that the burial rites were fully carried out by Joseph (15:46). Given the heat of the Middle East, it is hard to imagine that a body put to death on Friday would be fit for anointing (or anything else) on

Sunday. Matthew, trying to remove Mark's inconsistency, said they went "to see the sepulcher" (Matt. 28:1). Luke said they went to take "the spices which they had prepared" (Luke 24:1); so in Luke we are presumably back to embalming. John gave no reason at all why Mary Magdalene came to the tomb (John 20:1), for surely after "a hundred pounds of myrrh and aloes" and binding the body, "as is the burial custom of the Jews," there was no need for any further preparation. Perhaps John simply wanted to signal that Mary Magdalene occupied a special role in the Jesus movement.[2]

This means, of course, that we are relegating the tradition of the empty tomb, the visit of the women, the burial by Joseph, and the mention of Nicodemus to the realm of legend. Contemporary scholarship points in exactly that direction. The Joseph of Arimathea legend, in my opinion, was nothing but an attempt to give narrative form to a midrash tradition that shaped so many of the details of Jesus' passion. In my opinion, the details of the story of the crucifixion were actually written with Hebrew Scriptures open and under the primary influences of Psalm 22 and Isaiah 53. From Psalm 22 came the cry of dereliction: "My God, my God, why hast thou forsaken me?" (22:1), which both Mark and Matthew put into the mouth of the dying Jesus. Also from that psalm came the description of the crowd: "All who see me mock at me, they make mouths at me, they wag their heads; 'He committed his cause to the Lord; let him deliver him'" (Ps. 22:7, 8). To see the close connection with this psalm, one has only to read Mark: "And those who passed by derided him, wagging their heads. . . . 'He saved others; he cannot save himself'" (Mark 15:29, 31). Matthew added to Mark's story the line "He trusts in God, let God deliver him now if [God] desires him." It was, however, only one more almost verbatim line from Psalm 22.

This Psalm went on to use words that the early Christians interpreted to be descriptions of crucifixion. "I am poured out like water, and all my bones are out of joint; . . . my tongue cleaves to my jaws; thou dost lay me in the dust of death; . . . they have pierced my hands and feet—I can count all my bones . . . they divide my garments among them, and for my raiment they cast lots" (Ps. 22:14–18). The author of the fourth Gospel clearly had this part of the psalm in mind when he had Jesus say: "I thirst" (John 19:28). When John told the story of how Jesus managed not to have his legs broken, he actually quoted this psalm (John 19:32–36). There was also a reference to bones not being broken in Psalm 34:20. Finally, when John portrayed the soldiers dividing Jesus' garments among themselves, casting lots for his tunic (John 19:23, 24), he was clearly drawing from the resources of this psalm.

From Isaiah 53 came words so totally identified with Jesus on the cross that most people, even today, believe that they actually were written in that setting: "He was despised and rejected by men; a man of sorrows, and acquainted with grief; . . . he was wounded for our transgressions" (Isa. 53:3, 5). At the trial before the Sanhedrin and Pilate, Jesus was portrayed as keeping silent (Mark 14:51). Surely that was written under the influence of the words of Isaiah. "He was afflicted, yet . . . like a sheep before its shearers is dumb, so he opened not his mouth" (Isa. 53:7).

Similarly Mark wrote in his Gospel: "Those who were crucified with him also reviled him" (Mark 15:32). By the time Luke wrote, those crucified with Jesus had become two in number and a legend had developed about each of them—one penitent, the other not. But the germ of that story is found in Isaiah 53: "He was numbered with the transgressors . . . and [he] made intercession for the transgressors" (v. 12). When Luke expanded the legend by portraying the thief as one who not only defended Jesus but who also asked to be remembered when Jesus came into his kingdom, and he had Jesus respond with the words "Today you will be with me in paradise" (Luke 23:43), Luke was only making real the note of intercession found in the last part of Isa. 53:12, which Mark had ignored.

In a similar fashion the story of the burial by Joseph of Arimathea was created, in my opinion, to give narrative content to Isaiah's words that "they made his grave . . . with a rich man in his death" (Isa. 53:9). Joseph entered the tradition as "a respected member of the council," that is, one of the rulers of Israel. The rulers were both wealthy and influential.

The crucifixion of Jesus, I am certain, was a fact of history, but the details through which the story of that crucifixion were carried into history were surely the creation of the midrash tradition that fed the developing legends about this Jesus. The tomb of Jesus was unknown because, in all probability, there was no tomb. There was no tomb because he was buried as a common criminal in a common grave, which was the hint of truth found hidden away in a sermon attributed to Paul and found in a text in the Book of Acts.

THE WOMEN AT THE TOMB

But is there no germ of truth, no historical reality, in the account of the women's visit to the tomb, which every Gospel contains? I believe there is, but, in my opinion, the women's visit had nothing to do with the first Easter. My conviction about this rests first on the premise that the discovery of the empty tomb would never have issued in an Easter faith. If there had been a tomb, and if that tomb had been found empty, it would have meant only that one more insult had been delivered to the leader of the tiny Jesus movement. The disciples, whoever they were, would have concluded that not even the dead body of this Jesus had been spared degradation. No Easter faith would have resulted from an empty tomb. Therefore such a tradition could not have been primary. It was but a story incorporated later into the narrative.

Second, the visit of the women to the tomb was related to the literalized tradition of the third day, which I have already dismissed as a chronological measure of time. So if the burial tradition, the empty tomb, and the third-day tradition were not originally part of the Easter experience, there is little room for the women's visit, which depends on all three traditions to be more than just another facet in a developing legend.

Third, the visit of the women to the tomb was attached to the Jerusalem resurrection tradition, which was a later, secondary development. What, then, was the germ of truth that ultimately caused the visit of the women to the tomb to be incorporated into the Easter story?

The one consistent person in all of the empty tomb stories is Mary Magdalene. The fourth Gospel said that Mary Magdalene went alone. I suspect that in that detail lies the originating germ of truth. Mary Magdalene was clearly a significant person in the Christian story. She certainly had prominence and access not just to Jesus but also to the disciples (John 20:1–4), and in this Gospel is portrayed as the chief mourner, who even asked for access to the body of Jesus (John 20:11–18).[3]

Since the Gospels make it clear that following Jesus' arrest the disciples forsook him, no one was around to know what transpired in either his death or his burial. Mary Magdalene went, I would suggest, after the Sabbath, to locate the place of his burial. She discovered not the empty tomb but the reality of his common grave. No one could identify the place. The plaintive cry, "They have taken away my Lord, and I do not know where they have laid him" (John 20:13), has the ring of authenticity. In that bit of history, I believe the tradition of the women at the tomb was originally located. Other elements were later fed into the developing empty tomb story, as I shall try to demonstrate.

When Peter reconstituted the disciples in Galilee and they returned to Jerusalem, Mary's story of not being able to find where they had buried Jesus was then, in time, incorporated into the resurrection tradition. A similar fate had enveloped the unknown place of Moses' burial (Deut. 34:6). Exactly how that visit by the women and the legend of the empty tomb were incorporated into the developing tradition is the story that I have yet to tell.

For now, the clues are complete. Easter occurred first in Galilee. It focused primarily on the experience of Peter. It had something to do with the reenactment of the common meal. The symbolic terms "after three days," "on the third day," and "on the first day of the week" came out of the Jewish apocalyptic tradition and were not a measure of chronological time. Finally, the story of Jesus' burial and the tomb itself were midrashic attempts to cover the embarrassment of both apostolic desertion and Jesus' burial in a common grave. It remains now to put these clues together to re-create, if possible, the narrative of the first Easter moment.

Part Five

Reconstructing the
Easter Moment

Chapter 19

But What Did Happen?
A Speculative Reconstruction

"They all forsook him and fled" (Mark 14:50).

"Simon, Simon, behold, Satan demanded to have you, and when you have turned again, strengthen your brethren" (Luke 22:31).

But what really happened? It is not enough to say what did not happen. It is easy to identify the legendary elements of the resurrection narratives. Angels who descend in earthquakes, speak, and roll back stones; tombs that are empty; apparitions that appear and disappear; rich men who make graves available; thieves who comment from their crosses of pain—these are legends all. Sacred legends, I might add, but legends nonetheless.

To dismiss these familiar biblical details as legendary does not end our search for the truth of what happened, it only drives us to another level where we ask a different question. What happened that gave birth to the legendary details that gathered around the moment of Easter? Why did they gather? Hundreds of millions of people have lived and died on this earth—some of them famous, powerful people—and no similar legends gathered around them. Why this one man, at this time, in this place? Who was and who is Jesus of Nazareth? Why did the events that occurred after his death possess such power? What could account for dramatic changes such as transformed lives, the lifting of despair, new courage, the redefinition of God, new worship patterns? What happened that caused people to begin to say of Jesus of Nazareth, with awesome conviction, that "death cannot contain him! We have seen the Lord"?

We have, as I suggested we would do in the opening lines of this book, pressed to enter into those nascent moments of our faith story, the "big bang" beginning of Christian history. We have looked for and found a new lens, the lens of midrash, with which to read our sacred narratives. We have tried to experience and to feel the problems that first-century writers had as they sought to convey, well after the fact of Jesus' earthly life, the power and meaning present in the critical moment in which Christianity was born. We have tried to embrace with our twentieth-century minds the reality of a world in which the Gospels were written, where there were no books, newspapers, photographs, libraries, radios, television sets, reporters, and certainly no living eyewitnesses.

We saw how Christianity was changed in 70 C.E. by the Roman army's destruction of Jerusalem, the Jewish center of Christianity. We noted some of the transitions that occurred as this faith story, so deeply Jewish, began to float freely in a sea that was primarily gentile, where no knowledge of the founding traditions, or of the original worldview, existed. We saw experiences that were common to Jewish people become distorted when they were transposed into a non-Jewish setting and were misinterpreted by non-Jewish minds. We felt the pain of broken communications when a Christian gentile world, profoundly ignorant of the Jewish way of writing and understanding Scripture, proceeded to impose upon their now-misunderstood holy words the authority of inerrancy. We watched as the Christian faith story got embellished, as the miraculous elements became heightened, and as the legends grew. When we can see these patterns developing so obviously even in the written works that we possess, composed between 70 C.E. and 100 C.E., then we can begin to comprehend that the same thing must have occurred between 30 C.E. and 70 C.E., when there were no written records. How in that unexplored tunnel of time did the facts get embellished, the miraculous get heightened, and the legends grow? When we wandered through such a process it felt like there was little solid ground, much quicksand, and slippery slopes down which slid our fragile grasp on reality and faith.

We looked at the biblical texts themselves. They proved to be quite untrustworthy if what we were seeking was objective facts and consistent details. The resurrection narratives of the Gospels agree on little if one looks for literal facts. Yet, amid this confusion of detail, there remains a powerful witness to a certain reality that was proclaimed with a peculiar intensity: "Death cannot contain him, we have seen the Lord."

Then we sought to enter the meaning of the words they used to capture the essence of the experience they had had and the meaning they found in this Jesus. We came to see how they interpreted him using the familiar Jewish images of prophet/martyr, salvific hero, atoning sacrifice, suffering servant, and son of man. But that still does not tell us why these words and images seemed appropriate to this life. So still we ask, What happened that caused these words and images to be applied to Jesus?

In our search for clues to help us enter the tunnel of darkness between 30 C.E. and the written texts of Easter, we must now draw some implications. I outlined the evidence that points strongly to the fact that Galilee, not Jerusalem, was the primary setting in which the moment of Easter was born. Once that was established, many other things fell into place. If Galilee was primary, then the angels of the empty tomb, the tomb itself with its massive stone and its female visitors, to say nothing of the entire burial tradition, must all be dismissed as not factual.

These parts of the tradition were quite simply the myths and legends that arose later in a Jerusalem setting from a people who were not capable of narrating in any other way the transcendent meaning that had grasped and resurrected the very core of their lives. To press this even further, the primacy of Galilee means that all of the appearance narratives that purport to be the physical manifestations of the dead body that somehow was enabled to be revivified and to walk out of a tomb are also legends and myths that cannot be literalized. The risen Jesus did not literally eat fish in Jerusalem. Thomas did not touch the physical wounds. Resurrection may mean many things, but these details are not literally a part of that reality. To affirm Galilee as the primary locale in the experience of Easter is a radical step, but it is nonetheless a step that the Bible itself seems to acknowledge.

Our second clue was that whatever Easter was, Peter stood as the primary person at the heart of the experience. Once again the Gospels themselves seem to bear witness to this in profound and obvious ways. This fact forced upon us the probability that many of the things said to and about Peter, including the change of his name from Simon, were post-Easter, not pre-Easter, stories.

Our third clue pointed out the strange and enigmatic connection of the resurrection with food. Broken bread in a primary way, and poured-out wine in a secondary way, were uniquely and consistently attached to the Easter experience. This means that every meal, every feeding story, in the New Testament might well be a post-Easter, not a pre-Easter, story.

Our fourth clue was to see that all literal time references attached to the phrase "the third day" must be dismissed. We watched that symbol grow from "after three days" to "the third day" under the influence of other phrases, "on the first day of the week," and "the day of the Lord." We identified that phrase with a later developing Jerusalem tradition. We thereby separated the moment of Easter from any references to time so that it could float freely in timelessness before it was set into a specific reference.

Finally we looked at the burial traditions of the New Testament and dismissed the Joseph and the Nicodemus stories as developed legends out of the Jerusalem tradition. However, we discovered that in the Book of Acts, in a speech attributed to Paul, there may well be that bit of remembered, factual truth that did not finally die. Jesus was buried by those who executed him, as was the fate of convicted criminals, and that would have been especially true for Jesus, since all of his disciples had forsaken him and fled.

So we come through these clues back to the moment of Jesus' death, a moment that seemed to be connected with the celebration of Passover, though exactly how it was connected is a source of conflict within the Gospels themselves. Here I will try to re-create the moment, enter the experience, and seek the reality that broke upon the world and that changed the face of human history. What in fact did happen?

THE ULTIMACY OF CONVICTION

Let me first state the obvious: No one can finally do anything other than speculate! Ultimately one comes to a point in this search where one must say either yes or no to Jesus, and yes or no to the ultimate significance of his life. That line is drawn, and we must decide whether we will step over it in faith or, by refusing to step over, turn and walk away from this tradition. No matter how deeply we search the Scriptures, no matter how profoundly we probe the text for literal details, no matter how many questions we raise, finally the Christ must either be the source of resurrection that lies within us or we are forced to admit in honesty that we have become the faithless ones.

Speculation about what happened cannot replace the conviction that something real transpired. But speculation can serve as a helpful means for encouraging and inviting others to journey with us into the possibility of a meeting with the risen Christ, and for that purpose I offer this proposed reconstruction. I am one of those people who has an abiding sense of inquiry, which continually plagues my mind. I want to put things together so that I can approach, in some rational form and through some rational procedure, the ultimate place of mystery. I recognize that my rational processes can take me only to the edges and never into the heart of the mystery. But at the very least, I want to walk to the threshold of ultimacy and say either a resounding yes, which will cause me to continue my journey into God, or a resounding no, which will force my efforts to cease.

I cannot say my yes to legends that have been clearly and fancifully created. If I could not move my search beyond angelic messengers, empty tombs, and ghostlike apparitions, I could not say yes to Easter. I will not allow my twentieth-century mind to be compromised by the literalism of another era that is not capable of being believed in a literal way today. If the resurrection of Jesus cannot be believed except by assenting to the fantastic descriptions included in the Gospels, then Christianity is doomed. For that view of resurrection is not believable, and if that is all there is, then Christianity, which depends upon the truth and authenticity of Jesus' resurrection, also is not believable. If that were the requirement of belief as a Christian, then I would sadly leave my house of faith. With me in that exodus from the Christian church, however, would be every ranking New Testament scholar in the world—Catholic and Protestant alike: E. C. Hoskyns, C. H. Dodd, Rudolf Bultmann, Reginald Fuller, Joseph Fitzmyer, W. E. Albright, Raymond Brown, Paul Minear, R. H. Lightfoot, Herman Hendrickx, Edward Schillebeeckx, Hans Küng, Karl Rahner, Phyllis Trible, Jane Schaberg, D. H. Nineham, Maurice Goguel, and countless others. These are scholars of great personal integrity. They do not literalize the Easter narratives, but they also do not abandon the worship of Jesus as their Lord.[1] Neither do I.

There is no exodus of this group from the Christian church because we are convinced that the reality of Easter is not captured in the words of the developing Christian legends. We can reject the literal narratives about the resurrection and still not reject the truth and power of the resurrection event itself. That is the distinction that must be made. We would not have the legends unless there had been a moment so indescribable that legends became necessary to explain it. We would not have an Easter tradition unless there had been an experience so real that earthbound words could not capture it. Easter points us to a dimension of life that became so visible that ecstatic silence was originally the only appropriate response.

For me the Gospel traditions are pointers toward the truth. They are not the truth. I stretch back from their accounts only by theory toward the moment of the birth of Christianity in the same way that physicists and astrophysicists stretch back by theory toward that instant so small that clocks cannot measure it; the millionth of a second at the very beginning of creation in which is contained the ultimate secret of how the universe came into being. I trace the development of our Christian tradition from our first moment the way physicists and astrophysicists trace the development of the universe from its first moment. Theory after theory has been discarded as inadequate, as new knowledge has been discovered. Clues are found in electromagnetic waves, radio beams, and light at the edges of space, which demand that new theories be formulated. But no one doubts the reality of the universe that continues to beg for some explanation.

Similarly I do not doubt the reality that appeared in time and history that we call resurrection. There have been measurable effects stemming from that moment that demand explanation. Various explanations have been offered in the history of Christianity. Some of the earlier ones appear in the biblical texts. Those explanations are not sacred, but the moment that gave rise to them is. That moment was, in my opinion, not in time or history. That moment did not occur inside our concept of space. Neither did creation. Time and space both are the properties of the universe. The creation occurred before there was either time or space. To suggest that the resurrection was a reality that could not be contained in time or space, however, does not mean that the resurrection was not real any more than it means that the big bang, which inaugurated both time and space, was not real. It does mean that I do not bind either the reality of the universe or the reality of the resurrection inside the categories of time and space.

But enough of this! What happened that caused the Christian movement to explode in time and to be carried for two thousand years in history? What is my best guess, my educated speculation?

THE CRUCIFIXION AS IT MAY HAVE HAPPENED

Jesus was arrested. He had made himself anathema to the entrenched religious authorities. He had relativized the claims of the law, introduced competing values, broken the power of religious controls, and threatened the nation with religious anarchy. He was a threat to religious power, order, and authority. Since one of the historical functions of religion was to keep anxiety in check, to keep unanswerable questions from being asked, and to play the game called "Let's Pretend That We Can Control Our World," the threat from this man was intolerable. So the religious leadership working with the Roman officials brought about his death.

That execution occurred during the feast of the Passover. The population was agitated and restless. The yoke of foreign domination was heavy. The religious hierarchy had worked out a modus operandi with the Roman authorities. The empire that ruled Judea also secured the power and influence of the Jewish priesthood, but inside a severely restricted area of operation. It was limited power, but it was power that was precious to them nonetheless. This man Jesus threatened that power. If he loosened the control of the religious system, if religious anarchy became commonplace, the Roman authorities would impose total control. The high priest himself served at the pleasure of the Roman authorities. Hence Jesus, the prophet from Galilee, had to go.

A sign of the powerlessness of the temple priesthood was seen in the need to have the cooperation of Rome in capital cases. This was achieved quite easily, for Roman officials did not encourage rebellious religious leaders for very long. The details of this execution may well lack literal historicity. Surely the story about Pilate releasing a notable prisoner named Barabbas, which means the son of God (Bar = son, Abba = God as Father), was legendary. The fact remains that Jesus of Nazareth was executed, and when he was dying it was clear that his movement was crushed, for "they all forsook him and fled." The story of Simon's denial undoubtedly contains some thread of history, but even those details should not be literalized. It must be noted, however, that a movement does not normally invent hostile stories about its leaders. But the story of the beloved disciple at the foot of the cross, told only in the Book of John so that Jesus' mother could be commended to his care, was the very stuff of self-serving legend, created by the members of the Johannine community to enhance yet again the reputation of their mentor.

The overwhelming probability is that the uncompromising truth was expressed in the phrase "they all forsook him and fled."

Jesus died alone. He died the death of a publicly executed criminal. His body probably received the typical treatment given to those so unfortunate as to fall into that category. He was removed from the instrument of execution, placed into a common grave, and covered over. No records were kept, for no value was attached to those who had been executed. Bodies did not last that long in their graves anyway. Burial removed the stench of decaying flesh, and in a very short time only some unmarked bones remained. Even the bones were gone before too long. Nature rather efficiently reclaims its own resources.

No one knows the exact date on which the crucifixion occurred. The synoptic Gospels and the fourth Gospel locate it near the time of Passover. I see no reason to doubt that. There is, however, too much agenda in both the synoptic's attempt to identify the Last Supper with the Passover feast, and the fourth Gospel's attempt to identify the day of crucifixion with the day on which the Paschal Lamb was slain, for me to take either assertion literally.

How long was Jesus on the cross before he died? I do not think anyone knows. Remember, those who might have noticed and relayed that information had all forsaken him and fled. The appearance of Joseph of Arimathea, the darkness over the land, the split in the temple veil, the ecstatic cry of faith from the centurion—all were elements of the developing legend. The hasty burial before the Sabbath was but a part of the burial legend. Thus no one knows how long Jesus lived on the cross, how he died, when he was taken down, or where he was buried, "for they all forsook him and fled." That means there was no first-day-of-the-week visit to the tomb by the women to anoint him, since there was no tomb and no sense of when he died or of where he was buried.

As I mentioned earlier, I think it quite possible that Mary Magdalene at some point did seek to discern the final resting place. But she was unsuccessful, for it was not a marked grave. They took away Jesus' body, and Mary, the chief mourner, was unable to locate the place where, as the text says, "they have laid him." Mary could have made that inevitable journey of the mourners, for I believe that there is a strong possibility that the woman who came to be called Magdalene was the same Mary who lived with her sister

Martha in Bethany, only a few miles from Jerusalem in a house that Jesus frequently visited. I argued that possibility and tried to build that case in a previous book (*Born of a Woman*, HarperSanFrancisco, 1992).

THE DISCIPLES' RESPONSE TO CALAMITY

But to where did the apostles go when they fled? "You will all be scattered, every man to his own home" (John 16:32). These words in John are a wonderfully preserved clue. That is, these words say that the disciples went "each to his own home." And to Simon, who would someday be called Peter, and probably to every other disciple, home was Galilee. Since the record appears to indicate that Jesus and his disciples came from Galilee to Judea by way of the desert east of the Jordan River to avoid the dangers of Samaria, my hunch would be that the disciples returned home by the same route. That would mean that Bethany, to the east of Jerusalem, would be on their way. Since they had stayed in Bethany, according to the biblical texts, during the week before the arrest of Jesus, it would be natural to go there following his death, especially since it was on their way back to Galilee.

I have no idea how many disciples went in that direction, but I am confident that Simon did. I suspect that it was in that home on that night that Simon's denial was admitted, and for which he received the bitter feelings of those in grief. Grief and anger are closely connected emotions, and that connection would be particularly so if this house contained one who was the woman closest to and most esteemed by Jesus. Surely such a person would not spare Simon's feelings if she felt him to be responsible in any way for Jesus' death.

There are many elements in this story that cause me to wonder about the historicity of Judas Iscariot. Was his betrayal invented to make the behavior of the other disciples seem less shocking by comparison? Judas seems likely to be a creation of midrash. Even the reason Jesus had to be betrayed is not clear. Was he that difficult to locate? Then the details of the thirty pieces of silver that can be found in the prophet Zechariah (11:12), the two contradictory accounts of his death (Matt. 27:5; Acts 1:18), the story of bread dipped in the bowl at the Last Supper (John 13:26; Mark 14:20; which reflects Ps. 41:9), and finally the name Iscariot itself, about which there are so many explanatory theories, none of which really satisfies—all of these details cast doubt for me on Judas's historicity.

I am also aware that the fourth Gospel in particular portrays Mary Magdalene as having a close and trusting relationship with both Simon and the beloved disciple. I do not mean to literalize the narrative that tells of that relationship, but I do want to register the insight that these people knew each other well, even intimately (John 20:3). I should note, too, that every time the women were listed in the Gospels, Mary Magdalene was given the priority position of being named first. I do not believe that is either accidental or coincidental. Women in the first century took their status from the status of the male to whom they were related. I find this a significant detail.

So on the night of the crucifixion I place Simon in the home in Bethany of Mary called Magdalene and her sister, Martha. I envision a scene in which trauma, grief, anger, and despair were all present, to say nothing of fear. As soon as possible, I suspect, Simon continued his journey. He had to get home, for the safety of Galilee and the healing sense of yearning to be among familiar things beckoned him. Nowhere else would seem tolerable in this moment of his life. So into the desert he trudged, making the long journey east of the Jordan. Sometimes it took a week to ten days to travel this distance by foot. One could not walk during the heat of the day, or in the darkness of night, so travel was limited to the hours from dawn to early morning and from sunset to nightfall. There was little to fear during this journey, however, for anonymity was the reality for every traveler. Some number of days passed, therefore, before Simon made it back to Capernaum, or Bethsaida, and even more days (or possibly weeks) before the trauma wore off sufficiently for Simon to begin to put his life in order.

The impact of Jesus on Simon had to have been enormous. No one was sure, including the Gospel writers, just how long Simon's life had revolved around the life of Jesus. Simon had heard Jesus' teaching, he had watched his impact on others. Simon had seen the quality of Jesus' life, and perhaps, above all else, he had been privileged to live inside Jesus' relationship with God. Jesus had taught Simon to pray. Jesus had loved him into being loving. Jesus had called him across the barriers that prejudice had erected against Samaritans, against women, and even against such Gentiles as the Syro-Phoenician woman. Simon was stretched by each of these experiences. Jesus had talked about the kingdom of God breaking into history, about the final judgment, and about the end of time. Simon had sensed from his words that Jesus' very life was in some way related to that kingdom and its coming. Perhaps Jesus was a sign of it; maybe he was the agent of it; or perhaps even the secret of his life was that he was somehow incorporated into the meaning of that kingdom.

Simon had seen in Jesus a rare personal integrity that was displayed in the courage to be himself in all circumstances. When the masses came to hear Jesus and even to laud him, his head was not turned by their acclaim. When the forces of hostility closed in upon him, his face was not hidden in fear and his spirit was not embittered with rage. Jesus seemed to be free of the need to be defined by the responses of others. Simon yearned to possess that freedom.

Jesus also seemed to know how to be present to others. He engaged each moment and each person with the intensity of eternity. When he was with one called the rich young ruler, who carried the signs of earthly power, and when he was with the woman taken in adultery, with no power except the plea for mercy, the attention, the gaze, and the presence of Jesus to that person was portrayed as total. That person was perceived as being the only person in Jesus' life at that moment. In that manner he seemed to challenge with his very life the hierarchy of values by which human beings judged one another. To Jesus, each person bore God's image, each person was worthy of God's love, and therefore each person had the potential to grow into the full life of God's Spirit.

In the common folklore of that day, sickness and disease were thought of as the punishment for a sinful life, yet Jesus embraced the lepers. Immorality was a sign of rebellion against the ways of God, but Jesus reached out to the woman of the street who anointed him and called to discipleship those who cheated others in their careers as tax collectors. In a society that suggested that women were not fit creatures with whom to converse, Jesus was portrayed as talking with the woman by the well, taking her questions seriously, and offering her new insights. When guileless children came to him, he was pictured as welcoming them and rebuking those who felt that children were not fit to make demands on his time. Simon saw all of these things and many more. They were not only things of which he was conscious, but they also surely began to sink into the layers of his subconscious mind and to be registered simply with the phrase "that is just the way he is."

God, for Jesus, was a powerful reality, and Simon was in a position to share in that reality. God, to Jesus, was "Father," with the Aramaic word *Abba* standing behind that concept, filled with connotations of intimacy, caring, love, forgiveness. God, for Jesus, was like a father who welcomed his wayward son, a shepherd who searched for a single lost sheep, or a woman who swept diligently until she found a lost coin. To this God all could come and pour out their hearts and express their needs, no matter how petty those needs might be. One might have been taught by this Jesus to say to God, "Give us our daily bread" or "Deliver us from the evil one" (Matt. 6:7ff; Luke 11:3); or one might have been encouraged to emulate the clamoring widow who would not stop knocking on the door until her desires were met (Luke 18:3–5). But one could also pray for the coming of God's kingdom or for a forgiveness so gracious, constant, and limitless that it reached toward infinity. Simon could not have escaped some participation in these realities.

Simon was also aware that there was about Jesus' life a sense of power that caused hints of miracle and even magic to enter not only his life but into other people's talk about him. How to find the germ of truth in these narratives is difficult for us today, but something was clearly there. Perhaps to Simon and to those who knew him best, Jesus seemed larger than life, which made him appear to them to have the power to control those forces before which most human beings feel helpless, such as the wind and the waves. Perhaps it was that in the storms of life Jesus was always a center of calm, so that in time those around him came to externalize his calmness onto the world itself. Perhaps it was that Jesus fed those near him so deeply with spiritual food that they began to envision great hosts of people sharing in that spiritual banquet, at which there was always more food than could be digested, no matter how large the crowd.

Perhaps Jesus' presence was so great and his wholeness so apparent that he did effect cures in people. Perhaps some people needed only to touch the hem of his garment; others needed only to draw on his presence to find the courage to take that first step into wellness; and still others needed only to know of God's love and forgiveness in a society that had taught them that pain, sickness, and tragedy were signs of God's judgment and, therefore, of their sinfulness. But whatever the explanation, the life of Jesus seemed to call people into wholeness and wellness. That was surely the experience for Simon. If that was so, it should surprise no one that stories grew up around this Jesus that explained these phenomena as only first-century people could explain them. I suspect Simon heard these explanations; indeed he may even have participated in creating them.

Simon also saw in Jesus a man who had a mission. I suspect that Simon was not certain what that mission was, but its reality was never in doubt. The world has a way of standing aside in the presence of a person who knows where he or she is going, and Simon was part of Jesus' world. When people came to write their understanding of Jesus, they portrayed him as one who had a rendezvous with destiny. The word *hour* was attached to that sense of rendezvous, either by Jesus himself or by others. It matters little how the connection came into being, the concept was surely thought to be appropriate to Jesus' life. He would not be prematurely pressured into his "hour." It could not come until he was ready. How his "hour" came to be connected with what the Scriptures called "the day of the Lord" is not exactly clear, but such a concept added to his mystique and in time caused many parts of the Hebrew tradition to be attached to this Jesus in the search for an adequate explanation.

The one thing that was certain was that the city of Jerusalem was involved in that "hour," and that this city drew Jesus magnetically. I suspect that, contrary to the synoptic Gospels' conception of his life, Jesus had journeyed a number of times to that holy city. I am confident that Jesus was executed in that city. I am all but persuaded that the most important journey that the Jesus movement made to the city of Jerusalem came after Jesus' crucifixion and not before it, despite the biblical story of the Palm Sunday procession. The reason for making so strange a statement cannot yet be chronicled, so I file it here with the promise to return to it. Suffice it now to say that Simon saw mission, mystique, destiny—all somehow associated with the meaning of Jesus, and these things made an indelible impression on this fisherman.

These and probably countless other experiences played across the stage of Simon's mind as he journeyed, following the crucifixion, first to Bethany and then on his long trek back to Galilee. Simon was doing the work of a grieving person. He was recalling episodes in the life of the deceased Jesus, isolating them for a moment so that he could relive them in his mind. Simon would lift each remembered event out of his stream of consciousness, turn it from side to side, seeking new angles so that he could understand that particular moment in some new way or find in it some new dimension. Grief work is always painful, because each moment, after examination and a time of reliving, falls back ultimately into the blackness of an unrelieved sense of loss. Jesus was dead. He had been killed. The dream, whatever it was that had been connected to the life of Jesus, could be no more. For days, weeks, even months, this thought occupied Simon.

I suspect Simon did not engage in this grief alone. There is every reason to believe that James and John, the sons of Zebedee, who were friends of Simon's before Jesus came into their lives, were with Simon in his time of grief. They all shared the fisherman's trade.

They all worked around the Sea of Galilee. They would surely be in contact now, as would the colorless person of Andrew, who suffered the fate of being identified only as "the brother of Simon." Perhaps there were others, but these four surely talked together and grieved together. Together they processed their experiences and wondered what it all meant. Together they felt the void of darkness. The sense of meaninglessness was almost like a physical presence among them. The clouds did not lift with the passing of time. The intensity of one person's presence in another person's life is equaled only by the intensity of absence when that person is gone. Jesus, the intensely present one in the consciousness of this little band, was now the intensely absent one in the very being of those who tried to put their lives back together in their homes in Galilee.

Economic necessity and psychological health both demanded that they return to their means of securing a livelihood. Fishing was all they really knew; so after the passage of some weeks or even months, I believe, they returned to their trade. The note in John 21 that has Peter say, "I am going fishing" and portrays the others as responding, "We will go with you," has about it the ring of historical authenticity. One cannot be immobilized forever by grief. My guess is that they once again took up fishing as the crew of the same boat. It was still important to them to be surrounded by those who understood the defining trauma of their lives. So Simon, James, John, and Andrew went back to the world of fishermen, plying their skills in the dark hours of the night before the dawn broke on the Sea of Galilee.

Fishing in this manner is both busy and boring. The best catches were just before the rising of the sun. That was also the time to market the catch. The midday meal in that society was the primary meal. Only the development of electricity has transformed dinner into lunch, and supper into dinner. The nets had to be cleaned and properly repaired or they were ineffective, and the daylight hours were used for that work. Mostly dependent on the wind for choice positions in the twelve-mile-wide sea, the manpower required to row the boat could be quite demanding. Lowering the nets while either at anchor or drifting in relatively still waters could make hours seem endless. All in all, there was much time to talk.

248

These waters were also filled with memories. It was at this lake where these fishermen first met Jesus of Nazareth. He had taught crowds by this lake from their boat. They had journeyed across it in his company. Perhaps they had even endured a storm on these waters when he was on board. The surrounding villages—Bethsaida, Capernaum, Chorazin, and Gennesaret—were familiar names associated with the memory of Jesus. Nothing they did allowed them to escape his presence in their memories. For them, Jesus was still everywhere.

When dawn began to crack, these fishermen would head for shore, dragging their catch with them. Once on shore they would secure the catch, and before taking it to the market, they would eat together by the lake. The menu was fish—freshly caught, cleaned, and broiled on an open fire at the lakeside—and bread brought with them from home earlier that day. While they ate they would again talk. Jesus remained the content of their conversations.

There were times in that early darkness that the mist on the lake looked like apparitions. Grieving people do tend to see forms that speak to their grief. Simon once thought he saw a ghostlike figure walking on the sea. It was so real that he actually rose and walked out into the water to get a better view. When he was waist-deep in the water, the misty apparition seemed to evaporate, so Simon returned to the beach, shaken, and wondering why his mind played tricks on him.

Every Jewish meal, even bread and fish eaten by the sea in the early hours of the day, was a liturgical event. The meal symbolized the eschatological feast that occurred on the day of the great banquet that would inaugurate the kingdom of God. At this banquet, the mythology suggested, people would come from north, south, east, and west to sit at Abraham's table. So at every meal Jewish men and women prayed for the kingdom to come. The meal began with the ceremonial blessing over the bread. The head of the house would lift up the bread and pray words generally like these: "Blessed are you, Lord God, King of the universe, who causes grain to come forth from the earth to nourish our bodies."

Day after day this little band of fishermen would perform this routine blessing, perhaps by rote, and they would break their fast of the night with bread and fish. Wine was not used at most meals, especially in the dawn hours. Wine was costly, and it was also ceremonial. For the poor, wine was an element only of the special feasts. It was bread and fish that were the diet by the Sea of Galilee in John 21. It was bread and fish that were the provisions of the feeding-of-the-multitudes stories.

Surely every time they blessed the bread to begin this early morning meal their minds recalled another meal held in Jerusalem in an upper room on a strange and fateful night. Fear, anxiety, and melancholia abounded that night. It was so dramatic. Jesus took bread, broke it, and identified it with his broken body. It made no sense, but it seemed to say that disaster loomed ahead. That disaster was in every part of that evening. But the meal and all that happened afterward on that night had the effect of stamping every blessing over the bread at every meal with an indelible meaning and an indelible memory. So it was that morning after morning by the Sea of Galilee fishermen who had been deeply touched by Jesus of Nazareth, now thought of as "the crucified one," began their morning meal by taking bread, blessing it, breaking it, and remembering.

These themes must have played over Simon's unconscious mind in those quiet moments when he allowed himself the luxury of reminiscing. Bread broken—"This is my body broken." Did Jesus command them to break bread in memory of him when they gathered? Or did they begin to do it and then proceed to justify that tradition by reading the command to do so back into the mouth of Jesus? Did Jesus say, "As often as you eat this bread and drink this cup you show forth the Lord's death until he comes" (1 Cor. 11:26)? Or did the disciples slowly begin to see the connection between bread, taken, blessed, broken, and shared, and the life of Jesus that had been taken, blessed, broken, and given? How long did it take for this new possibility to emerge, or this new understanding to rise?

The death of Jesus was incontrovertible. The meaning that death brought in that instance was not pleasant. Jesus had been executed upon a cross of wood. The Torah, so sacred to every Jewish man and woman, called one accursed who was hung upon a tree. What arrogance it would take for unlearned fisherfolk to suggest another alternative. Jesus was accused of blasphemy. No power intervened to save him. Death became God's "no." That "no" had been engineered by the highest religious authorities of the land. The chief priests spoke for God. Jesus had been condemned by God's earthly representatives. How could those who were not educated in either the Torah or the traditions of God's people stand with credibility in opposition to that?

Each day these themes played their point and counterpoint in the minds of these disciples, and, I suspect, especially in the mind of the one called Simon. On one side there was the experience that they had had with Jesus that called them out of the old and into the new in their understanding of God. On the other side, Jesus was dead, and this new understanding had not prevailed. It was the old and not the new that had proven victorious. The words of condemnation, spoken by the high priests, were reinforced when the high priest was thought of as God's anointed one. The condemnation was reinforced by the quoted texts of sacred Scripture, through which, they were taught to believe, God had spoken in every age and in which they searched to discern God's will for all time. The religious hierarchy were the survivors, the victors. Jesus was the deceased, the vanquished. The minds of those like Simon had to begin to wrap themselves around the inevitability of those conclusions. Jesus must not have been of God. Jesus must have been wrong. Jesus had to have been guilty of blasphemy. He was dead, and they had to begin to accept the fact that they had been misled, duped, and therefore they also were guilty.

These conflicting thoughts about Jesus preoccupied Simon. How could the messiah be killed? No one had ever heard of a dead messiah, an executed messiah, a messiah hung upon a tree! I wish I could have told him that, Simon must have said to himself again and again. Yet try as he would, Simon's inevitable conclusions just did not fit. How could God say no to a message of love and forgiveness and still be God? How could God deny one who had reached across every human divide to enhance all those whom God had created? How could one be so completely an agent of life and not at the same time be an agent of God? How could one give his life away so totally and still be thought guilty of a capital crime? It did not add up in Simon's mind. How he wished it would! How deeply he yearned to put these ideas behind him, not to engage this tortuous process any longer, to resolve the tension, and to get on with his life.

But Simon had drunk too deeply from this fountain of living water. He had been fed too deeply with this spiritual bread that seemed to meet life's deepest hunger. He could deny it again and again, but he could not make his denial stick, even in his own mind. So Simon wrestled, day after day, week after week. He fished and he shared bread and fish by the lake with his friends as the dawn broke through the dark Galilean sky. The weeks added up to months and still there was no resolution.

In the Jewish liturgical year the great festival that rivaled, and perhaps even surpassed, Passover in popularity was called the feast of the Tabernacles, or Booths. It came in the fall of the year. Among the Jewish people this festival was also known as Sukkoth or Sukkot. Large numbers of people journeyed to Jerusalem for this feast, just as they did for Passover. But Tabernacles was much more a festival of celebration. No paschal lamb was slain. No memories of slavery were recalled. No pain of recognizing that Jewish people still lived in bondage to a foreign power needed to be part of this celebration. This feast was all about the joy of the harvest, about the freedom they had known in the wilderness wanderings when they lived in temporary shelters or booths, when even the sacred scrolls of God's presence were carried in a mobile tabernacle.

Like all Jewish festivals, Tabernacles had been caught up in the yearning for a messiah, for God's kingdom, and for God's reign. The liturgy of Tabernacles was built around readings from Zechariah, chapters 9 through 14, and parts of Psalm 118, which were chanted in this celebration by the people as they proceeded to and around the altar of the temple. The Tabernacles' liturgy also focused on the symbols of light and water. Israel was to be a light to the nations of the world, and out of Jerusalem would flow fountains of living water, which was a symbol for the Spirit that was to rule the world when God's kingdom came.

As the time for the festival neared, its content quite naturally entered Simon's mind, and he began to associate it with his constant attempt to make sense out of Jesus' death. Familiar phrases from the liturgy of Tabernacles were called to mind: "I shall not die, but I shall live and recount the deeds of the Lord. . . . The Lord has chastened me sorely, but he has not given me over unto death. Open the gates of righteousness that I may enter through them and give thanks to the Lord. This is the gate of the Lord, and the righteous shall enter through it. . . . The stone which the builders rejected has become the head of the corner. This is the Lord's doing; it is marvelous in our eyes. . . . Let us rejoice and be glad in it." These were the familiar words of Psalm 118, a psalm completely identified with the celebration of Tabernacles. This was the psalm always used in the procession to the altar that marked the feast of Tabernacles. This prophetic word spoke of the time when "the Lord your God will come [to Jerusalem] and there shall he be continuously." The lesson read each year at Tabernacles was from Zechariah 14. It also spoke of "living waters" that would one day flow out of Jerusalem. On that day, Zechariah asserted, "the Lord will become king over all the earth." These words were as familiar to Simon as the words concerning the birth of Jesus are to Christians today, since they are read again and again at our Christmas celebrations. So Simon allowed these words to enter his mind, dwell there, and then depart as he contemplated the possibility of returning to Jerusalem to join in the celebration of the Sukkoth feast of Tabernacles.

Simon thought that enough time must have passed since the execution of Jesus to make it safe to return as just one more face in a host of pilgrims. He also wanted to reestablish contact with those to whom he had once been so close. He thought of Mary Magdalene in particular. There was still the pain of their unresolved conflict that weighed heavily on Simon. Perhaps there were also other disciples who had stayed in Jerusalem. Simon discussed his budding plans with his fishing mates. Since the festival was a fortnight or so away, no immediate decision needed to be made.

In the synagogues on the Sabbaths prior to Tabernacles, other parts of the prophet Zechariah were read. There was the account in chapter 11 where the rulers of the temple paid thirty pieces of silver to rid themselves of one whom God had appointed to be shepherd of Israel (11:7ff). This was followed by the divine promise that "I will pour out on the House of David and the inhabitants of Jerusalem a spirit of compassion and supplication, so that when they look on him whom they have pierced they shall mourn for him as one mourns for an only child and weep bitterly over him as one weeps over a firstborn." It spoke of the divine plan to "strike the shepherd that the sheep may be scattered." All of this was preamble to the account of Tabernacles in Zechariah 14, which looked to that time when "the Lord will become king over all the earth."

Simon discussed these passages, too. Even when he heard the sacred Scriptures read, they seemed to shout to him of Jesus. Simon's mind continued to be unsettled. He was restless and agitated. The images kept fighting one another. Insight collided with a grotesque sense of the impropriety of his thoughts. No one would ever have regarded a simple fisherman as a source of theological wisdom. That was the task of the high priest or the learned scribes who regularly pronounced on the truth or falsity of religious ideas. They had rendered their judgment on Jesus of Nazareth. Yet, proper or not, the truth that was taking hold of Simon could not be denied. Every day these possibilities dawned anew in his mind. Somehow he knew himself to be grasped by a love that would not let him go.

But while Simon's mind wrestled, he also worked. Each night meant another trip on their boat after midnight into the center of the lake in search of enough income to buy yet another day's bread. On this night before his proposed journey to Jerusalem they had a particularly large haul of fish. On a hunch, Simon changed the nets from one side of the boat to the other, with strikingly good results. They hauled their catch ashore in the lightened mood of success. It would be a fine breakfast by the lake that morning.

A charcoal fire was prepared already. Perhaps other fishermen also had a good catch and had come to shore ahead of Simon and the others. A piece of uneaten broiled fish was still on their primitive grill. When a catch was good, such wastefulness could be tolerated. In his exuberance Simon had actually jumped into the sea to swim ashore so that he could help bring the boat safely ashore with its large catch. He felt a bit of his spirit returning after such a very long time of depression.

Once the catch was secured, they stoked the fire, cleaned the fish of their choice, and placed it on the hot coals to broil. The bread they kept on the boat was brought out. The meal was about to begin. Simon, as the oldest member of the group, did the ceremonial blessing. Images flowed together: the psalm of Tabernacles, "I shall not die but I shall live"; the words of Zechariah, "They looked on him whom they pierced"; and that awful night when Jesus took bread, blessed it, broke it, and gave it to them, calling that bread his body. As was the custom among the Jews, Simon verbally put these images into the ceremonial blessing, and he broke the bread.

Suddenly it all came together for Simon. The crucifixion was not punitive, it was intentional. The cross was Jesus' ultimate parable, acted out on the stage of history to open the eyes of those whose eyes could be opened in no other way to the meaning of Jesus as the sign of God's love. God's love was unconditional, a love not earned by the rigorous keeping of the law. God's love was beyond the boundaries of righteousness, a love that demanded nothing in return. Jesus' death was the final episode in the story of his life. It demonstrated as nothing else could or would that it is in giving life away that we find life, it is in giving love away that we find love, it is in embracing the outcast that we find ourselves embraced as outcasts. It was a love that allowed us to stop pretending and simply to be. Simon saw the meaning of the crucifixion that morning as he had never before seen it, and Simon felt himself to be embraced even with his doubts, his fears, his denials in a way that he had never before been embraced. That was the dawn of Easter in human history. It would be fair to say that in that moment Simon felt resurrected. The clouds of his grief, confusion, and depression vanished from his mind, and in that moment he knew that Jesus was part of the very essence of God, and at that moment Simon saw Jesus alive.

It was as if scales fell from his eyes and Simon saw a realm that is around us at every moment, a realm of life and love, a realm of God from within which Jesus appeared to Simon. Was it real? Yes, I am convinced it was real. Was it objective? No, I do not think it was objective. Can it be real if it is not objective? Yes, I think it can, for "objective" is a category that measures events inside time and space. Jesus appeared to Simon from the realm of God, and that realm is not within history, it is not bounded by time or space. Was it then delusional? I do not think so, but there will always be those whose eyes are not opened and those who will never see what Simon saw, so they will always think it is a delusional claim.

There will also be some who accept this definition and then pretend that they do see, even when they do not. They will insist that they have concrete evidence. Many of them will occupy high positions in ecclesiastical circles. But the proof of the vision or lack thereof will be seen in what happens in their lives. Do they become Christlike, open, accepting, loving, and the feeders of the hungry sheep of the world? Or do they become righteous, eager to enforce their understanding of truth on others, judging and rejecting those who, by their standards, are inadequate believers or inadequate human beings?

"Simon, if you love me you will feed my sheep." This was the meaning that Simon seemed to hear again and again as he tried to make sense out of his experience in Galilee; that is, the risen Christ will be known when his disciples can love as Jesus loved, and when they can love the ones whom Jesus loved, namely, the least of God's children. In time this truth would be incorporated into a parable and put onto the lips of Jesus, who would at that time be portrayed as the Son of man who came in the clouds of glory to judge the earth (Matt. 25). The message was simple. When you feed the hungry, you feed Christ; when you give water to the thirsty, clothing to the naked, comfort to the distressed, companionship to the rejected and the imprisoned, you are giving to Christ himself. God had in fact come out of heaven to dwell in Jesus. Jesus, now seen to be the essence of God, had come to dwell in the least of these our brothers and sisters. It was, in the words of later Christian theology, a new incarnation. God in Christ, Christ in the least of these. Yes, Simon saw Jesus alive in the heart of God.

THE VISION OF CHRIST THAT STARTED THE CHURCH

What did that seeing look like? I will never know. I do know that, as we discussed in the chapter on Paul, when the first disciples tried to say this in human language, they used the word *ōphthē*, which is the same verb used in Isaiah's account of the moment when he "saw" God high and lifted up (Isa. 6:1) and when Paul wrote, "Have I not seen Jesus the Lord?" (1 Cor. 9:1). What does this seeing mean? Why did Luke have Simon named Peter, now as a leader of the church, say, "God made Jesus manifest not to all the people but to us who ate and drank with him after he rose from the dead" (Acts 11:41)?

Simon saw. He really saw. Jesus had been lifted into the living God. It had nothing to do with empty tombs or feeling wounds. It had to do with understanding that Jesus made God real and that God had taken the life of Jesus into the divine nature.

With a burst of animation Simon tried to bring his breakfast mates into his vision. He tried to open their eyes. His tortured mind poured out his words in torrents. The bread in his hand was broken over and over until light dawned in James, John, and Andrew.

None of these fishermen had the tools necessary to develop the elaborate Christologies that would mark the Christian future. All they knew, and they knew it profoundly, was that God had claimed the life of Jesus and that this life, now part of God, was available to them forever, as God. They also knew that they now had to be agents of this life, giving it away. They even seemed to realize that no matter how many people there were to whom the gift of the Christ would be given, there would always be infinitely more to give. Baskets of scraps from the unending table of God's bountiful love were forever being symbolically gathered after all "had eaten their fill."

Simon finally understood that death could not contain the one whom he now knew to be the Christ of God. This was the Holy One of God who, for Simon, had the words of eternal life. Simon had seen the Lord. The risen Christ had appeared first to one whom the church began to call Cephas in Aramaic, the Rock, Petros, in Greek. Simon saw. Simon opened the eyes of others to see. Simon was the rock upon which the community of Christians came into being. It was that community which renamed him Peter. It was that community which, in their sacred narratives, portrayed Jesus as saying to Simon, "You are 'Petros' and on this rock I will build my church."

So Simon rallied his mates with his vision, and together they decided that now they must go up to Jerusalem for the feast of Tabernacles, and in that setting they must share this vision with others so they also might see. Simon Peter first reassembled his partners James, John, and Andrew, and they made the journey to Jerusalem. Later Peter would reassemble the Jerusalem disciples.

The journey back to Jerusalem for Peter and his mates was, in my opinion, not only a triumphant journey, but it became The Triumphal Journey. Theirs was, I believe, the Palm Sunday procession that was later read back into the precrucifixion life of Jesus, but that precrucifixion chronology, I am now sure, was not an accurate bit of history. The resurrection of Jesus was proclaimed in Jerusalem during the feast of Tabernacles in the fall of the year some six months after the crucifixion, and the details of the feast of Tabernacles, as I shall now try to demonstrate, determined the shape and the content of the Jerusalem Easter legends.

I think these clues are visible to us today in ways that they have not been before for three main reasons. First, we have in the past been Gentiles trying to read a Jewish book with no real concept of midrash. Second, we have, by and large, been ignorant of the content of the festival of Tabernacles. Finally, we have been prisoners of a mind-set that read the Gospels as biographies inside the framework of linear time. But now, recovering midrash, recovering Tabernacles, and being freed of linear time, we can see that every journey from Galilee to Judea has been overlain, in the developing tradition of the Christian people, with the content of every other journey.

The journey of Simon and his associates, returning from Galilee to proclaim the living Christ in Jerusalem during the festival of Tabernacles, was incorporated into an earlier journey by Jesus and his disciples to Jerusalem at the time of the Passover, to die. One wonders how that earlier journey could have been called triumphant? It ended in disaster. One also wonders how branches of greenery including palm got connected with that springtime Passover visit, since such branches and shouts of "Hosannah to the one who comes in the name of the Lord" are a regular part of the feast of Tabernacles, which comes in the fall of the year. One wonders how that strange story of the fig tree, which Jesus cursed after finding no fruit on it, got attached to Passover, which is a season of the year when no fruit tree was bearing. But fig trees were in full fruit at the feast of Tabernacles, for that was the harvest season when fruit was expected on every fruit tree in Palestine. One also wonders how the legend of the tomb got created, but in the feast of Tabernacles a tomblike structure, used only for temporary housing, was part of the liturgy. The worshipers in that liturgy carried boxes of sweet-smelling leaves and fruit of the citron tree to that "booth" as part of the ceremony. Tabernacles also was a festival of seven days in its earlier forms, and eight days in its later forms, and I think that by superimposing that time pattern on Passover, the church created a holy week of eight days beginning with the procession of the palms and culminating on the first day of the week, which came to be the day to which the liturgy of Easter was ultimately attached.

I am suggesting that Simon's vision of Jesus alive came as much as six months after the death of Jesus by crucifixion, and that this vision occurred in Galilee; that Simon then opened the eyes of his fellow Galilean disciples so that they, too, could see Jesus risen; that they then journeyed to Jerusalem at the time of the feast of Tabernacles, and gathered together the Jerusalem disciples to share their faith; and that inside the liturgy of the celebration of Tabernacles, the story of Easter unfolded. In this manner, I will seek to demonstrate that the traditions of Tabernacles became the content of the development of the Easter narrative, giving us Palm Sunday, the cleansing of the temple, the first day of the week, the empty tomb, the spices carried to the tomb, and even the angelic messenger. Here the narratives were developed and here the legends grew.

But truth was not at stake in either the narratives or the legends. The truth of Jesus alive and available created the narratives and the legends—not the other way around. Narratives and legends can be dissected, rearranged, interpreted, and even cast aside, without threatening either the integrity or the reality of the experience that forced both into existence.

If my re-creation has validity beyond simply an interpretive speculation, then we should be able to find hints of it in the biblical texts, for narratives and legends always contain clues pointing us to their origins. I think we can find these hints in the seventh chapter of John, in the story of Palm Sunday, in the story of the cleansing of the temple, and even in those strange accounts we call the story of the transfiguration. But none of these hints were visible to me until I discovered the feast of Tabernacles and began to look for it in the Gospel record. To that story I now turn.

Chapter 20

Grounding the Speculation
in Scripture

One of the three great pilgrim feasts of the Jewish people in the first century C.E. was the festival of Tabernacles. Most Jews of that era in fact deemed this celebration to be the greatest, the most welcome, and the most fun. Tabernacles had many themes. It was a harvest feast to give thanks for the bounty of the earth, not dissimilar from the American celebration of Thanksgiving. But it was also a time to pray for rain, to acknowledge the light of God, and to remember the wilderness wandering era of Jewish history. Tabernacles also came in the same month as Rosh Hashanah, the Jewish New Year, and Yom Kippur, the solemn Day of Atonement. The contrast with these more somber liturgical traditions only acted to heighten the sense of joy and happiness that marked the festival of Tabernacles.

Yet, despite its enormous popularity in the period of history when Jesus of Nazareth lived, the festival of Tabernacles was not once mentioned in the synoptic Gospels of Mark, Matthew, and Luke. It found its only overt New Testament reference in chapter 7 of John. One cannot help but wonder where so important a festival—as important to Jews as Christmas or Easter is to Christians—went, or how it was avoided.

THE CONFUSING CHRONOLOGY OF THE GOSPELS' HOLY WEEK

The Gospel records concentrate very intently on the week during which Jesus' betrayal, Last Supper, trial, crucifixion, and resurrection were assumed to have taken place. A primary obsession in the telling of this Christian story was with the Jewish celebration of Passover. Jesus met his death during the festival of Passover, it was asserted. To this placement all of the Gospels seem to be in agreement. Jesus, therefore, was linked quite early in Christian memory with the image of the paschal lamb. This lamb was sacrificed, according to the Exodus story, on that night when the angel of death was to pass over the land. This was the final plague on the Egyptians and was identified as the death of their firstborn child. According to the tradition, by placing the blood of the paschal lamb on the doorposts of Jewish homes, the firstborn of Jewish families would be spared (Exod. 12:21–42). The final events of Jesus' life, which also involved the death of one known as God's firstborn, were told in terms of the liturgy of the Passover. Every other Jewish festival is missing from the synoptic tradition.

Jesus obviously had to go up to Jerusalem to be present at the time of the Passover. This had been a requirement of Jewish worship since the Deuteronomic reforms of the early years of the seventh century B.C.E., which mandated that the Passover celebration would be held exclusively in the Jewish holy city. Jesus' journey to Jerusalem was thus placed into the narrative by the Gospel writers just one week prior to his crucifixion/resurrection so that the drama could build. It began with something Christians now call the triumphal entry, which came to be celebrated under the title Palm Sunday. Holy Week became the liturgical name of those final eight days that began on Palm Sunday and concluded on the first day of the week, with Easter.

There are many problems, however, with the association of the Palm Sunday procession with Passover in the spring of the year and, therefore, with locating it as a prelude to the crucifixion. Mark, for example, seemed to tell his Holy Week story in two sections that were not well related to each other. He had a clear unit that described activities from the day of the procession through the apocalyptic teaching about the end of the world in chapter 13. Then it was as if a new unit of time began, as Mark introduced the Passover with the words "It was now two days before the Passover" (Mark 14:1).

Moreover Mark separated the triumphal procession into Jerusalem from the episode known as the cleansing of the temple so that these two events occurred on two different days of that final week. The device he used to separate them was a bizarre one, to say the least. As the divider Mark inserted the story of Jesus cursing the fig tree. On Palm Sunday, according to Mark, Jesus entered Jerusalem and went to the temple and "when he had looked round at everything, as it was already late, he went out to Bethany with the twelve" (Mark 11:11). The next day, on the journey back to Jerusalem, Jesus "was hungry," said the text. "And seeing . . . a fig tree in leaf," he went in search of its fruit. But there were no figs to be found, for, said the text, "it was not the season for figs" (11:12, 13). Nonetheless, despite the inappropriateness of looking for fruit in March from a tree that bears its fruit in September and October, Jesus laid a curse on the fig tree: "May no one ever eat fruit from you again" (11:12–26). The party then proceeded toward Jerusalem, where Mark made the cleansing of the temple the primary event of that second day. When the disciple band returned that night to Bethany, Mark used that journey to narrate the conclusion of his fig tree story. Once again it was a strange episode in the New Testament.

The disciples came upon the fig tree as they walked. It had now withered all the way down to its roots. Peter called that to Jesus' attention. "Master, look!" he exclaimed. "The fig tree you cursed has withered" (11:21). To this opening, Mark had Jesus respond with some teaching about moving mountains and the efficacy of prayer. It was a positioning for these two texts that did not fit the context well. The next day, Mark had Jesus return to the temple to teach, artfully dodging the question about his authority that was put to him by the chief priests and scribes. This section concludes with Jesus sitting down "opposite the treasury"—that is, in the same place from whence he drove the money changers the day before. Here he watched the poor widow make her offering of two copper coins. It appears that the treasury was back in business after its dislocating experience of the day before. This section appears to conclude with the long, apocalyptic chapter 13, on the signs of the end of the age.

Mark then started his next unit with the previously mentioned time marker "It was now two days before the Passover" (14:1). By continuing his counting process, the first unit of three days is added to these two days to reach the total of five days, unless this time reference was set on the third day of the first unit, which appears to be the implication of the word *now*. That would mean that the Passover meal, which for Mark was the Last Supper, would take place on the fifth day, the crucifixion on the sixth day, with Easter day being the eighth day of Mark's scheme, and also the first day of the week. So Mark came out with an eight-day week, but it was made up of two parts, which do not seem to be totally related to each other. For our purpose, it is worth noting that an eight-day celebration is the time frame associated most often with the feast of Tabernacles.

The mystery thickens when both Matthew and Luke refused to separate the Palm Sunday triumphal entry from the cleansing of the temple, placing the two events together in sequential order on the same day and, therefore, ruining Mark's arrangement of timing (Matt. 21:12ff; Luke 19:45ff). To make things even stranger, the fourth Gospel placed the cleansing-of-the-temple story at an earlier celebration of the Passover (John 2:13ff), near the beginning of his public ministry, when Jesus was also said by John to have gone up to Jerusalem. In John's scheme, this event was separated from the last week of Jesus' life by as much as two years. So, from several angles, the time references that circulate around both Palm Sunday and the cleansing of the temple appear to be confused.

But recall that Mark used the cursing of the fig tree story to divide the entry into Jerusalem from the cleansing of the temple. It was an episode that has become the expositor's nightmare. This narrative raised embarrassing questions. What kind of man is this Jesus that he would curse a fig tree for not bearing figs when, as Mark said quite implicitly, "it was not the season for figs" (11:13)? Matthew felt this embarrassment enough to put the story together in one episode so that the curse immediately resulted in the withering of the tree (Matt. 21:18–21). Luke omitted the story altogether, but he did include in his Gospel something called the parable of the fig tree (Luke 13:6–9). In Luke's parable the owner of a vineyard came to a fig tree, seeking its fruit. Finding none, he ordered his vinedresser to cut down the tree, since for "three years I have come seeking fruit on this fig tree, and I find none." The vinedresser interceded and proposed a more conservative route. Let us wait a year, let me dig around it, put on fertilizer, and see if it will bear fruit next year. If not, then we will cut it down.

Perhaps this parable, and whatever lay behind Mark's story of Jesus cursing the fig tree, had a common root in the oral tradition and developed in different directions. I have argued in a previous book that this might well have been what happened with Luke's parable of Lazarus and the rich man, and John's story of the raising of Lazarus, for both stories turn on what effects the return of Lazarus from the dead would have on the people.[1]

CLUES THAT POINT TO TABERNACLES

But I want to look at this strange fig tree episode from yet another point of view. Is this reference to the figs' not being in season a clue to a totally different setting in time that might have been the original context for both the triumphal-entry story and the cleansing-of-the-temple story? Can we speculate that, before these episodes were drawn into the Passover orbit, both the narratives, of Palm Sunday and of the cleansing of the temple, were located in a quite different season of the year? Identifying the triumphal procession with branches of greenery, and locating it near the Passover season as a prelude to the crucifixion, would indeed mean that it was not the season for figs. It might well have not been the season for greenery either. Passover was in the early spring month of Nisan (March to early April). Fig trees bore fruit in Judea during the month of Tishri (mid-September to mid-October). Suppose that this story was originally one in which a fig tree did not bear fruit when in fact it was due to bear fruit, and therefore was taken down as not worthy of continued life? That would suggest that the original location for this story was in the fall of the year, but it would also make Jesus' response less startling and more in character.

If we could disconnect from the strange idea that fig trees are subject to being cursed for not producing figs even when it is not the season for figs, and put the story into a proper context, it would, at the very least, be easier to understand. Then we could build on the connection that Mark makes so overtly between the fig tree and the temple. Both are supposed to fulfill their proper function—to produce figs, in the case of the tree, and to promote proper worship, in the case of the temple. Failing to do what one is created to do would properly be punished—by having the offending tree or the offending temple destroyed. So the connection between the cursing of the fig tree and the cleansing of the temple would make sense, and the fig tree episode could be a form of parable about the temple.

But in the middle of this episode a note was introduced about it not being the season for figs, and that idea destroyed all parabolic meanings. Because that line appears to be so out of place, we might conclude that it was a gloss, added by a later editor. Yet there is no evidence in any manuscript that this line was not from the hand of Mark.[2] Failing that, we might suggest that this line is a hint that the time, originally associated with this narrative of both Palm Sunday and the cleansing of the temple, had originally been in the fall rather than in the spring. Or to say it liturgically, perhaps it was originally associated with the feast of Tabernacles, a harvest celebration that came in the fall of the year, and not with the feast of the Passover, which came in the early spring. When that original setting was changed, this explanatory line had to be added. It is a clue worthy of filing while we look for others that might strengthen such a possibility.

Other clues are not hard to find. The feast of Tabernacles was marked by liturgical practices that almost surely suggested that this was the original setting of both Palm Sunday and the cleansing of the temple. The cries of hosannah that we think of as part of the Palm Sunday procession were in fact an important part of the Tabernacles liturgy, deriving from Psalm 118, which was the psalm almost exclusively associated with Tabernacles in Jewish liturgical usage. *Hosannah* is a Hebrew or Aramaic word, transliterated into English. It literally means "save us." "Save us, we beseech thee, O Lord" (Ps. 118:25) was the constant refrain of the people in the liturgy of Tabernacles when that psalm was read. Psalm 118 also contains, interestingly enough, the phrase "Blessed is he who comes [enters] in the name of the Lord" (Ps. 118:26), which is, of course, almost a direct quotation from the cry of the crowd given in the synoptic account of Palm Sunday.

This psalm had other Palm Sunday connections. It went on to say, "Bind the festal procession with branches, up to the horns of the altar" (118:27). In the festival of Tabernacles, branches of greenery, composed of myrtle, willow, and palm (called the lulab), were bound together and carried in the right hand to be waved at the appropriate time in the procession while the psalm was being chanted. The feast of Tabernacles consisted of a procession for days around the altar in the midst of the temple by people waving palm branches and shouting hosannah, and chanting, "Blessed is he who comes in the name of the Lord." So closely were the words of Psalm 118 associated with the waving of palm branches as part of the celebration of the feast of Tabernacles that the sprays themselves came to be called in the vernacular "the hosannahs." It is apparent, the more one learns of the liturgy of Tabernacles, that the content of Palm Sunday was originally shaped in almost every detail by this fall festival.

The rest of Psalm 118 exalts the temple, those who come to it, and, most especially, the king messiah, who would someday come in the name of the Lord. This psalm also contains other themes of the festival of Tabernacles. It celebrates light (v. 27), and it refers to the dwelling in tents (v. 15), a reference to the wilderness phase of Israel's history that Tabernacles celebrated. It also contains words that were later specifically incorporated into the Christian story of Jesus. "The stone which the builders rejected has become the head of the corner" (v. 22) was quoted in Matt. 21:42, Acts 4:11, and 1 Pet. 2:7. The phrase "This is the day which the Lord has made, let us rejoice and be glad in it" (118:24) became attached to the Christian day of worship and was used from early times at the beginning of the Eucharist on the Christian holy day, the first day of the week, known as "the day of the Lord."

There are also references in this psalm to the gates of the righteous that God would open so that his people might enter those gates and give thanks. On one level these gates were clearly the gates of the temple, but on other levels the reference was clearly to the gates of heaven, which God would open to receive the righteous one, the king, the messiah. The early Christians found themselves using Psalm 118 in a regular fashion, and we need to be aware that this was a psalm whose very identity was attached to its use in the fall festival of Tabernacles. This psalm meant Tabernacles to Jewish people just as surely as "O Come All Ye Faithful" means Christmas to Christians.

Two other Tabernacles customs need to be mentioned, for they also played major parts in the liturgical celebration. First, while the lulab, the branches of greenery, were held in the right hand by the festival marchers in procession, a box, called the ethrog, was carried in the left hand. In this box were placed the core and the blossom of the citron fruit. Both outward beauty and sweet fragrance were thought to be captured by this symbol.

Second, it was the custom for a Jewish family to erect a booth, called a sukkoth, for the celebration of Tabernacles. This booth was a temporary shelter for use during this feast, to stand symbolically for those days when the people of Israel wandered in the wilderness without a permanent home. Abraham E. Millgram, a Jewish historian, describes the sukkoth as it came to be envisioned in Jewish tradition.[3] It was to be a temporary abode. In height it was to be "not less than ten hand breadths, nor more than twenty cubits." No limit to its length was stated. Its roof was to be overlaid with materials that grew from the soil. The roof was not supposed to be so heavy as to block the worshipers' view of the stars. Indeed the lulab could be used after the procession as part of the covering for the booth, and the ethrog could be used to give the booth a special fragrance. In this booth the Jewish faithful were supposed to dwell symbolically for the seven days of the festival as a reminder of their days as a homeless people in the wilderness. All the people would emerge liturgically from these booths on the eighth day for a solemn assembly.

It was particularly important during the seven days of symbolic habitation in the booth that at least one symbolic meal be served inside the sukkoth. This meal would normally begin in the home with the kindling of the festival lights by the mother. Then would come the recitation by the father of the traditional blessing, the kiddush. It was at this point that the family would move to the booth to eat the token meal, with the blessing of the temporary structure following immediately upon the blessing over the bread. Amid all the ceremonies was the prayer that the day of the Lord would come, that the Lord would suddenly appear in his temple to begin his glorious rule at the birth of the new kingdom.

In addition to Psalm 118, the other work from the Hebrew Scriptures primarily associated with the feast of Tabernacles was the Book of the Prophet Zechariah. This book was written in two segments. The prophecies take up chapters 1 through 8. The final segment, chapters 9 through 14, appears to be from a different pen in a later period of Hebrew history. First-century Jews, however, probably read it as a single book, much as they read the Book of Isaiah as the words of one prophet even though its words came from the hand of at least three different authors. Biblical criticism is a discipline that had not yet been born.

In the first eight chapters of Zechariah, the prophet described two people who were "anointed" by God, "who stand by the Lord of the whole earth" (4:14). We need to be aware that the word translated "anointed" carried with it in the later Jewish world the concept of messiah. This became an evocative text for early Christian readers because Zechariah named the two "anointed ones" as Zerubbabel and Joshua. Zerubbabel was the anointed governor, and Joshua was anointed priest. These were the two figures referred to in the Book of Ezra as the leaders of the second return from exile (Ezra 3:2). Two things must be noted here. Joshua, or Yeshua, was written "Jesus" in the Greek Septuagint translation of the Hebrew Scriptures. In Ezra he was referred to as Yeshua (Jesus) and was called both priest and the son of Jehozadak, a name too close to Joseph to be ignored by Jewish Christians trained in the method of midrash (Zech. 7:11). Of this Joshua (Jesus), Zechariah wrote that God would set before him a single stone with this inscription upon it: "I will remove the guilt of this land in a single day" (Zech. 3:9). These words, associated with the sacrifice on the Day of Atonement, and now related by the prophet to one called Joshua (Jesus), would almost surely have been seen as a midrash brought to new fulfillment in Jesus of Nazareth.

This segment of the book concluded with the divine promise "I will return to Zion and will dwell in the midst of Jerusalem" (Zech. 8:3), and because of this presence of the Lord in Jerusalem, people of all the nations should come to Jerusalem to seek the Lord of hosts, for they would say, "We have heard that God is with you" (Zech. 8:23). I have little doubt that this passage helped to influence Luke's story of Pentecost, to which I shall turn in a moment, but, for our purposes now, even more dramatically did this passage set the stage for the feast of Tabernacles. During the seven days of that feast seventy bullocks were sacrificed on behalf of the seventy nations of the world, to remind the worshipers that on the day of the Lord all nations would gather against Jerusalem. Jerusalem would be saved, for all nations would be defeated by the coming of the Lord. Following that, year by year the survivors of these defeated nations would come to Jerusalem to worship the king and to keep the feast of the Booths or Tabernacles. A single bullock was offered on the last day, the eighth day, for the unique nation of Israel.[4] At this point the first section of Zechariah came to an end.

In the second section of Zechariah, chapters 9 through 14, Joshua and Zerubbabel are no longer the leaders. The atmosphere is not of peace and rebuilding but of expectations of warfare and siege. The governors are unnamed "shepherds." This portion of the book refers to the Greek period of the fourth and third centuries B.C.E. rather than to the Persian periods of chapters 1 through 8. But it was this segment that became the primary passage of Scripture read during Tabernacles, in the century before the destruction of the temple.[5] Perhaps that was because this segment was climaxed in its closing chapter by a narrative of this feast itself. Certainly this segment of Zechariah was also well known in early Christian circles, for it was referred to time and again in Christian texts with both direct quotations and in clearly influenced words.

In the opening chapter of this segment is found the story of the king coming to Jerusalem, triumphant yet lowly, riding upon a young ass. He was portrayed as the prince of peace (Zech. 9:9–11). This text was quoted as part of the Palm Sunday preparation in Matt. 21:5 and in John 12:14, 15, and it was alluded to in Mark 11 and Luke 19. But in the Hebrew Scriptures it was a story associated with Tabernacles, not with Passover. Its inclusion in Christian Scripture as a preparation for the crucifixion indicates that it was moved from its original setting.

In chapter 11 the story was told of Israel paying thirty shekels of silver to rid itself of the good shepherd God had appointed to rule over them (vv. 7ff). This shepherd, upon appointment, was said to be doomed to be slain by those who trafficked in sheep—those who bought and sold animals. Suddenly we see the story of the cleansing of the temple coming into focus. Surely it was also originally a part of the fall festival of Tabernacles. The thirty pieces of silver were cast into the temple treasury (Zech. 11:13), which clearly shaped Matthew's story of Judas throwing his thirty pieces of silver into the temple (Matt. 27:5). So here we see still another element of the passion story that originated in Tabernacles but was transferred to Passover.

In Zechariah 12 we are told that when Jerusalem "looked on him whom they have pierced, they shall mourn for him as one mourns for an only child and weep bitterly over him as one weeps over a firstborn" (vv. 10–11). Each family shall mourn alone, "by itself," said the text (12:14). Surely that was a picture of the earliest reality that followed the crucifixion, for the now-familiar words of chapter 13, which said, "Strike the shepherd that the sheep might be scattered," became a text put into the mouth of Jesus by both Matthew (26:31) and Mark (14:27).

Finally, this book of Zechariah was concluded with a picture of the day of the Lord coming in the midst of the celebration of Tabernacles. The time would be marked by continuous day, for even "at evening there shall be light" (14:7). It would also carry the note of the perennial hope of "living waters that shall flow out from Jerusalem" in an unending stream (14:8). Under the influence of these words it is easy to see how John, the only Gospel writer to mention the feast of Tabernacles, could suggest that Jesus, immediately after participating in this celebration, referred to himself as "the light of the world" (John 8:1), and during the feast itself as "living water" (John 7:38). Finally, the climax of the celebration would occur when the people of the world came to Jerusalem "to worship the King, the Lord of hosts, and to keep the feast of booths" (Zech. 14:16). His story concluded, "And there shall no longer be a trader in the house of the Lord of hosts on that day" (14:21). This is further emphasized in the next book in the Bible, Malachi (3:1ff). On the day after the king came to the city, he would come to his temple and cleanse it by making way for the nations to come and worship.

Again and again in this passage from Zechariah, which is set in the context of the festival of Tabernacles, we see the themes that early Christians associated with the story of Palm Sunday and the cleansing of the temple. When the Book of Zechariah is combined with Psalm 118 and augmented by the Book of Malachi, we have the following elements of the passion story:

- the ride of the king into Jerusalem on a donkey
- the waving of palm branches
- the shouts of hosannah
- the payment of thirty pieces of silver
- the cleansing of the temple
- the people looking upon the one they had pierced
- the Lord suddenly coming to his temple
- the nations gathering to receive the waters of life,
  which was a synonym for the Spirit

In these segments of Hebrew Scripture, we have the outline of our Lord's passion narrative from Palm Sunday to Pentecost. Yet somehow all of these aspects of the feast of Tabernacles were transferred in Christian writings to the feast of Passover. We continue that mistaken association despite the presence of scholarly research, made available first by Professor Charles W. F. Smith of the Episcopal Divinity School in Massachusetts in articles written as early as 1960, that demonstrates the obvious connections with

Tabernacles. I suspect we continue to do this because linear time has bound us so tightly that we have not dared to follow where the evidence points, so let me propose another possibility.

THE GOSPELS' CONFLATION OF TWO TRIPS TO JERUSALEM

The first thing to be noted is that, despite the synoptic Gospels' silence on the Jewish feast of Tabernacles, the echoes of this great festival are heard throughout the story of the passion. This drives me to suggest that there must have been two occasions when the disciples were thought to have gone up to Jerusalem with Jesus. One of those journeys resulted in Jesus' crucifixion. The other journey, however, which must have been located during the feast of Tabernacles, was associated with his triumph over death. The second thing to note is that John's Gospel did record the visit to Jerusalem at Tabernacles, but this Gospel writer portrayed that journey as an event that occurred early in Jesus' earthly ministry. To John's account of the feast of Tabernacles journey I now turn to explore what is to be found there.

I begin this analysis by lifting up one Haggadic principle used by the rabbis for studying the Jewish sacred story. "There is no before and after in Scripture, for chronological arrangement was only one of many possibilities."[6] In this context I listen to the words of R. H. Lightfoot, who said, "The Festival [of Tabernacles] was regarded as a foreshadowing of the Day of the Lord, or the messianic age, since popular sentiment connected it not only with the harvest and vintage now completed, but with a future, very different harvest, that of the final ingathering or harvest of the nations in the days of the Messiah."[7]

The Johannine narrative of Jesus' journey to Jerusalem for the Tabernacles celebration is filled with strange words and enigmatic symbols. The portrayal of Jesus is, at one and the same time, both historical and mythical. Jesus journeyed not only to the holy city in physical time and space, but he also took, in this narrative, the place of the temple and became the source of living water for all the world. History and nonhistory, limited time and timelessness, humanity and divinity flow together in strange ways in John's account.

John opened the episode by announcing that the feast of Tabernacles was at hand and that Jesus was in dialogue with "his brothers." Were these his earthly blood brothers, named in Mark 6? Or was the word *brothers* but a synonym for the disciples? Later in this Gospel John did use the word *brethren* to refer to his disciples (20:17). But the burden of the text was that "the brothers," whoever they were, were in Galilee and "did not believe in him" (John 7:5). I have suggested that this was exactly the situation following the crucifixion. Tabernacles was a prelude to the day of the Lord, when the messiah would suddenly come out of the heavens to his temple. So Jesus urged his brothers, "Go to the feast yourselves; I am not going up to this feast, for my time has not yet fully come" (John 7:8). Jesus remained in Galilee, requiring his "brothers" to go up without his physical presence. It was again, it seems to me, a glimpse into the postcrucifixion reality. But this narrative then says that after his brothers had gone, he also went up, in private. The words *going up* and *went up* are the same words used later in John's Gospel to describe Jesus' ascension [*anébesan* (7:10), *anébē* (7:14), and *anebébēka* (20:17)]. In Greek the phrase carries a double entendre that is not capable of being captured in the English translation.

Meanwhile, at the Jerusalem feast, Jesus was the source of much debate centering on the questions "Where is he?" and "Who is he?" Both are postcrucifixion questions, I submit, read back into this episode. They are the questions that most plagued the Galilean disciples in the weeks and months that followed the crucifixion. "About the middle of the feast," the text now says (John 7:14), Jesus suddenly appeared in the temple. The exact words are: "Jesus went up into the temple." (Once again *anébē* is the word used.) Was this a hidden, enigmatic reference to his exaltation into heaven? The language lends itself to that possibility. Did the reference to "the middle of the feast" cause the seven- to eight-day celebration time to be squeezed down into the popular resurrection symbol of three days? I think that case can also be made.

The conversation rolled on in this dual manner with two levels apparent in almost every word—one in time and history and one beyond time and history. "Are you angry with me because on the Sabbath I made a man's whole body well?" Jesus asked (John 7:23). Was this a reference back to the man healed of his paralysis on the Sabbath, who then, in violation of the Sabbath, took up his pallet and walked (John 5:1–9)? If so, it was a strange placement, coming two chapters later in the text and following the miraculous feeding of the multitude, which, like the crucifixion, culminated in yet another episode of desertion by the disciples. On that occasion, when the disciples "drew back and no longer went about with him" (John 6:66), Jesus asked the twelve, "Do you wish also to go away?" And it was Peter who answered, "Lord, to whom shall we go? You have the words of eternal life" (John 6:68). Then Peter acknowledged Jesus as "the Holy One of God" (John 6:69). That was and is an equally strange placement of a confession of faith by Peter, who was, in chronological time, yet to forsake Jesus, to deny him, and to be restored to him by the Galilean seaside (John 21:1ff). When this passage is located in history as an episode in Jesus' earthly life, problems abound. Such a placement is strange. Such a context is nonsensical.

But now look at these narratives from the perspective of post-Easter. Is it possible that then words about making a man's "whole body well on the Sabbath" could be a reference to the one who, between Friday and the first day of the week, was believed to have been restored to new life? When the paragraph ends with Jesus saying, "Do not judge by appearances but judge with right judgment" (John 7:24), the inner logic of the words becomes even more confusing in the historical context; but they open up to new levels of meaning in the postresurrection context.

Again the debate was joined about whether he was the Christ. It was said, "When the Christ appears no one will know where he comes from" (John 7:27). Would that not certainly be true if people thought they had killed him, only to discover that he was alive in God's eschatological kingdom from which he would appear as the Son of man when the feast of Tabernacles was concluded?

In John's rendition of the feast of Tabernacles, the authorities then tried to arrest him. The chief priests and Pharisees sent officers to remove him. That sounds to us like literal behavior inside literal history. But Jesus responded to this crisis with words that were not temporal or bound in history and that make the most sense in a postcrucifixion time sequence. "You will seek me but not find me. Where I am you cannot come" (John 7:34). John's story then moved on to the last day of the feast—a day it called, provocatively enough, "the great day"—and the text announced that "Jesus stood up and proclaimed" himself to be the source of living water, which the Gospel writer interpreted to be "the Spirit, which those who believed in him were to receive" (John 7:37–39). Please note again the dual meanings here. On "the great day, Jesus stood up"! The word translated "stood up" is related to the verb used elsewhere in the Gospel for the resurrection (John 20:19; Luke 24:8). Was the reference to "the great day" a reference to the last day of Tabernacles or to the day of the resurrection? Or was it deliberately written to refer to both? In either case, was it this historical Jesus or the glorified Christ who became the source of the Spirit? John would say later that the risen Christ breathed on his disciples, and they received the Holy Spirit (John 20:22). But here we are told that on the great day Jesus "stood up" and became the source of "living water."

This resulted, according to John's story, in even more division over Jesus. Was he the prophet? Was he the Christ? But he was from Galilee, not Bethlehem! When Nicodemus tried to enter the conversation, he was ridiculed, and the Pharisees said to him, "Search and you will see that no prophet is to rise from Galilee" (John 7:52). Once more that was a double meaning, for did "rise from Galilee" mean originate in Galilee, or did it mean "be resurrected for seeing" by those who were in Galilee? There are far too many double meanings in this chapter, and far too many powerful symbols, to be ignored.

The feast of Tabernacles clearly was related in some now lost way to the story of Easter. John alone has preserved the festival itself, but, as we have noted, signs of the feast of the Tabernacles are all over the synoptic accounts of the passion. Indeed the connections are overwhelming—so overwhelming as to reveal that the feast of Tabernacles could have been at the beginning the primary context for the proclamation of the risen Christ and that, in time, this connection was lost and everything conspired to push the events related to the story of our Lord's resurrection out of the orbit of the festival of Tabernacles and into the orbit of the festival of Passover.

I wish to propose another possibility. Peter, having had in Galilee an experience of the inbreaking reality of God that he called resurrection, which included seeing Jesus of Nazareth as part of who God was and is, shared that experience first with his Galilean fishing partners James, John, and, maybe, Andrew. It was electrifying, and, though not clear to any of them, it was real. It had come in a combination of signs, grief, inner conflict, and the sacramental act of breaking bread and seeing through that symbol the body of Jesus broken on the cross as the ultimate sign of the infinite love of God. This compelled Peter and the Galilean group to go up to Jerusalem for the feast of Tabernacles, a journey that John placed into the historic life of Jesus, but he preserved the original, nonhistorical, context by writing the narrative in such a way as to be read on two levels at once. The synoptic writers, by contrast, simply attached to Jesus' final journey to Jerusalem, at the time of the Passover when the crucifixion occurred, all of the symbols of the later journey during Tabernacles. In fact, however, this journey to Jerusalem for the feast of Tabernacles took place, I now propose, some six months after the crucifixion and was led by Peter, not Jesus. But it was a Peter who believed himself to be carrying the undeniable message of his Lord risen and living to those in Jerusalem who had not yet seen the Lord risen and enthroned in heaven.

Sharing the story of what Peter called "the appearance of Jesus resurrected into the very presence of God" with his Jerusalem friends in the context of Tabernacles gave the whole experience a new and vital frame of reference. The newly gathered community of believers now joined the processions around the altar, waving their branches of palms and other greenery. They shouted their hosannahs and their liturgical refrain "Blessed is he who comes in

277

the name of the Lord." They built a sukkoth, or temporary shelter, that was later, I believe, incorporated into the Christian story as the temporary tomb in Joseph's lonely garden. They went to the sukkoth carrying the box called an ethrog, containing the fragrant citron fruit and blossom, which I am now convinced got incorporated into the later resurrection narratives as the spices carried by the women, but for a purpose that never was really clear. As the liturgy of Tabernacles developed under the impact of this Christian revelation, it included a procession to a tomb-like temporary dwelling, where one member of the community would dress in white to announce, as part of the liturgy, "He is not here, behold, the place where they laid him." In time that white-robed liturgical functionary was transformed by Gospel writers into the eschatological angel or angels who announced to the women the resurrection message that the tomb, which was a symbol for death, could not contain Jesus of Nazareth.

But above all else, I believe it was the ceremonial meal that was required to be eaten in the sukkoth that bound together forever the experience of the risen Lord and the reenactment of the common meal in which bread was broken and wine was poured. In that sacramental act eyes were opened to see the body of Jesus as the bread of life, broken for the world to feed the deepest human hunger for God, and hearts were opened by the blood of Jesus, understood as the atoning sacrifice that lifted human beings anew into God's presence. To feed the people of the world with this bread and this wine became the vocation of those who found their lives in this Christ.

The resurrection thus began with Peter, who finally understood that it was the duty of those who loved Christ to feed the sheep of Christ, but it soon journeyed to Jerusalem and found expression inside the Jewish festival of Tabernacles. That festival, lost by and large to the gentile consciousness after the fall of Jerusalem, was preserved in a single reference in John 7, but it was incorporated into the passion narratives by moving all of the symbols of Tabernacles into the dominant celebration of Passover. Passover was the time of crucifixion, but Tabernacles was the time when the story of Jesus' resurrection was finally proclaimed in Jerusalem. It was the symbols of Tabernacles that came to be thought of as the symbols of the Jerusalem resurrection tradition—a Palm Sunday procession, the cleansing of the temple, the empty booth, the sweet-smelling spices, the ceremonial meal, and the angelic messenger who announced the resurrection. All are symbols derived directly from the festival of Tabernacles.

I thus see two stages in the narrative of Easter that lie behind the biblical accounts, but both stages find expression in the confusion of the texts of the Gospel. Was it in Galilee or in Jerusalem that the primary moment of Easter occurred? My thesis is that the evidence points to Galilee, and to one called Simon. But this Simon then came to Jerusalem accompanied by his Galilean companions, who had been incorporated into this experience in their home region. In Jerusalem Simon shared his story with the Jerusalem community that had known and followed Jesus, and this sharing took place during the Tabernacles celebration so that the shape of the Easter narratives found in the Bible was, in fact, determined by the symbols of the Tabernacles celebration. In time even the historic detail of the futile search for the tomb of Jesus by Mary Magdalene shortly after the crucifixion was incorporated into the Easter story, making the women at the empty tomb the focal point of that narrative in each of the canonical Gospels.

There are two other possible references to a Tabernacles framework in the synoptic Gospels, both of which I think add mightily to the persuasiveness of this argument. First, there is the strange and difficult-to-interpret story of the transfiguration. It is found in Mark (9:2–8), Matthew (17:1–8), and Luke (9:28–36). Interestingly, the fourth Gospel, which alone of the Gospels gives us the Tabernacles tradition, does not include an account of transfiguration.

But the accounts in the synoptic Gospels are all similar. The transfiguration occurred in Mark and Matthew "after six days," and in Luke "about eight days" after certain events that Luke had just been describing. Tabernacles was a seven- or eight-day festival, with the added eighth day coming later in Jewish history. The time references in the Gospel narratives of the transfiguration make little sense except when these narratives are placed in the context of the festival of Tabernacles, where surely they once resided. The next feature that locates these narratives in Tabernacles was the proposal of the erection of three booths—one for each of the principals in the narrative. The heavenly voice's rejection of this proposal, first made to Peter, represents, in my opinion, a growing realization in the earliest Christian community of the uniqueness of the Jesus experience.

The other two principals in the story of the transfiguration, Elijah and Moses, were both believed to reside in heaven by God's direct action, as we have noted earlier. The resurrection of Jesus was thought in the primitive tradition to be similar to the mythology surrounding Elijah and Moses. Jesus, too, was taken into God. A booth, therefore, should be built at the feast of Tabernacles for all three. That may well have been Peter's first conclusion, for he was portrayed in the transfiguration story as the one who made this suggestion, for as the text states, Peter "did not know what to say for they were exceedingly afraid" (Mark 9:6). But the voice from the cloud of God spoke to Peter and said, No, Peter, this is my Son, my special emissary, a part of my very being. Listen to him.

It is interesting to note that the transfiguration is set in Galilee before the disciples and Jesus began what the synoptic Gospels all call the first journey to Jerusalem. My reading, however, would locate this narrative in the postcrucifixion period, but still in Galilee before the disciples, led by Peter, began the real triumphal procession to Jerusalem. It was, I believe, a procession that took place during the feast of Tabernacles some six months after the crucifixion, when a tiny band of perhaps as few as four disciples, led by Peter, began the journey to Jerusalem. That journey would change the face of human history, for they journeyed inside the experience of having seen the living Lord, exalted into the very presence of God, having become part of what God is, and now available to them as life-giving Spirit. They went to proclaim that death could not contain him. They went to bear the witness, "We have seen the Lord!" They went to open the eyes of others so that they, too, might see and believe and thus might have life in his name.

The second reference in the synoptic Gospels that I believe was also shaped by the Tabernacles tradition was the appearance of the risen Lord to two disciples in the village of Emmaus, told only by Luke (24:13ff). In this story both history and context were, I believe, confused.

Clopas and his partner left Jerusalem in disillusionment after the crucifixion. They appear to have been made aware that the grave had not been located (Luke 24:23). Those are the echoes, I am now convinced, of the original tradition. But when they arrived in Emmaus, there was some confusion in the text about whether that was home or a temporary dwelling, perhaps a booth. They invited their traveling companion to come in with them. He accepted. Yet, despite the fact that he was the guest, he took over the role of host. He said the blessing after taking the bread. Then, breaking the bread and sharing it with them, he vanished. It had all the markings of the ceremonial liturgical meal shared inside the sukkoth, or temporary dwelling, as part of the celebration of the festival of Tabernacles. When we add to this narrative the concluding proclamation that Jesus had been made "known to them in the breaking of the bread" (Luke 24:35), the case seems to me to be significantly made.

Finally, we add to this reconstruction the Lucan story of Pentecost, which also had major Tabernacles themes, but which Luke had set at the time of Shavaut, a different Jewish festival from Passover. That combination creates, for me, the final clue that makes valid my proposed reconstruction.

Luke seemed to be aware that an event took place in Jerusalem some time after the crucifixion. Since the resurrection was located by Luke on the first day of the week following Good Friday, Luke decided that the second, later, Jerusalem event had to be identified with the outpouring of the Holy Spirit. Since Passover was the context of the first experience and since the tradition suggested that the second Jerusalem experience was associated with a later Jewish festival, Luke chose Jewish Pentecost, or Shavaut, as his setting to tell his story of the coming of the Holy Spirit. Thus the Christian festival of Whitsunday, or Pentecost, was born. But Luke, not familiar with Jewish liturgical practices, I now suggest, chose the wrong festival. He chose Shavaut instead of Sukkoth. It was not a bad guess on Luke's part. Shavaut was also a harvest festival among the Jews, albeit only a harvest of grains that marked the first fruits of the harvest season. The celebration of Shavaut was also associated with loaves of bread made from the newly cut grain. Since both first fruits and bread were familiar symbols among Christians by the time Luke wrote, my guess is that it seemed to Luke to be an appropriate choice. Yet the symbols Luke employed in his Pentecost story were overwhelmingly not the symbols of Shavaut but rather those of the later festival of Tabernacles. The nations being gathered and the outpouring of the Spirit in the form of living water indicate that Luke simply chose the wrong festival as the basis for his second Jerusalem narrative.

The gospel of Easter and Jesus as the exalted one, living with God, dawned, I believe, in Galilee with Peter at its heart. Peter then opened the eyes of the other Galilean disciples to see what he saw. They took this faith to Jerusalem during the feast of Tabernacles some six months after the crucifixion. That was the real triumphal journey. That was the original Palm Sunday. In Jerusalem they made known their faith in the risen, living Christ; and in time the Jerusalem setting for the resurrection became the primary one. However, almost every symbol of the Jerusalem Easter tradition can be identified as part of the celebration of Tabernacles. This largely lost Jewish celebration was the setting in which the Easter tradition was finally told, and that is what we have in the various narratives of our Lord's resurrection. Our great failing was that we did not know anything about midrash, so we literalized narratives that were not intended to be literalized. The Jerusalem Easter legends are not to be dismissed as untrue. They are meant to be probed for clues, as I trust I have done adequately. Behind the legends that grew up around this moment, there is a reality I can never deny. Jesus lives. I have seen the Lord. By that faith and with that conviction I live my life and proclaim my gospel.

Chapter 21

Life After Death—This I
Do Believe

All of my adult life I have wanted to write a major book on life after death. I wanted to make the case for its reality to modern folk like myself. I have thrown myself into this task with great energy. There was a time when I thought that this was the Rubicon line, and unless I crossed it all else would crumble. I have done massive research on the subject. For an entire year I studied the concept of life after death in the Hebrew Scriptures. I learned some fascinating things in that study—for example, that life after death did not appear as a major category in Hebrew thought until a concept of individualism was formed around the sixth century B.C.E. It did not gain much shape or power until about two centuries before Jesus' birth, and then it grew out of the pain of oppression and the heroic, sacrificial deaths of Jewish folk who put devotion to their understanding of God's truth ahead of their personal safety. These were interesting insights, but they led to no conclusions.

I spent another whole year looking at the understanding of life after death in the Christian Scriptures. I again learned some fascinating things. Every writer in the New Testament seems to have believed something different about the afterlife. There is no hell, for example, in Paul's writings. Paul mentions only the hope of life in Christ or the absolute annihilation of life in a timeless death. Most of the hellfire references in the New Testament are Matthew's gifts to Christianity. He was particularly obsessed with that idea. If Matthew had never written his Gospel, the revivalist preachers on the sawdust trail who trafficked in guilt and fear, and whose oratory has regularly stoked the fires of hell, would have had almost no biblical basis for their fulminations.

I spent another significant period looking at the various shapes the idea of life after death took in Western history, and the way that idea affected human beings, particularly in times of total belief. Peter the Great of Russia, for example, would visit the site of the execution of one whom he had condemned to death, to console his victim with vivid heavenly assurances. I began to understand how the concept of life after death had acted as a deterrent to any passion for building a just society. Life after death made the unfair world appear to be fair, for it represented justice delayed, not entirely denied. Karl Marx, who rejected the realm of heaven altogether, suggested that such a religion, built on such an idea, was properly recognized as nothing but an opiate of the people.

I also began to document the historical and political reality that when belief in life after death began to fade in Western civilization in the late nineteenth and early twentieth centuries, it was replaced by liberal politics. Indeed liberal politics were born, I would argue, to fill the vacuum created by the denial of a belief in life after death. Everything—from Marx to the varieties of European socialism including something called "Christian" socialism, to the New Deal, the Fair Deal, the New Frontier, the Great Society, the war on poverty, the Labour Party in the United Kingdom, and the role of organized religion in the civil rights movement, the peace movement, the women's movement, and the gay movement—was an unconscious response to the loss of a sure conviction in regard to life after death. The hope for life after death in a believing age took care of the human need to be assured that God and life were fair. When the hope that fairness awaited us in the afterlife waned in our unbelieving age, the need to make fair the unfair world was keenly felt and found expression in the political arena. Liberal politics came into being with that as its single basic agenda. If fairness was not destined to be achieved in an afterlife, a passion to achieve it in this life must be served. That was the first political response, I believe, to the loss of faith in God and the loss of a hope for heaven.

The second political response to this loss was not near so noble. When the secular spirit won the day, the drive to serve God by creating fairness on this earth lost momentum. When it did, liberalism became a bad word. Then the obsession to create earthly fairness was replaced by a spirit of greed and amorality in the political arena. In the United States this amoral greed was born, in my opinion, when President John F. Kennedy was killed in 1963. He was, for many, one who articulated the final glimmering ideal of hope for a better and fairer life in our world. This is not to say that President Kennedy necessarily embodied those ideals in his personal life, but it is to say that these were the symbols and legends that gathered around his person, and upon his death these values, which form his legacy, entered the realm of mythology.

Following that death, however, American political life was marked by one final attempt to build a fair world called "the great society." But that effort was marred by self-serving greed that stretched from the way Lyndon Johnson's personal wealth was created to the way various people made fortunes. The desire to assist the unfortunate was derailed by misuses of appropriated monies. In the Johnson years, however, people still had a sense that they were doing something wrong, no matter how well their behavior served them. But Johnson was followed in office by Richard Nixon, whose years were marked by a shift in attitude from immorality to amorality. The Nixon administration seemed incapable of seeing or knowing the difference between right and wrong. This movement culminated in the Reagan years, when the tax code was adjusted to allow capital to flow away from the poor and the middle class to this nation's wealthiest people. The twin realities of extreme wealth and rising homelessness became two sides of the same coin in the 1980s and 1990s in the United States.

In the United Kingdom similar phenomena of greed and legal class warfare marked the long reign of England's Iron Lady of politics, Margaret Thatcher. In that administration also the rich got richer and the poor got poorer.

If heaven did not make fair our unfair world, and if that was also not able to be achieved politically, then fairness as an ideal began to fade. People in what were once the leading Christian nations of the West started to act as if they could do whatever they wanted to do in order to get their share in the jungle called life. No one else really mattered. It was an ominous turn in values. Tracing this trend made me aware of how important the idea of fairness associated with life after death had been in the history of our civilization.

So it is that in much of the West in the last decade of the twentieth century, a time that has also witnessed the death of communism, a political system based on fairness is no longer considered a realistic possibility. A dawning sense exists that a new basis and a new value system for human life must be found.

Next I sought to understand life after death in the other religious traditions of the world. Nirvana, reincarnation, the transmigration of souls—all engaged my attention, titillated my interest for a moment, but then finally lost their appeal. I read widely in parapsychology. There is an amazing amount of material in this area of human speculation. There are also striking claims and fascinating "coincidences" that cry out to be explored. There are provocative hints about levels of communication that, by our standards today, are nonphysical. But no emerging or real consensus exists. Perhaps there are telepathic messages that human beings can pass one to another, but the data is so chaotic, so lacking in verification, as to be untrustworthy. I keep an open mind, but I remain an agnostic on this approach.

Finally I sought to analyze the images of both heaven and hell that have been dominant in the Judeo-Christian tradition. Hell has been a place of separation, a place of punishment, and a place of nothingness. Each of these concepts plays on something deep in the human psyche—our need for intimacy, our sense of guilt, and our quest for meaning. Hell in its various forms speaks to each of our distorting fears.

The concept of Heaven also grew out of something deep within the human being. To wilderness wanderers heaven was "a land flowing with milk and honey." To a church living in persecution, heaven was a place where there was no sorrow or sadness and no separation. To medieval peasants, who worked at physical labor from sunup to sundown six days a week, with only Sunday to recuperate and restore their energy, heaven became the eternal Sabbath, the heavenly rest. Basically, beneath the images, people were saying that hell was the ultimate symbol of that which threatened their humanity, and heaven was the ultimate symbol of their dreams and their vision of human fulfillment.

But above all it was clear that heaven and hell have been used by both church and society as a method of behavior control. A member of the British Parliament actually suggested, as late as the early 1990s, that we should revive the idea of hell to be a weapon in our fight against crime and drugs. This M.P. naively observed that in those eras when hell was taken seriously, we had less crime and less drug abuse. His conclusion could hardly be faulted, but the way he got to his conclusion was marvelously self-serving and ignorantly bizarre.

Nonetheless, heaven became the ultimate reward for good behavior, with God being cast as the rewarding parent, and hell became the ultimate parental punishment for evil behavior, with God being cast as the punishing judge. Heaven and hell, ultimate reward and ultimate punishment, were just another step increase from that era in which peerages were handed out to extraordinary citizens for exemplary contributions and where the whipping post was the threatened destiny for social derelicts, drunks, petty thieves, and debtors.

THE MERGING OF TRANSCENDENCE AND IMMANENCE

This study of life after death consumed as much as five years of my life. It fed many other things that I was doing, but the study itself seemed to lead me to no final conclusions. I do not today regret the years I spent on this subject. I treasure the insights I gained. But I will never write the book I set out to write, for I still do not know what to say or how to express my convictions on this subject except with a consuming vagueness.

I do believe that death is not the end of our lives. But I do not know how to talk about that. I have no words, I possess no concepts. I am reduced to silence before this ultimate mystery. But if someone were to ask me Job's ancient and searching question, "If a man (or woman) dies, will he (she) live again?" my answer would be "Yes." That is my conviction. That is what I believe. Yet there is so much about the traditional content of heaven and hell that I do not believe, that I can speak negatively far more easily than I can speak positively.

I do not believe in life after death as a method of behavior control. I have no interest in the reward/punishment aspect of the afterlife. In the honesty of one's heart of hearts, the person whose life is noble only for the sake of gaining the ultimate reward of heaven is immediately guilty of being self-serving. If one acts one way and not another only to get a reward, one's life becomes insufferably shallow and petty. I would not be drawn to anyone or to any religious system that approached life in such a way. I recall the hymn that says: "I love thee Lord, but not because I hope for heaven thereby, Nor yet for fear that loving not, I might forever die."[1] This hymn speaks to a higher good than that of the selfish person seeking a reward. It is my hope that Christianity will shed its reward and punishment motifs as a clear aberration in our understanding of the Gospels and as simply unworthy of the Lord we claim to serve.

I hope, too, that the church will someday reject the behavior control business as a blind and alien path that we have traveled in ignorance. The business of the church is to love people into life. When we confuse that and begin to think that our job is to judge one another, out of some self-imposed standard of righteousness, we have then, in my opinion, misread the whole message of the Gospel. To make moral pronouncements and to judge human life has become the favorite indoor sport of institutional Christianity, but it has never been of the essence of the Gospel. So I dismiss heaven as a place of reward, and I dismiss hell as a place of punishment. I find neither definition either believable or appealing.

Life after death must mean more than that. Talking about heaven is, for me, like talking about the resurrection. I no longer need to describe it. In this volume I have written about the resurrection of Jesus. I have dismissed many of the later-written details of Easter as legends, but I continue to cling to the core experience that inspired that legend. When I come to describe what actually happened on the first Easter, I find that I can talk about the effects that Easter had, the power it produced, the changes it wrought, the context in which it was experienced, and the results it created. But the moment itself? About that I discover that I am reduced to a profound, reverential silence. That moment was beyond time and space and, therefore, beyond the capacity of our language to capture or of our minds to understand. One has only to stand before that transcendent moment, containing that which the church has called the resurrection of Jesus, and there utter only a simple yes or no. In that silence I speak my yes, and then I seek to live into the power of that resurrection in my life.

In a similar fashion my years of study on the issues of life after death have given me no words with which to discuss the idea. For Jesus it seemed to mean something like communion with God. It meant being in touch with something that transcended all of one's human categories, including a transcendence of the self that one is. It meant having one's eyes opened to see dimensions of life not normally seen and to have one's ears open to hear melodies and harmonies not normally heard.

This means that now I no longer look for God or for ultimate meaning in some distant place beyond this world. I rather seek these realities in every moment and in every relationship. For me the transcendence of God is no longer something different from the immanence of God. Transcendence is always a dimension of the immanent. The immanent is the point of entry; the transcendent is the infinite depth capable of being discerned behind any moment, beyond any point of entry.

For me heaven is an invitation into life, which, when explored deeply enough, when lived fully enough, when engaged significantly enough, is a way of passing into transcendence. In this way finite moments slip into being infinite, timeless moments. I also believe that human life can be lived so deeply, that love can be experienced so powerfully, that incarnation in fact occurs again and again. God is not a heavenly man, an external force, or a judging parent. God is the creating spirit that calls order out of chaos. God is the life force that emerges first into consciousness, then into self-consciousness, and now into self-transcendence, and ultimately into we know not what. God is the love that creates wholeness, the Being at the depths of our being, the Source from which all life comes.

This is the God that I see in Jesus of Nazareth, and so I affirm that this life is the life of God being lived among us. His was a life not finally bound by human limits. When those whose fear of God's presence was so total that they struck back to kill him, they finally were forced to discover that all they actually did was to free the meaning of his life from the boundaries of finitude and to make him timeless, eternal, and ever-present. When the eyes of Simon finally saw the meaning of Jesus' life, when the ears of Simon finally heard the music of Jesus' life, then he stared across that invisible but ever-so-real barrier that separated time from timelessness, finitude from infinity, human spirit from Holy Spirit, and he saw Jesus inside the meaning of God.

How does one talk about that? Only symbolically, I assure you. First there was the ecstatic negative proclamation, "Death cannot contain him!" In time the ecstasy of that claim was turned into human stories about tombs being empty, stones being rolled away to allow the divine exit, grave clothes being placed so as to suggest that he rose out of them, and startled women conversing with him in the garden.

Next there was the ecstatic positive proclamation, "We have seen the Lord!" In time the ecstasy of that claim was also turned into human stories about heavenly apparitions that appeared inside sealed space, during a meal in Emmaus, by the Sea of Galilee, or in the upper room. To quell the doubts and to answer the questions, details were added. So we are told that Jesus ate a piece of broiled fish, that he spoke to them to interpret the Scriptures, that he invited the physical inspection of his wounds, and that he commissioned them to be his agents in all the world. It was not long before that transcendent moment in which meaning broke into the consciousness of those still living inside this world, meaning that was beyond this world, had been turned by human beings into a concrete fact of history, complete with magical details.

Such a transformation might be sustained in a premodern age of faith, but that kind of magic and sleight of hand will never survive in our contemporary world, where miracle and the supernatural are both suspect. If we insist that Easter's truth must be carried inside such a literal framework, we doom Easter's truth to the death of irrelevance. Yet to talk about ultimate moments is something that human beings must do, and to explain human experiences is a compelling human need. We need not apologize for that. We do need to apologize for the arrogance of those human beings who insist that we reduce all transcendent reality to an explanation, using literalized human words, and then claim ultimacy not for the experience but for the explanation. We do need to apologize for the human assumption that when we have explained something in understandable human language, we have established the objectivity of our explanation as the bearer of ultimate truth.

Because Jesus was the name given to a life of ultimate, transcendent meaning that emerged in a Jewish context, Jewish concepts were inevitably the first line of human explanation. We see the influences of the feast of Tabernacles and the feast of Passover. We see the interpretative power of such Jewish concepts as prophet/martyr, atoning sacrifice, suffering servant, and son of man. There was nothing any more literal about these explanations than there was about the narratives of empty tombs or apparitions. The former was an intellectual attempt to explain. The latter was a legendary attempt to understand. The truth of Easter lies beyond both of these interpretive efforts.

So also does life after death get twisted and tangled in the words used to convey it, and in the power that is thought to derive from it. I want to move beyond the pious sentimentality used in times of crises even by those who do not believe in God. I want to move beyond the immature assurances with which an adult consoles a child who has lost either a pet or a parent to death. I want to move beyond the institutional tactics of behavior control, of reward and punishment, that finally issued in the practice of the sale of indulgences, primarily on the Catholic side of Christianity, and the manipulation of human fear by extolling the punishing power of divine wrath, primarily on the Protestant side of Christianity. I do not want either the promise of heaven or the fear of hell to manipulate any person into doing anything. That may well be a proper function of society, of the laws that govern the social order, of civic awards and public praise on one side and civil fines and even penal incarceration on the other. But that is not the role of God, the vocation of the Christian church, or the function of heaven.

Life is finite. At least in every individual expression of that life, it is finite. It comes into existence at a particular moment. It lives out, more or less, its appointed span of days. It passes out of existence, and the elements that once coalesced to form that life return to the primal soup to be reformed as part of another entity. My affirmation is that only those creatures who have developed self-consciousness can, within their span of days, commune with that which is beyond our limits. When we commune with the limitless, the eternal, the ultimately real one, we share in those aspects of that reality with which our hearts and minds are bound. If one does that completely enough it could well be said of that one that his life had been incorporated into God at the moment of his death. If Jesus of Nazareth provided us with the means by which we can walk on his path into the same destiny, then it is easy to understand why some would claim that they heard him say, "I am the way, the truth, and the life. No one comes to the Father but by me"; or "I am the resurrection and the life, he [she] who believes in me, though he [she] die yet shall he [she] live."

So I stand before this portrait of God painted by Jesus of Nazareth and interpreted by the church. I recognize the legends, the accretions, the context of that ancient world which had the task of transforming the inbreaking reality into human words. I probe all of those elements until I get beyond them to the experience that produced them. Here words fail me. Silence engulfs me. I peer beyond the limits in which my life is lived, and I say my prayerful yes . . .

Yes to Jesus—my primary window into God;

Yes to resurrection—which asserts that the essence of Jesus is the essence of a living God;

Yes to life after death—because one who has entered a relationship with God has entered the timelessness of God.

These three yeses coalesce into being the defining experience of my life. Out of these affirmations I will live, I will love, and I will enter life deeply. I will scale life's heights and explore its depths. I will seek truth without fear, and when I find it, I will act on it regardless of the cost. I will never rank peace above justice or the unity of an institution ahead of the integrity of that institution. Those are just other ways of being faithless to the primary defining "yes" that lies at the center of who I am.

I will never again seek to speculate on the nature of life after death, the definition of heaven, or the arguments for or against its reality. Those books on life after death that I read in my earlier life will remain in a row on a shelf in my library. I will not open them again. I will treasure those persons with whom my life is emotionally bound today, and I will enjoy the expanding privileges of their friendship. When they die, I will grieve at the loss that my life will experience. I will not speculate on how, if, or in what form I might see them again. That is not my business. My business is to live now, to love now, and to be now. As I give my life, my love, and myself away now, I hope that others can be called into deeper life, greater love, fuller being, and that by expanding each other, we enter the infinity of what Paul Tillich called "the eternal now."[2] To live it, not to explain it, is my task and, I believe, the task of the Christ in this world and therefore the task of that group of people who dare to call themselves the body of Christ.

So let us live, my brothers and sisters. Let us even eat, drink, and be merry, not because tomorrow we shall die but because today we are alive and it is our vocation to be alive—to be alive to God, alive to each other, alive to ourselves.

"Choose ye this day whom you will serve!" As for me and my house we will serve the crucified/risen one, who said, "I have come that you might have life and that you might have it ABUNDANTLY," and I will live in expectant hope that where he is there will I someday be. That is quite enough for me.

Shalom.

Notes

Chapter 1. *The Method Called Midrash*

1. Jeffrey John, in conversation with the author, Magdalen College, Oxford, February 1991.
2. S. Aarowitz, from an article on Midrash in *The Jewish Encyclopedia* (London and New York: Funk and Wagnalls, 1904, 1916, 1925).
3. John S. Spong, *Born of a Woman* (San Francisco: Harper San Francisco, 1993).
4. Michael Goulder, *Midrash and Lection in Matthew* (London: SPCK, 1974).
5. Michael Goulder, *Luke, A New Paradigm* (Sheffield, UK: Sheffield Academic Press, 1989).
6. Dale and Patricia Miller, *The Gospel of Mark as Midrash on Earlier Jewish and New Testament Literature* (Lewiston, NY: Edwin Mellon Press, 1990).
7. George Carey, Archbishop of Canterbury, quoted in *London Times*, 19 April 1992.
8. Jaroslav Pelikan, *The History of the Christian Tradition* (Richmond: Univ. of Virginia Press, 1973), 9.

Chapter 2. *The Impact of Easter—A Place to Begin*

1. *London Times*, 18 April 1992; *Wall Street Journal*, 20 February 1991.
2. There are a few scholars that attribute 1 Peter to the apostle. They are a distinct and very small minority, however.

Chapter 3. *The Vehicle of Words—An Unsteady Ship*

1. Sigmund Freud, *The Future of an Illusion* (London: Hogarth Press, 1928).
2. Paul Tillich, *The New Being* (New York: Charles Scribner & Sons, 1965).
3. Albert Schweitzer, *The Quest of the Historical Jesus* (Tübingen, 1907; London: A & C Black, 1948).
4. Peter O'Donald, geneticist, in conversation with the author, Emmanuel College, Cambridge University, spring term 1992.

Chapter 4. *The Witness of Paul*

1. Reginald Fuller, *The Formation of the Resurrection Narratives* (New York: Macmillan, 1971), 203, n. 53.

2. Ibid., 41.
3. Ibid., 39. He argues that James got caught up in the pillar tradition because of his leadership role.
4. George Carey, Archbishop of Canterbury, quoted in *London Times,* 19 April 1992.
5. Another archbishop in the Anglican communion, whom I choose not to identify by name.

Chapter 5. *Mark: The Kerygma Is Joined to the Sepulcher*

1. Scholars universally dismiss any claims that vv. 9–20 of Mark 16 were originally part of the Gospel. They were added much later, and are not part of Mark in the most ancient manuscripts.
2. Edward Schillebeeckx, *Jesus: An Experiment in Christology,* trans. Hubert Hoskins (New York: Seabury Press, 1979), 334ff.

Chapter 6. *Matthew: Polemics Enter the Tradition*

1. Michael Goulder, *Midrash and Lection in Matthew* (London: SPCK, 1974), 3ff. First and Second Chronicles are a later version of the same material that appears in 1 and 2 Kings.
2. Ibid., 448.
3. Ibid., 449.

Chapter 7. *Luke: The Turn Toward Gentile Understandings*

1. Michael Goulder agreed with my conclusion in conversation at the University of Birmingham, England, July 1992.
2. Edward Schillebeeckx, *Jesus: An Experiment in Christology,* trans. Hubert Hoskins (New York: Seabury Press, 1979), 341.
3. Ibid., 343.
4. Recall that the fourth Gospel, which mentions one named Clopas, had not yet been written.

Chapter 8. *John: Sometimes Primitive, Sometimes Highly Developed*

1. Reginald Fuller, *The Formation of the Resurrection Narratives* (New York: Macmillan, 1971), 137.
2. Translation by Raymond Brown, *The Gospel According to John* (Garden City, NY: Doubleday, 1966, 1970).
3. Fuller, *Formation,* 134; and Raymond Brown, *The Birth of the Messiah* (Garden City, NY: Doubleday, 1977), 988.
4. This is revealed through the number of Passover celebrations Jesus went to in Jerusalem in the fourth Gospel. See John 2:13ff.
5. Fuller, *Formation,* 137.
6. I have developed this possibility in my book *Born of a Woman: A Bishop Rethinks the Birth of Jesus* (San Francisco: Harper San Francisco, 1992).

Chapter 9. *A New Starting Point*

1. The habit of recording every word spoken in the oval office by an American president did not begin with Richard Nixon. He only made that process famous.
2. Words of the Nicene Creed.

Chapter 10. *The Primitive Interpretive Images*

1. W. O. E. Oesterly, *The Jews and Judaism During the Greek Period* (London: SPCK, 1941).
2. Edward Schillebeeckx, *Jesus: An Experiment in Christology*, trans. Hubert Hoskins (New York: Seabury Press, 1979), 273–85.
3. "Q" community—the word *Q* comes from the German word *Quelle*, which means "source." Q material is assumed to be the non-Markan material common to Matthew and Luke. Those who dismiss the Q hypothesis do so by asserting Luke's dependence on Matthew.

Chapter 11. *The Atoning Sacrifice—The Image of the Book of Hebrews*

1. A ceremonial washing basin used by the priest in many liturgical traditions to symbolize an act of cleansing for priestly unworthiness.

Chapter 12. *The Suffering Servant—The Image of 2 Isaiah*

1. Dale and Patricia Miller, *The Gospel of Mark as Midrash on Earlier Jewish and New Testament Literature* (Lewiston, NY: Edwin Mellon Press, 1990).

Chapter 14. *The First Clue: It Occurred in Galilee, Not in Jerusalem*

1. I have developed these ideas in my earlier book *Born of a Woman: A Bishop Rethinks the Birth of Jesus* (San Francisco: Harper San Francisco, 1992) far more extensively.

Chapter 15. *The Second Clue: The Primacy of Peter*

1. Dale and Patricia Miller, *The Gospel of Mark as Midrash on Earlier Jewish and New Testament Literature* (Lewiston, NY: Edwin Mellon Press, 1990).

Chapter 17. *The Fourth Clue: The Third Day—An Eschatological Symbol*

1. Maurice Goguel, *The Life of Jesus,* trans. Olive Wyon (New York: Macmillan, 1933), 178.
2. Reginald Fuller, *The Formation of the Resurrection Narratives* (New York: Macmillan, 1971), pp. 23–30.

Notes

Chapter 18. *The Fifth Clue: The Burial Tradition As Mythology*

1. Reginald Fuller, *The Formation of the Resurrection Narratives* (New York: Macmillan, 1971), 54.
2. John S. Spong, *Born of a Woman: A Bishop Rethinks the Birth of Jesus* (San Francisco: Harper San Francisco, 1992).
3. Ibid., chap. 13, "Suppose Jesus Were Married?"

Chapter 19. *But What Did Happen? A Speculative Reconstruction*

1. Michael Goulder, of the University of Birmingham, England, is the only biblical scholar I know who has decided that his scholarship can no longer support his faith commitment. He has resigned from the Anglican priesthood and calls himself today a nonaggressive atheist. I have no desire to cast judgment on him. His scholarship has enriched me and deepened my faith. Indeed I have had the privilege of saying to Michael Goulder that God has spoken through him to me. I respect his honesty. I do not share his conclusion.

Chapter 20. *Grounding the Speculation in Scripture*

1. John S. Spong, *This Hebrew Lord* (New York: Seabury Press, 1974, revised 1992).
2. C. F. W. Smith, "No Time for Figs," *Journal of Biblical Literature* 79 (1960). It was this article by Dr. Smith that opened me to all these possibilities.
3. Abraham E. Millgram, *Jewish Worship* (Philadelphia: Jewish Publication Society of America, 1971), 314.
4. Smith, "No Time for Figs," 321.
5. G. F. Moore, *Judaism in the First Centuries of the Christian Era* (Cambridge, MA: Harvard Univ. Press, 1930), 2:298.
6. D. Daube, *The New Testament and Rabbinic Judaism* (London: Athlove Press, 1958), 408.
7. R. H. Lightfoot, *St. John's Gospel, A Commentary* (Oxford: Clarendon Press, 1956), 182.

Chapter 21. *Life After Death—This I Do Believe*

1. The Hymnal of the Episcopal Church, 1982, no. 682.
2. This is in quotes because it is the title of Tillich's book, published by Charles Scribner & Sons, 1963.

Bibliography

Aarowitz, S. from an article on Midrash in *The Jewish Encyclopedia*. London, New York: Funk and Wagnalls, 1904, 1916, 1925.

Addison, James Thayer. *Life Beyond Death*. New York: Houghton Mifflin, 1932.

Albright, W. F., and C. S. Mann. *Matthew*. Anchor Bible Series. New York: Doubleday, 1984.

Badham, Paul. *Christian Beliefs in Life After Death*. London: Macmillan, 1976.

Bailie, John. *And the Life Everlasting*. New York: Charles Scribner & Sons, 1936.

Balmforth, H. *The Gospel According to St. Luke*. Oxford: Clarendon Press, 1930.

Becker, Ernest. *The Denial of Death*. New York: Macmillan, 1973.

Becque, Maurice, and Louis Becque. *Life After Death*. New York: Hawthorne Books, 1960.

Bell, W. Cosby. *If a Man Die*. New York: Charles Scribner & Sons, 1934.

Bethune-Baker, J. F. *An Introduction to the Early History of Christian Doctrine*. London: Methuen Press, 1951.

Blunt, A. W. F. *The Gospel According to St. Mark*. Oxford: Clarendon Press, 1929.

Bonhoeffer, Deitrich. *Letters and Papers from Prison*. Edited by Eberhard Bethage. Translated by Reginald Fuller. New York: Macmillan, 1962.

Bonnell, John Sutherland. *Heaven and Hell*. Nashville: Abingdon Press, 1956.

Boros, Ladislaus. *The Mystery of Death*. Translated by Gregory Bainbridge. New York: Herder & Herder (Seabury), 1956.

Brown, Raymond E. "Apocalyptic Eschatology and the Transcendence of Death." *Catholic Bible Quarterly* 36 (1974): 21–43.

———. *The Birth of the Messiah*. Garden City, NY: Doubleday, 1977.

———. *The Gospel According to John*. Two volumes. Garden City, NY: Doubleday, 1966, 1970.

———. *The Virginal Conception and Bodily Resurrection of Jesus*. New York: Paulist Press, 1977.

Bruce, F. F. "To the Hebrews or to the Essenes." *New Testament Studies* 9 (1962–63): 217–32.

Brunner, Emil. *Dogmatics*. Vol. 3. London: Lutterworth, 1962.

———. *Eternal Hope*. Translated by Harold Knight. Philadelphia: Westminster Press, 1954.

Buber, Martin. *I and Thou*. New York: Charles Scribner & Sons, 1958.

Buchanan, George W. *To the Hebrews*. Anchor Bible Series. Garden City, NY: Doubleday, 1972.

Bultmann, Rudolf. *The Gospel of John: A Commentary*. Translated by G. R. Beasley-Murray. Oxford: Oxford Univ. Press and Basil Blackwell, 1971.

Burkitt, F. C. Hosanna. *Journal of Theological Studies*. Vol. 17, pp. 139–52. Oxford: Clarendon Press, 1916.

———. *Studies in the Western Text of St. Mark*. Journal of Theological Studies. Vol. 17. Oxford: Clarendon Press, 1916.

Cabiness, A. *Christmas Echoes at Paschaltide*. New Testament Studies. Vol. 9. Cambridge: Cambridge Univ. Press, 1962.

Caird, George B. *St. Luke*. Baltimore: Penguin Books, 1963.

Caird, George B., et al. *The Christian Hope*. London: SPCK, 1970.

Campbell, Joseph. *Myths to Live By—In Conversation with Michael Toms*. New Dimensions Foundations. Audiotapes. National Public Radio.

Campbell, Joseph, with Bill Moyers. *The Power of Myth*. Edited by Betty Sue Flowers. New York/London: Doubleday, 1988.

Campbell, J. Y. *Three New Testament Studies*. Translated by E. J. Brill. The Netherlands: Leiden Press, 1965.

Capra, Fritjof. "Physics, Mysticism, and Social Change." Lecture at the Univ. of Santa Barbara, CA., Mind Supermind Series, 1983.

Carrington, Philip. *The Primitive Christian Church*. Cambridge: Cambridge Univ. Press, 1952.

Cavalin, H. C. C. *Paul's Argument for the Resurrection of the Dead in I Corinthians 15*. Stockholm: C.W.K. Gleeruphund, 1974.

Cheek, Mary Tyler. *Death, the Key to Life*. Cincinnati: Forward Day by Day, 1982.

Conzelmann, Hans. *The Theology of St. Luke*. Translated by Geoffrey Buswell. London: Faber & Faber, 1960.

Cox, Harvey. *The Secular City*. New York: Macmillan, 1965.

Cullmann, Oscar. *Immortality of the Soul or Resurrection of the Dead*. London: Epworth Press, 1958.

Dahl, M. E. *The Resurrection of the Body*. London: SCM Press, 1962.

Dante. *The Divine Comedy*. Available in a wide variety of editions.

Daube, D. *The New Testament and Rabbinic Judaism*. London: Athlove Press. Univ. of London, 1958.

de Sargy, P., and P. Grelot, M. Carrez, and A. George. *La Resurrection du Christ et l'exegese*. Paris: Editions du Cerf, 1969.

De Sola Pool, David. *The Service of the Heart*. Hertford, UK: Stephen Austin & Sons, 1967.

———. *The Book of Prayers and Order of Service for the Feast of Tabernacles*. London: Oxford Univ. Press, 1960.

———, ed. *The Traditional Prayer Book for Sabbaths and Festivals*. Published by the Rabbinical Council of America. New York: Behrman House, 1960.

Dibella, Alexander A., and Louis F. Hartman. *The Book of Daniel*. Anchor Bible Series. Garden City, NY: Doubleday, 1977.

Dodd, C. H. *According to the Scriptures*. London: Nisbit, 1952.

———. *The Interpretation of the Fourth Gospel*. Cambridge: Cambridge Univ. Press, 1953.

———. *The Parables of the Kingdom*. New York: Charles Scribner & Sons, 1935.

Duthie, Charles S., ed. *Resurrection and Immortality: Selections from Drew Lectures*. London: Samuel Bagster & Sons, 1929.

Eusebius. *The History of the Christian Church from Christ to Constantine*. Translated by G. A. Williamson. New York: Dorset Press, 1965.

Fitzmyer, Joseph. *The Gospel According to Luke*. Vols. 28–28A. Anchor Bible Series. New York: Doubleday, 1985, 1987.

Fosdick, Harry Emerson. *Spiritual Values and Eternal Life*. Cambridge, MA: Harvard Univ. Press, 1927.

Freud, Sigmund. *The Future of an Illusion*. Translated by W. D. Robsom. London: Hogarth Press, 1928.

Fuller, Reginald. *The Foundation of the Resurrection Narratives*. New York: Macmillan, 1971. London: SPCK, 1972.

Geering, Lloyd. *Resurrection—A Symbol of Hope*. London, Auckland, Sydney, Toronto: Hodder & Stoughton, 1971.

Gelin, Albert. *The Religion of Israel*. New York: Hawthorne Books, 1958.

Gilkey, Langdon. *Naming the Whirlwind: The Renewal of God Language*. New York: Bobbs-Merrill, 1969.

Goguel, Maurice. *The Life of Jesus*. Translated by Olive Wyon. London: George Allen & Unwin, 1933; New York: Macmillan, 1933.

———. *The Primitive Church*. Translated by H. N. Snape. London: George Allen & Unwin, 1964.

Goulder, Michael D. *Luke, A New Paradigm*. 2 vols. Sheffield, UK: Sheffield Academic Press, 1989.

———. *Midrash and Lection in Matthew*. London: SPCK, 1974.

Grant, Robert M. "The Coming of the Kingdom." *Journal of Biblical Literature* 67 (1948): 297–303.

———. "The Resurrection of the Body." *Journal of Religion* 28 (1948).

Greeley, Andrew. "Are We a Nation of Mystics?" *New York Times Magazine*, 26 January 1975.

Green, F. W. *The Gospel According to St. Matthew*. Oxford: Clarendon Press, 1936.

Guy, H. A. *The Fourth Gospel—An Introduction*. London: Macmillan, 1972.
———. *The Gospel of Luke*. London: Macmillan, 1972.
———. *The Gospel of Mark*. London: Macmillan, 1968.
———. *The Gospel of Matthew*. London: Macmillan, 1971.
———. *The New Testament Doctrine of the Last Things*. London: Oxford Univ. Press, 1948.
Hartman, Louis, and Alexander Dibella. *The Book of Daniel*. Anchor Bible Series. Garden City, NY: Doubleday, 1977.
Hartshorne, Charles. *The Logic of Perfection and Other Essays in Neo Classical Metaphysics*. LaSalle, IL: Open Court, 1962.
Hendrickx, Herman. *Infancy Narratives*. London: Geoffrey Chapman, 1984.
Hennecke, E., and W. Schneemelcher. *New Testament Apocrypha*. Philadelphia: Westminster Press, 1963.
Hick, John. *Death and Eternal Life*. New York and San Francisco: Harper & Row, 1976.
Hocking, William Ernest. *Thoughts on Death and Life*. New York: Harper & Brothers, 1937.
Hoskyns, Edwin C. *The Fourth Gospel*. Vols. 1 and 2. London: Faber & Faber, 1940.
Hultkrantz, A. K. E. *Conceptions of the Soul Among North American Indians*. Stockholm: Caslon Press, 1953.
Jung, Carl. *Memories, Dreams and Reflections*. New York: Vintage Books, 1965.
———. *Psychology and Religion*. New Haven: Yale Univ. Press, 1938.
Justin Martyr, Saint. *Dialogue with Trypho*. Excerpts from the Works of St. Justin. Edited by G. J. Davey and A. L. Williams. St. Charles, IL: St. Charles House, 1973.
Kaufman, Gordon. *Systematic Theology, A Historicist's Perception*. New York: Charles Scribner & Sons, 1968.
Keck, Leander. *Paul and His Letters*. Philadelphia: Fortress Press, 1979.
Kelly, J. N. D. *Early Christian Doctrines*. New York: Harper & Row, 1960.
Kelsey, Morton. *The Other Side of Silence*. New York: Paulist Press, 1976.
Kepler, Thomas, ed. *Thinking About Paul. An Anthology*. New York/Nashville: Abingdon Press, 1940.
Koester, H., and J. M. Robinson. *Trajectories Through Early Christianity*. Philadelphia: Fortress Press, 1971.
Kübler-Ross, Elisabeth. *On Death and Dying*. New York: Macmillan, 1970.
Küng, Hans. *Eternal Life?* Translated by Edward Quinn. Garden City, NY: Doubleday, 1984.
Lake, Kirsopp. *The Historical Evidence for the Resurrection*. London: Williams & Norgate, 1907; New York: G. P. Putnam & Sons, 1907.
———. *Paul, His Heritage and Legacy*. London: Christopher Press, 1934.

Lamont, Corliss. *The Illusion of Immortality*. London: Watts, 1952.

Lamp, G. W. H., and D. M. Mackinnon. *The Resurrection*. London: Mowbrays, 1966.

Lightfoot, R. H. *St. John's Gospel, A Commentary*. Oxford: Clarendon Press, 1956.

Loofs, Frederick. *What Is the Truth About Jesus Christ?* New York: Charles Scribner's, 1913.

McCool, Gerald A., ed. *A Rahner Reader*. New York: Seabury Press, 1975.

MacGregor, G. H. C. "The Eucharist in the Fourth Gospel." *New Testament Studies* 9 (1962–63): 111–19.

MacQuarrie, John. *Christian Hope*. New York: Seabury Press, 1978.

———. *The Faith of the People of God*. London: SCM Press, 1963.

———. *Principles of Christian Theology*. New York: Charles Scribner & Sons, 1966.

———. *Twentieth Century Religious Thought*. London: SCM Press, 1963.

Mann, J. *The Bible as Read and Preached in the Old Testament*. Vol. 1. New York: KTAV, 1971.

Manson, T. W. "The Cleansing of the Temple." *Bulletin of the John Rylands Univ. Library of Manchester* 33 (September 1950): 271–82.

Martelet, Gustave. *The Risen Christ and the Eucharistic World*. New York: Seabury Press, 1976.

Martin, James. *Did Jesus Rise from the Dead?* London: Lutterworth Press, 1956.

Miller, Dale, and Patricia Miller. *The Gospel of Mark as Midrash on Earlier Jewish and New Testament Literature*. Lewiston, NY: Edwin Mellon Press, 1990.

Millgram, Abraham E. *Jewish Worship*. Philadelphia: Jewish Publication Society of America, 1971.

Moloney, Francis J. *Beginning the Good News*. Homebush, NSW: St. Paul's Press, 1992.

Moltmann, Jürgen. *Theology of Hope*. New York: Harper & Row, 1965.

Montefiore, Hugh. *The Womb and the Tomb: The Mystery of the Birth and Resurrection of Jesus*. London: Harper Collins, 1992.

Moody, Raymond R. *Life After Death*. New York: Bantam Books, 1975.

Moore, G. F. *Judaism in the First Centuries of the Christian Era*. Vols. 1 and 2. Cambridge, MA: Harvard Univ. Press, 1930.

Moule, Charles F. D. *The Origins of Christology*. Cambridge: Cambridge Univ. Press, 1977.

———, ed. *The Significance of the Message of the Resurrection for Faith in Jesus Christ*. Part 1 by Willi Marxen. Part 2 by Ulrich Wilckens. London: SCM Press, 1968.

Nineham, D. E. *St. Mark*. Baltimore: Penguin Books, 1963.

———. *The Use and Abuse of the Bible*. London: Macmillan, 1976.

Noss, John B. *Man's Religion*. London: Macmillan, 1949.

Noth, Martin. *The History of Israel*. London: A. C. Black, 1960

Oesterley, W. O. E. *The Jews and Judaism During the Greek Period*. London: SPCK, 1941.

Ogden, Schubert, M. *Christ Without Myth*. New York: Harper & Brothers, 1961.

———. *The Reality of God and Other Essays*. New York: Harper & Row, 1966.

Orr, James. *The Resurrection of Jesus*. Cincinnati: Jennings & Graham, 1907.

Otto, Rudolf. *The Idea of the Holy*. Oxford: Oxford Univ. Press, 1926.

Pagels, Elaine. *Adam, Eve, and the Serpent*. New York: Random House, 1988.

Pannenberg, Wolfhart. *The Apostle's Creed*. London: SCM Press, 1972.

———. "Did Jesus Rise from the Dead?" *Dialogue* 4 (1965): 18–35.

———. *Jesus: God and Man*. London: SCM Press, 1964.

———. *Theology of the Kingdom of God*. London: SCM Press, 1964.

———. *What Is Man?* London: SCM Press, 1962; Philadelphia: Fortress Press, 1962.

Pelikan, Jaroslav. *The Emergence of the Catholic Tradition 100–600*. Volume 1 of The Christian Tradition Series. Chicago and London: Univ. of Chicago Press, 1971.

———. *The History of the Christian Tradition*. Richmond: Univ. of Virginia Press, 1973.

Penfield, Wilder. *The Mystery of the Mind*. Princeton, NJ: Princeton Univ. Press, 1975.

Perkins, Pheme. *Resurrection: New Testament Witness and Contemporary Reflection*. Garden City, NY: Doubleday, 1984.

Perrin, Norman. *The Resurrection According to Matthew, Mark, and Luke*. Philadelphia: Fortress Press, 1977.

Perry, M. C., ed. *Historicity and Chronology in the New Testament*. London: SPCK, 1965.

Pike, Nelson. *God and Timelessness*. London: Routledge & Kegan Paul, 1970.

Pittinger, Norman. *After Death*. New York: Seabury Press, 1980.

Prat, Fernand. *The Theology of St. Paul*. Westminster, MD: Newman Press, 1950.

Price, Samuel. *Outlines of Judaism*. New York: Bloch, 1946.

Pringle-Pattison, A. Seth. *The Idea of Immortality*. The Gifford Lectures, 1922. Oxford, UK: Clarendon Press, 1922.

A Rahner Reader. Edited by Gerald A. McCool. New York: Seabury Press, 1975.

———. *On the Theology of Death*. New York: Herder & Herder, 1961.

Ramsey, A. Michael. *The Resurrection of Christ*. Philadelphia: Westminster Press, 1956.

Rauthings, Maurice, M.D. *Beyond Death's Door*. Nashville: Thomas Nelson & Sons, 1960.

Richardson, Alan. *An Introduction to the Theology of the New Testament*. New York/London: Harper & Row, 1958.

Robinson, H. Wheeler. *Inspiration and Revelation in the Old Testament*. Oxford: Clarendon Press, 1946.

Robinson, John A. T. *The Human Face of God*. Philadelphia: Westminster Press, 1973.

———."The Relation of the Prologue to the Gospel of John." *New Testament Studies*. Vol. 19 (1962–63): 120–29.

Ross, D. M. *The Spiritual Genius of St. Paul*. London: Hodder & Stoughton, 1925.

Rowell, Geoffrey. *The Vision Glorious*. London: Oxford Univ. Press, 1983.

Russell, D. L. *The Method and Message of Jewish Apocalyptic*. Philadelphia: Westminster Press, 1964.

Schaberg, Jane. *The Father, the Son, and the Holy Spirit*. Chico, CA: Scholars Press, 1982.

———. *The Illegitimacy of Jesus*. San Francisco: Harper & Row, 1987.

Schillebeeckx, Edward. *Jesus: An Experiment in Christology*. Translated by Hubert Hoskins. New York: Seabury Press, 1979.

Schneemelcher, Wilhelm, ed. *New Testament Apocrypha*. Translated by A. J. B. Higgins et al. Philadelphia: Westminster Press, 1963–66.

Schoenfield, Hugh C. *The Passover Plot*. New York: Bantam Books, 1967.

Schultz, Jürgen, ed. *Jesus in His Time*. Translated by Brian Watchorn. Philadelphia: Fortress Press, 1971.

Schweitzer, Albert. *The Quest of the Historical Jesus*. Tübingen, 1907. London: A & C Black, 1911, 1926, 1948.

Selby, Peter. *Look for the Living: The Corporate Nature of Resurrection Faith*. Philadelphia: Fortress Press, 1976.

Selwyn, Edward Gordon. *The Resurrection. From Essays Catholic and Critical*. New York: Macmillan, 1926.

Sheehan, Thomas. *The First Coming: How the Kingdom of God Became Christianity*. New York: Random House, 1986.

Simon, Ulrich. *Heaven in the Christian Tradition*. New York: Harper & Brothers, 1958.

Slattery, Charles Lewis. *Life Beyond Life*. London: Longmans Green, 1911.

Sloan, Harold P. *Eternal Life*. Philadelphia: Methodist Book Room, 1948.

———. *He Is Risen*. Nashville: Abingdon-Cokesbury, 1952.

Smith, C. Ryder. *The Bible Doctrine of the Hereafter*. London: Epworth Press, 1958.

Smith, C. W. F. "The Horse and the Ass in the Bible." *Anglican Theological Review* 27 (1945).

———. "No Time for Figs." *Journal of Biblical Literature* 79 (1960).

———. "Tabernacles in the Fourth Gospel and in Mark." *New Testament Studies* 19 (1962–62).

Spong, John S. *Born of a Woman: A Bishop Rethinks the Birth of Jesus*. San Francisco: Harper San Francisco, 1992.

———. *The Living Commandments*. New York: Seabury Press, 1977.

———. *Living in Sin? A Bishop Rethinks Human Sexuality*. San Francisco: Harper & Row, 1988.

———. *Rescuing the Bible from Fundamentalism: A Bishop Rethinks the Meaning of Scripture*. San Francisco: Harper San Francisco, 1990.

———. *This Hebrew Lord: A Bishop's Search for an Authentic Jesus*. San Francisco: Harper San Francisco, 1993.

Stendahl, Krister, ed. *Immortality and Resurrection. Four Essays*. New York: Macmillan, 1965.

Stott, Wilfred. "The Conception of Offering in the Epistle to the Hebrews." *New Testament Studies* 9 (1962–63).

Taylor, A. E. *The Christian Hope of Immortality*. New York: Macmillan, 1947.

Taylor, Vincent. *The Atonement in New Testament Teaching*. London: Epworth Press, 1940.

———. *The Gospel According to Mark*. London: Macmillan, 1953.

Teilhard de Chardin, Pierre. *The Future of Man*. London: Collins, 1964.

———. *Hymn of the Universe*. New York: Harper & Row, 1961.

———. *The Phenomenon of Man*. London: Collins, 1950.

Tillich, Paul. *The Courage to Be*. New Haven: Yale Univ. Press, 1952.

———. *The Eternal Now*. New York: Charles Scribner & Sons, 1963.

———. *The New Being*. New York: Charles Scribner & Sons, 1965.

———. *Systematic Theology*. Vol. 3. Chicago: Univ. of Chicago Press, 1963.

Unamuno, Miguel de. *The Tragic Sense of Life*. Translated by J. E. C. Flitch. New York: Dover Press, 1954.

Von Campenhausen, H. *Traditions and Life in the Church*. Philadelphia: Fortress Press, 1968.

Von Hugel, F. *Eternal Life*. Edinburgh: T. & T. Clark, 1912.

Von Rad, Gerhard. *Old Testament Theology*. Translated by D. M. G. Stalker. Two volumes. New York: Harper & Row, 1962, 1965.

Warner, Marina. *Alone of All Her Sex*. New York: Alfred A. Knopf, 1976.

Weatherhead, Leslie D. *After Death*. London: James Clark, 1953. New York: Abingdon Press, 1936.

———. *The Case for Re-Incarnation*. London: City Temple, 1957.

———. *The Resurrection*. Nashville: Abingdon-Cokesbury, 1951.

Werner, E. "Hosannah in the Gospels." *Journal of Biblical Literature* 65 (1946).

Westcott, B. F. *The Gospel of the Resurrection*. London: Macmillan, 1898.

———. *The Revelation of the Risen Lord*. London: Macmillan, 1898.

Whitehead, A. N. *Process and Reality*. New York: Macmillan, 1930.

Whiteley, D. E. H. *The Theology of St. Paul*. Philadelphia: Fortress Press, 1964.

Williams, H. A. *Jesus and the Resurrection*. London: Longmans, 1957.

Yarnold, G. D. *Risen Indeed: Studies in the Lord's Resurrection*. New York: Oxford Univ. Press, 1959.

Index